EX LIBRIS
TSM

American Story

Memories and
Reflections of Bruce Gould
and Beatrice Blackmar Gould

American Story

Harper & Row, Publishers

New York, Evanston,

and London

To my wife, who has brought me joy, who has made my life a living hell when she thought I was on the wrong track—and who has, since our first meeting, never been uninteresting.

To my courageous husband, amused by life, so, steadily amusing; to whose good temper, firm patience, and magnanimity with a volatile, often capricious companion I owe much.

"The sum which two married people owe to one another defies calculation," Goethe says. "It is an infinite debt, which can only be discharged through all eternity."

Contents

❦ *Illustrations*

Illustrations

American Story

*The whisper of a pretty girl can be heard
farther than the roar of a lion.*

—ARAB PROVERB

1

Once Upon a Time

When I met my wife—she was twenty—she had the most joyous smile I had ever seen. It flicked dimples in her cheeks and lit even the dark of her eyes, which seemed to shine only for me.

A pretty girl, I suppose, always seems like a miracle to a young man—I was twenty-one—even more so if she happens to be looking straight up at him, smiling.

I quipped some nonsensical thing.

I liked the instant way she laughed. She didn't need signposts.

Her mind, I soon discovered, was as honest as her laughter. She could knock your idea out of the ball park before you had really unwound if you were not careful. Maybe, I thought, I have reached the end of the rainbow.

But this girl at the State University of Iowa was so serenely her own mistress—responsive and gay, indeed, but in possession of herself—it was a long time before that first impression crystallized into serious thought.

1

In his remarkable autobiography, *Memory Hold-the-Door,* John Buchan says of his marriage:

> In the autumn of 1906 my unsettled years came happily to an end, for I became engaged. . . . I had no longer any craving for a solitary life at some extremity of the Empire, for England was once more for me an enchanted land, and London a magical city. . . . I found the perfect comrade. I have been happy in many things, but all my other good fortune has been as dust in the balance compared with the blessing of an incomparable wife.

And then he mentions her not again.

But mentioning Beatrice not again would destroy this book. She not only has brought enchantment and delight into our life together, she has been a partner in work, stimulating, original, quirky, and humorous. And I have always thought a man was a compass seldom pointing true north unless corrected quietly, firmly, gaily, by the sometimes sound, sometimes amusingly feminine deviations of the woman at his side.

In that casual meeting on Iowa's autumnal campus in 1919, I, of course, had no intimation of the future. This laughing girl, her skin, quite literally, an astonishing Raeburn pink and pearl, just looked like a possible date. I couldn't have imagined—it would have been too wildly implausible to imagine—that either of us, much less both of us, would ever be editors of the *Ladies' Home Journal* for twenty-seven unbroken years from July, 1935, to April, 1962.

The *Journal* was a publication I did not know. If I had any feeling at all about that magazine, I in young insouciance rather despised it. *Vanity Fair, Smart Set, The Yellow Book* were my admirations. The *Saturday Evening Post* and all such bourgeois publications for the complacent middle-aged were to be condemned airily, especially unread. So tightly was my mind constricted by the binding integument of George Jean Nathan's and Henry L. Mencken's prejudices that I was, like most collegiate intelligentsia of my time, more given to decrying than to praise. The theatre was my goal; playwriting my aim; fame, fortune, and gay bachelorhood in foreign capitals the stuff of my daydreams.

But if I had been seeking a perfect editor for the future *Journal*

I could, that year, have sifted through all the golden girls on all the bright campuses of the Midwest and not found one whose background, intelligence, and, most importantly, practical ideals fitted her better to help edit a great mass magazine for women.

Though we had never met before I had, of course, for some time been distinctly aware of this butterfly. Somewhere in the Indian-summer sun she had been just dizzily glittering, the way women sometimes do for reasons of their own. Though I was not in my bumptious youth noticeably warped by an inferiority complex, this delightful coed seemed a little out of my orbit. She was one of Kappa Kappa Gamma's outstanding girls. I was a "Barb."

At Iowa, in John Held, Jr.'s Jazz Age, a Barb was way off in outfield. A man, to rate, drove a Stutz Bearcat. He owned a raccoon coat, sported a silver hip flask. I had none of these things. I didn't even drink. I was destined to remain a Barb until Kappa Sigma cautiously took me in—I suppose because I was finally becoming a sort of Big Man on the Campus.

But being a Barb wasn't my important hurdle with Beatrice. I was later to realize, and be guided all my life by the knowledge, that Beatrice had an uncanny intuition. About people she had extrasensory perception—or else saw like the relentless child who noticed the king wore no clothes. Some sagacious ancestral voice whispered to me to move with caution, bade me mind my tongue. With a flip of her hand, Beatrice drifted off, but our lives had just that instant been joined in a single strand—a daughter with beauty and integrity and five handsome grandchildren are today's proof of it.

Fortunately, I was born overconfident. My early, to me magnificent, successes—spelling down even Virgil Still, contributing at thirteen from a paper route to the family grocery fund, ranting Macbeth and Petruchio in high school to a discomfited audience, ruthlessly editing the high-school paper—such achievements gave me the swollen self-confidence often mentioned by well-meaning friends as not being entirely a social asset. My bumptiousness I recognized with occasional, but perhaps insufficient, regret. A boy rattling his stick along the picket fence of life rather glories in the clamant noise.

Something—poets rhyme about it—brought Beatrice and me together. It hasn't been all beer and skittles, of course. I don't believe any man, any aspiring man, even a lucky man like me, has ever lived who hasn't at some moment faced freezing despair. There were to be never more than just Beatrice and me paddling our occasionally sinking canoe—Beatrice and me and the benevolent gods protecting drunks, fools, and the very young.

. . . the battle of the sexes can be a most enjoyable scrimmage
If you'll only stop trying to create woman in your image.
                              —OGDEN NASH, "Marriage Lines"

2 🐚

Men and Women Are Different

The question "How do you two manage to work together?" (without flying apart, they mean) has been perhaps the only really interesting thing, to others, about Bruce and me. No newspaper interviewer has failed to ask that question—nor have most of our friends.

Marriage is potentially explosive—collaboration notably so. Gilbert and Sullivan's alliance shattered. Most playwriting teams have reshuffled partners with regularity, usually with acrimony as well. Shake marriage and career together and you have the makings of a minor fission.

Men query my husband with obvious incredulity, as though saying, "Isn't the strain of marriage enough—without bringing it into the nice, unemotional office?"

Women's questions have sometimes hinted of envy, implying, perhaps, "How did you manage to work your way into that stimulating man's world, and have a woman's life as well?"

Both men and women have suggested a constant threat, a sword over our heads, suspended by a hair. How right they were. Perhaps these very differences have kept our working life together so absorbing.

My answers have been various. Usually, I speak of my husband's magnanimity. He gives generous, overrunning credit to the enrichment a woman's mind and experiences can bring to thought on almost any problem. I've never heard him belittle women, unless he is making a joke so obvious even, as he says, a woman would see the humor of it. He never competes with women. He likes them too much. Competitive by nature, he directs all his combativeness toward men.

So I say to my women friends, "Bruce praises me for what I do—and helps me do it. When our daughter needs me as baby-sitter, he takes over my job as well as his."

Perhaps this is the heart of the truth. Bruce has always been explicit and overgenerous in his estimation of my share. And when I slip away—involved with child or grandchildren, or merely take a trip to Paris to see Dior plain—he simply shrugs and smiles at feminine ways. He has never, thank goodness, tried to make me think like a man or act like one—and doesn't tag me as capricious or unreasonable because I don't.

Bruce is not notable for calm, nor am I, and our partnership, like our marriage, has been tempestuous. The hair suspending the sword above our heads has perilously stretched. "That's terrible" has been one of our milder comments on the other's work. Many a tender idea has been decapitated like Lewis Carroll's Jabberwock:

> The vorpal blade went snicker-snack!
> He left it dead, and with its head
> He went galumphing back.

Tears on the Reading Railroad while we were commuting to Philadelphia or New York, haughty stalkings from the conference room, considerable door banging, torn-up manuscripts have punctuated our joint career.

Our differences have not been wholly professional. After the threatened packing of the Supreme Court and before Roosevelt's third-term election, dinner-table arguments waxed so intense that our daughter, with the equanimity she blessedly possesses, finally rose from the table plate in hand saying, "I think I'll have dinner in the playroom and listen to *The Lone Ranger* till after the election." And did.

But our disputes, in the main, have been heat lightning on a lovely summer evening. Fortunately, the lightning has rarely struck anything precious—and thunder can clear the air and lend brilliance to the later sunshine.

Two people could scarcely be more different in all small matters of living. He hates to get up. I spring cheerfully from my bed with the light. Since we like to have breakfast together—I drink coffee, he takes tea—this is still a source of contention after forty years. I am conventional. He breaks all the rules. To me, mealtimes are sacred—he is always late. He can come in, innocent as a lamb, after a cheese soufflé is spoiled and ask what time is lunch. (The hour does not vary.) Or he can blandly suggest at six we have a quick snack and go to an early movie just when a browning roast in the oven has passed the point of no return. He enjoys the society of artists, bohemians, newspapermen, raffish characters of all sorts, politicians if they don't consider themselves statesmen. I prefer as companions courteous people who customarily comb and brush their hair and keep their shoes and fingernails reasonably clean—fishermen, children under seven, and picnickers I exclude from this stringent rule. An astonishing number of responsible, well-mannered people are also witty, amusing, perceptive, and continuously engaging company. Such persons are my heart's love. I make friends slowly and cherish them. He is more amused than I by life's passing show—the pageant of character and personality; he would have enjoyed Chaucer and his company. Fortunately, where loyalties are involved, with friends and working associates, our views usually harmonize.

Bruce always wanted to write plays. I guess I always wanted to do what he did.

An incident of our early collaboration comes back to me. It was a fine breezy June day in Maine, 1927. We were working outdoors with clipboard and pencils at a kitchen table on an isolated piny point jutting into Long Pond, near Soamesville. Across the ruffled lake two peaks of Mount Desert formed the splendid backdrop for the play we were hopefully concocting.

We had had our usual breakfast of bacon and eggs cooked on the old wood-burning range in the kitchen–living room of our rented cabin. Our running water we ran out to the lake to dip. After our morning contentions, we would row a mile across the deep lake, climb the hill another mile and buy, at a farm, young frying chickens, rhubarb, and maybe vegetables, arguing all the way whether rhubarb pie or apple pie was better, Ibsen a better playwright than G.B.S.

We were starting a new play, our second. Our earlier one, *The First Gentleman of Her Time,* had surprisingly been optioned by Ethel Barrymore (an option for six months paid $500) and that sum enabled us to take the summer off from our respective newspaper jobs on the New York *World* and the New York *Evening Post* to write a new play. Our money had to be stretched, so we had traveled to Maine two in a lower berth—the $500 made us so rich we needn't scrimp with a shared upper. We had chosen this island cabin on lovely Long Pond because it was cheap and we could be absolutely alone. We did not, at the time, feel it was a capricious choice, though we had to row a mile to reach any human habitation (we were even then seven miles from a town and a doctor) and our first child was due in early October.

On that lovely, windy, mackerel-clouded day we were almost at the end of Act I. After a more than usually querulous warmup session, my husband said: "I think it would be funny if he would ask her, 'Why is it a young woman in love dreams more about houses and babies than about the man she's in love with? That leaves so many openings for an efficient mistress.' "

I fear I looked at him rather coolly.

"That would be unexpected. . . ."

My pencil did not move.

"Humor at that point would be poignant."

Usually we laughed at each other's wit, even though feeble. My eyes remained glazed.

"What is the matter with you this morning?"

"Isn't it perhaps wrong for such an emotional moment?" I ventured.

Collaborations are always risky, as has been suggested. The ego is involved. A criticism of one's newborn thought seems a criticism of one's entire artistic being. Frequently wit is the tenderest child of all.

My husband rose, his face looking somewhat swollen. "You are the most imperceptive person I can imagine. You have no sense of humor. It is no good trying to work with you."

The finished sheets were violently torn across and then again across. Act I was caught by the breeze, scattered with the wind over the thickets of our point.

Our lunchtime cocoa and sandwiches were consumed in chilly silence.

"I don't feel like walking today," I said. "I think I'll read in the hammock. We can have baked beans for supper."

That afternoon my husband stolidly rowed across Long Pond to get the milk and the mail. He seemed to be making faster time than usual, his oars flailing the unoffending wavelets to a froth.

Though somewhat corpulent, being six months gone, I retrieved every piece of paper from the blueberry bushes and the brambles. All except one, drowned in Long Pond.

Next morning, pieced together with paper and glue—except for a hole in Scene 2—Act I lay on the table. We resumed our work.

My husband apparently was born without the ability to say, "I am sorry. I was wrong." Trollope says men never can; that women rather like being abject. At least not until he had been softened by twenty years of marriage do I remember ever hearing Bruce say it— and then rarely. Precious comedy lines lost in Scene 2 were reconstructed from memory and we went on collaborating. The play, *Man's Estate,* was eventually produced by the Theatre Guild and earned us enough money to help pay for the farm at Hopewell where we now live.

This sounds as though I were long-suffering, noble, patient—a put-upon and subservient wife. Not at all. I am merely, like most women, practical. The $500 which bought that free summer was infinitely precious. When might we have in hand, at one time, a like sum again? No one could foretell whether the unpredictable Barrymore would renew her option, produce the play, or let it drift into that oblivion where the hearts of unproduced authors are broken. In the autumn I would have a child, and even if the rent and groceries were paid for, these long, carefree mornings for work would be hard to come by.

Our newspaper jobs paid us barely enough to live. A play—a successful play—was our hoped-for road to fame-and-fortune, the best way to achieve the triumph whose expectation had brought us— or at least Bruce—to New York. It would not only buy shoes for the baby and a crib, but would give us leisure to write another play.

Perhaps, too, as a young undisciplined wife, I felt the fragility of a relationship whose future value I dimly discerned and which has been the sustaining joy of my life. Quarreling seriously with my husband and collaborator, I decided, might be fun on a short-term basis, but did not make sense in the long run, for a woman who wanted to tag along.

"Men and women are different" was one of the *Journal*'s slogans —not merely to be taken in its explicit sense, so dear to the French with their "Vive la différence!" Our long years with women editors, millions of women readers, confirmed constantly its deeper meaning.

Women are simply not little men, or equal men, or heaven forbid, bigger men—in mind or spirit—though they may luminously possess both. Since they walk such different paths, women's reactions to daily life are different and will be until IBM puts out a child-bearing, child-rearing machine, and household helpers miraculously reappear on earth to nurse the young and old, to cook and to comfort. If men and women thought too much alike they should be alarmed. Since both views are simply two parts of a picture puzzle, why deny the pleasure they give?—the chance to look at each thought, each person, each sentiment, each house, with *different* eyes. As the stereopticon gives depth in a view, so in marriage nothing need be flat. Perhaps Bruce and I represent the extreme of the opposite principles; this would explain both our disagreements and our harmony.

My share in this book will be what it has always been in our work —the woman's point of view. That is because the only parts of my life that seem real to me, as I look back on them now, are the events of a woman's life. I feel great kinship with Queen Victoria, who found her true self in marriage rather than in the responsibilities and rewards of her position.

My relationship with my husband, infinitely varied, intensely surprising after forty years, often tumultuous and unreconciled as in our earliest knowledge of each other, is yet reconcilable ever into something that perhaps could not always be called harmony but is the constant joy of my days. Our daughter (before whose kindness, perception, and balance I am in awe), our grandchildren, pretty, gay, and curious to learn, are the very earth on which I stand. They are part of its green and flowering, its changing sun and shadow. Summing up in his autobiography, Trollope said that he found "*joy* in his work—comfort in loved ones." To many women, and to me, this seems an odd inversion.

A play produced in New York, Paris clothes, membership on committees, palaces visited, curtsying to queens: these have been changing ripples on the surface of a quiet lake; events, interesting enough —some of them ordeals, some of them rewarding—which came to me because of our work, really Bruce's work, in which he wanted me to share.

We ran the *Journal* as two people. We agreed we would never clash publicly, however much fun it would have given our delighted staff and expectant ears straining on other floors. We formulated and often repeated at moments of stress a rule for the times we did disagree: If we both like it, it's probably good. If one of us doesn't, let's not fight it out now, but wait for time to tell.

Bruce is mad about flying, the theatre, art, satire, and caricature. Satire for women, I usually doubted; my "doubt" sometimes had the force of a veto. Aviation crept into the *Journal*, perhaps more often than it should, in several thrilling stories. I, for some reason, have a passion for Proust, but I did not insist that his involuted sentences, his shadowy recollections, his unusual affections would be the right thing for the *Journal;* nor did I feel that we compromised or lowered our standards by not publishing for the precious few.

We both like to dance, to swim, to travel, to read, to watch sunsets and sunrises, eat good food and drink good wine, play or, increasingly, watch tennis, go to the theatre, spoof each other without malice, divert ourselves with children and talk to intelligent grownups. We both like each other but, happily, for different reasons.

It's not an easy thing to reminisce about one's life. Bruce says it's a bit like undressing in Macy's window, and he's not sure he has the figure for it, though, standing six feet one, he still weighs around 180. (I must, at five feet seven, cut down to one piece of breakfast toast with honey and an egg to avoid creeping up to 130.)

As you will see, some of the chapters have been set down by just one of us; some were jointly written. Together, we hope they make an agreeable, interesting whole. If not, we have only each other to blame.

You can preach a better sermon with your life than with your lips.

—OLIVER GOLDSMITH

3

The Woman in My Life

Whether my mother, Edna Earle Gould, was beautiful or not, I don't know. With her red hair, she had the delicate fair skin, almost translucent, that redheads sometimes have. Her eyes, green, deep-set, often stern, limited their concern to what was happening to her family; what was happening in the outer world hardly interested her, then or later.

Almost more than my mother's dark red hair I remember her hands. Waking in the middle of the night with a croupy cough is an early memory—sleepily feeling the rasping caress of my mother's long, rough fingers rubbing my chest with turpentine and lard. I have no copy of Dürer's prayerfully clasped hands, nor do I need one. They are so imprinted on my mind that I could almost etch both from memory—Dürer's hands or my mother's—so loving, so much alike.

There was nothing namby-pamby about my mother's devotion. She loved you; she was a loving person. She expected to be obeyed. And was. Like Dorothy Canfield Fisher, she believed that "Mother is not a person to lean on but a person to make leaning unnecessary."

13

But she had infinite patience with the complicated problems of a boy growing up. She seldom reached behind the door for the old-fashioned clothesline you knew was there for use. She preferred love, as long as it worked—but was prepared for action when needful.

When I was growing up in early Iowa, some sixty years after it entered the Union in 1846, everyone, it seemed to me, was poor. Ironing and mending were done after dark. I would stumble off to bed unable to keep my eyes open another instant over another book and see my mother just setting up her ironing board beside a wicker basket piled high with damp clothes. Daylight hours were for harder work—scrubbing, baking, washing for a family of seven. In his moving and immensely entertaining autobiography, *Act One,* Moss Hart dwells on his East Side Jewish family's dire poverty—"the dark brown taste of being poor," he quotes Ruth Gordon's phrase. Poverty became Hart's personal villain. When he finally struck it rich with *Once in a Lifetime,* you stood up and cheered. You hoped he would never be poor again.

I didn't feel dismally impoverished as I grew up. As a boy I wasn't, I guess, too concerned with money matters, though in our home there was always an awareness of the never-ending struggle between Capital—a bloated man with $ signs on his vest, according to my father's favorite newspaper, *Appeal to Reason*—and Labor— a put-upon, muscled giant who was only belatedly to learn his own strength.

But I never took in the fact we were actually poor until it was past mattering. When it rained, and the roof leaked, it was exciting to set out pots and pans to catch the drips. I guess I thought we were lucky to have enough pots and pans. And when, about nine, after closely watching the shoemaker, while ostensibly listening to what he was saying about the shortcomings of marriage, I taught myself to half-sole my own shoes with discarded belting from my father's creamery, the pride of achievement was even greater than the pleasure of saving fifty cents.

Perhaps it's valuable to have been born poor, in the middle-class Midwest, to understand, even a little, this diverse country engaged, as Lincoln said, on the most radical political experiment known to man—an attempt to run a continent on Christian principles, by common consent. Many if not most successful editors of large-circulation periodicals have had parents who were in some form churchmen or educators. This gives them the necessary evangelical touch that sparks the drive to remake the world nearer the heart's desire. You have to truly believe the world can't get along without you to be a successful editor, politician, actor, or happy baby.

George Horace Lorimer, DeWitt and Lila Wallace, Bernard Kilgore, Henry Luce had teaching and preaching backgrounds. Mike Cowles' father was an Algona, Iowa, teacher before he turned successful publisher. The defect of Mike's inherited wealth may have slightly stood in his way, but not seriously enough to prevent his being about as successful an editor as boys lucky enough to start right at the bottom.

The Gould family's original American ancestor, Zaccheus, a middle-class emigrant from Ipswich, England, had helped establish, in 1638, Topsfield and Ipswich, Massachusetts. With his brother Daniel and half a dozen other Englishmen Zaccheus staked his life on America's future. Fortunately, his given name did not descend in the family, but, according to Beatrice, some of his worst characteristics have. Notably independent and stubborn, he was fined for sitting in church with his back turned to the minister, of whose ideas he apparently disapproved.

He is described as "a man of exceptional liberality in his theological ideas; maintaining friendly relations with Quakers and with Baptists although both were proscribed." Harboring a nephew, an outlawed Quaker, cost him another penalty in sterling. He "became probably the largest landowner in the region, his property at the time of his death being estimated at not less than 3,000 acres." But from earliest times these Ipswich men were willing to fight and risk for democracy.

From North Adams, Massachusetts, by that time peppered with Goulds, my own sturdy grandfather, Charles Wilbur Gould, ran away at ten to the Erie "Canawl," seeking fame and fortune. In a measure he found them. Early establishing the Elgin, Illinois, Board of Trade, which set commodity prices for butter, eggs, cheese, and milk thereabouts, he became comparatively wealthy in the burgeoning dairy business when nineteenth-century trusts were just emerging in that state. My father had thus grown up with his own sailboat and racehorse, with enough ready money so "Billy" Gould could pick up the tab. After graduation from Elgin Academy he had wanted to go on to Harvard to study law. With an excellent mind, a philosophic disposition, and a lifelong intellectual bent, he would have profited. But self-made Grandfather Gould thought my father shouldn't waste time at college. He should set up as a commodity broker in Chicago and start becoming rich. It was only when my grandfather, brashly and a little too heroically in the overweening pride of his personal success, entered the arena against the Chicago Bordens, and found himself suddenly with broken lance, pierced armor, and cut purse, that my father renounced trade, turned an intellectual socialist and remained one the rest of his life.

Of my grandfather I remember an unworried old gentleman with a kindly white beard carrying a gold-headed ebony cane I'm hoarding for my arthritic years. In his capacious side pocket a striped paper sack overflowed with jelly beans and corn candy available to the reaching hand of any child. He lived to eighty-six, maintaining the equanimity under stress which Beatrice says characterizes my family —which she blesses in our daughter.

Following my grandfather's financial collapse, my father, Wilbur Samuel Gould, precipitately retreated to rural Iowa, there to meet my red-headed mother, eight years younger. Singing contralto in Cascade's Methodist choir, dancing as long as there was music, and generally enjoying life, she seemed to be just waiting for him to come along. Dutifully Father joined the church, married, and, after two older sons were born, launched me on life's exciting roller coaster July 28, 1898, in Luana, Iowa, a village then and now of three hundred people.

I loved my huge father, respected and admired him, but I never quite understood him and his quiet, uncompetitive ways. In his calm temperament there was something too acquiescent, too philosophically acceptant of whatever the world poked into his hand.

As I grew old enough to be impertinent, my father's almost deliber-

ate refusal to use his considerable brain to compete actively in the
world struck me as odd. It seemed an actual betrayal of his obligation.
I once asked him why he had not exerted himself more to make
money.

"When I die," he said, finally, "I'll have as much as any man. Six
feet of earth."

Actually, my father needed a bit more than six feet if he weren't to
be crowded in death as, during his lifetime, lack of money constricted
his movements—he was six feet one and weighed in mint condition
210 pounds.

Perhaps, like Camus, he may have thought, "What better can a man
wish for than poverty? . . . With the possibility of activity in leisure?"

Younger, perhaps my father had not been so philosophical. He had
wanted to join the Gold Rush to Alaska but my mother put her foot
down—whether it was adventure or money that tempted him I don't
know. I do know that when her seafaring father, Sidney Walton Davison, who had a roving foot—he had gone to sea from Calais, Maine,
at twelve—tried to persuade my father to desert Iowa and take over
a coffee finca he had acquired in South America, my mother would
have none of that, either. She wanted her children, she said, "brought
up in the good old U.S.A."—and would not be budged. My mother
was fearfully set in her ways, which were Methodistically moral, intel-
ligently basic, and generally pretty sound. Perhaps they were limiting,
too, to her husband's wider interests, but if so he never complained.

Chromos of Eugene V. Debs and William Jennings Bryan dec-
orated our family's sparse walls. Between them hung the picture of
an even more outspoken reformer of that day—Teddy Roosevelt, a
political radical from the wicked East, where, I was led to believe,
the streets of Hell ran straight into the canyons of Wall Street. These
three mavericks were my father's political heroes. He believed that
the radical legislation Debs, Bryan, and Teddy then advocated would
soon become the law of the land. It took longer than he, who truly
believed in the Rights of Man, thought—for many it is still taking
longer.

When I was a boy I did feel sometimes that my mother was deprived. When I grew up and got rich I intended to make it all up to her. I'd buy her all the silk dresses she could wear. And I did. Apparently more than she actually needed. The first one I ever bought, green-blue silk with a lace collar, I found practically unused, neatly creased, among her effects when she died at the age of ninety-five.

In all my life at home I never heard a cross word between my parents. If my mother swore, it was only with her flashing eyes. "Rats!" was my father's most explicit expletive; it meant his temper had really been roused. The memory of his huge hand connecting with the seat of my small clothes, when he caught me cajoling my sister into swallowing a spoonful of mustard, reminds me still of his dislike of cruelty.

My two older brothers were athletes, robust, courageous fellows, stout football, basketball, and track men in their high school and college years, with only mildly scholarly interests. One was as English in temperament as the other pure Irish. They were my tormentors during much of my youth. I was not notably athletic, reading much, and fond of using long words I did not wholly understand. They thought my pastime putting on airs. Fortunately, the two younger members of the family, Ruth and Kenneth, were less contentious. Or maybe I was bigger than they were.

The Irish came from my mother, through a Raferty grandmother.

[Beatrice interpolates: Once sitting at a luncheon in Washington next to the wife of our just-appointed ambassador to Ireland, Bruce said to her that he had an Irish grandmother, a Raferty. "One of the Pittsburgh Raffertys?" she politely asked, being from Sewickley. "No, I think one of the Riff-Raffertys," he replied, so endearing himself to her that she promptly invited us to Ireland for a visit.]

My early years like any Midwest, semi-rural boyhood were punctuated by boys' battles, chips placed on shoulders, bloody noses. In east Des Moines, where we moved when I was four, we swam all summer at the third sandbar in muddy Brook's Lake. When circuses came to town and the roustabouts took over, we made sure we all swam and left in a body. They seemed like a pretty tough crowd to us decently brought-up youngsters. Their bawdy, obscene language was hardly fit even for the pages of a modern bestseller. By the age of six or eight I knew more about sex than I know now. I've found it isn't as simple as some of my early teachers made out. I remember one professor of applied sex, a gigantic Negro circus hand. A stolen suitcase, ripped by his huge knife, gaped open beside that sprawling, nude body. Drunk and garrulous, enjoying the summer sun, he filled our tender ears with details of his activities—he was an early advocate of integration. Talking with Dr. George H. Gallup once about our respective Iowa boyhoods, I found we agreed that by the time a small-town Iowa youngster was eight or nine he knew as much about the facts of life as he could later discover from Havelock Ellis, Krafft-Ebing, or even Ian Fleming—that is, if he'd hung around an Iowa livery stable and barbershop early on.

Despite all the external evidence to the contrary, my mother urged me to believe that the world was mine, if I'd but work hard. If you wanted to succeed, she said, you had to have "sand." Stick-to-it-iveness was all. Hang on and redouble your efforts. I heard all about Robert Bruce—and it was somehow mysteriously conveyed to me, without words, that I was perhaps Bruce's namesake, and probably in the direct line.

I suppose I could and should have considered myself an underprivileged child—though I doubt Huck Finn did and there was still, in those moneyless days in the Midwest, much of Huck and Tom Sawyer in our simple upbringing.

The Des Moines Public Library was the magic casement, swung wide by courtesy of Andrew Carnegie, which opened the world to my provincial eye. Borrowing my two older brothers' unused library cards, I lugged home six books at a time, all my skinny arm could carry. Father observed this with a mildly disturbed eye.

"I don't object, Bruce, to your reading such stuff," he admonished me. "But you must read good books as well."

We struck a bargain. For every two books of trash, I would read one good book, the austere librarian to be arbiter.

I was quite willing to read any number of good books as long as my endless supply of trash was not cut off. I couldn't kick that habit abruptly, without suffering excruciating withdrawal pains. Every available fairy tale, everything by Henty, Alger, and Conan Doyle, *The Liberty Boys of "76,"* I zipped through.

I gained an early degree of independence, basic knowledge of commerce, and a widening of my education through my paper route. The first drug addict I ever met was a customer. A pallid-faced widow in worn cotton dress, often under the influence of laudanum, she was good pay when not in a stupor. I knew what the two merry sisters, buxom in pinks and reds, with so many larky men friends, were up to long before the owner of the respectable apartment house they had invaded caught on. A college president customer shared his wisdom. Education, he said, would take me anywhere. I should look ahead and plan. I should be honest. The same things my mother and father persistently dinned into my ears.

And I learned at about the age of eight something of the dangers of sudden wealth when an older cousin, hearing that my father presented a dollar to each son on his birthday, took a sudden intense interest in me. He unselfishly helped me celebrate that glorious day, beginning with a bubbling chocolate soda; a double straw conserved our means for the splendid pleasures later offered by the Olympia Candy Kitchen's rainbowed gumdrops, sticky molasses kisses, walnut-coated nougat rolls, luscious maple creams, ending gloriously with sugar-crusted cream puffs and double banana splits. I returned home, completely penniless but completely happy, at dusk. I told my father how my cousin had even, as a final token of friendship, let me buy, on time, a wonderful pearl-handled penknife he had long treasured. But since I was now completely out of funds I didn't have to pay for it right away. My father turned the knife over in his huge hand, making no comment on the broken condition of the smaller blade.

"Bruce," he did say, finally, "if you want to buy this knife, after you have earned the money to pay for it, you may do so. You can't

Bruce's mother, Edna Earle (Davison), just before her marriage.

Beatrice's mother,
Mary Kathleen (Fluke),
at twenty.

Bruce, at four,
curls scissored by his own hand.

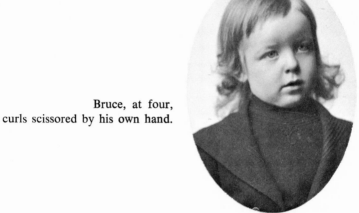

Beatrice's beady, exploring eye at two-and-a-half forecast her never-failing interest in life. Her sister, Florence, is at right.

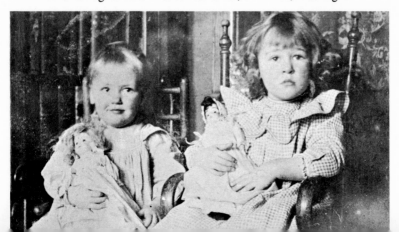

Bruce, a pensive high-school graduate at sixteen.

Pin-ups from the theatre and art world enlivened Bruce's student room.

Bruce's skinny Petruchio nearly collapsed carrying a hefty Kate.

Wings and gold stripe proved he was a naval aviator, but the war had ended.

buy it without funds. Return it with the explanation that I will not let you buy anything until you can pay for it."

Later, I remember proudly showing my father a suit bought with my own paper-route profits. He reminisced: "When I was your age, my clothes were always made for me."

I doubt he was doing more than remembering, but I suddenly saw my ill-fitting off-the-shelfs for what they were. My overweening boyish pride of achievement—the curse of the self-made man—was cut down to size. At a later day, when I walked across London's streets from Claridge's to Savile Row to be fitted by George VI's tailor, I'm sure I got a special bang out of the experience because of my father's early scorn of clothes off the rack. Contrast is the art of life as well as the life of art.

My father died at eighty-four, felled by a cerebral hemorrhage. As my mother left the hospital one evening, the last words she heard him say were "Goodnight, sweetheart."

Shakespeare somewhere says, "What a piece of work is a man!"

Thinking of the great women I have known—first, my mother, my wife, now my daughter, not to mention her budding darlings, Kathleen, Alison, and Susan, as well as the many other remarkable women who have crossed my path—I can't help saying: What a piece of work is woman! Each day rebuilding those she loves with food from breast and hand, she nourishes the strong, sustains the weak, raises the defeated when all seems lost. Giving life in the beginning, she gives faith at noontide, and love and comfort to the end.

I know I am full of sentiment. And what joy it has brought. I have had the rewards of my sentiment—or call it sentimentality, if you will.

I don't believe woman came from Adam—that rib is just one of man's feebler jokes; more likely Eve created Adam in the time-honored way and then dutifully, and more or less cheerfully, has been taking care of the lucky fellow ever since.

4

From Whence I Came

My mother had a leaping imagination and a more romantic attitude toward life than Bruce's mother. When my father moved to Emmetsburg, Iowa, where I was born, he fulfilled a promise: that when he attained the magnificent salary of $1,000 a year he would buy my mother the most beautiful silk she could find. The silk was rich blue moiré, thick and lustrous, the dress made by her high of shoulder, draped of skirt, ornamented (perhaps from *Ladies' Home Journal* fashion plates) with delicate hand-made ruchings of the silk. At her first party in Emmetsburg, where my father was now superintendent of schools, teacher of history and political science, my mother wore her new dress proudly, its color, I imagine, setting off her fair rosy skin, her shining brown hair, her lively blue eyes.

And this was her fascinating tale. At the same party was another dress, worn previously when its owner had been presented at the Court of St. James's. The other dress, whispering of queens and palaces, was neighbor to her own. How could life in our small frame house on a rutted Iowa street be dull, brushing as it did close to royal scenes across the sea?

But my mother was no idle daydreamer, longing for the unattainable. She intended to make life interesting and did. Daily tasks were speedily over; but, she said, "It takes integrity to make a bed." Tasks more challenging roused her spirit—a paper for the Browning Club, requiring much study ("There is no excellence without great labor"), or the creative triumph of the blue silk dress.

My mother, I think, awakened every morning with gratitude for the wonders that day might hold—changes in sky and weather, melting snow in the woodpile, the red bud on a maple, foretelling spring's wild birth, summer's opulence.

My earliest memory is of being snatched back from the soft, pleasant dust of our road, dangerous because at any moment a team might come trotting by, before a shiny black surrey or a farm wagon rolling cordwood to town. Soon would come the joyous sound of schoolchildren, freed at noon, scuffling, chattering, magic tall beings who could jump rope, roll hoops, go to school.

They announced my father, walking home with head erect and springy step—my good-looking father, with his high crisp curl of black hair, his red cheeks, his gray eyes, which could be so stern or so kind. When my father was in sight, I was allowed to run down the sidewalk like the big children and, holding his hand, walk comfortably into the house for noon dinner.

The round table in our dining room was the center of family life three times a day as I was growing up. (I never remember a meal in the kitchen except an occasional breakfast, later, during college vacations.) Everyone talked. My mother told of the washlady speaking of marriage: "It's like a jug handle—all on one side"; of the janitor admiring the creamy content of his pail after he had stripped the cow, "You won't find a catfish in this milk!" As soon as a child could toddle he was allowed to set knives, forks, and spoons, sometimes proudly carry in the pumpkin-pie dessert.

At the table we children were later encouraged to tell "Why I like *Ivanhoe*" or "The most interesting thing that happened to me today." We were even permitted to argue, provided it was about books, or the Civil War, and not the endless " 'Tis," " 'Tis not," of childhood. My father had been a formidable debater at college, where his purpose was to win; it took some years and my husband's humor to teach me that the dinner table should not be a debating society also. We talked politics. Woodrow Wilson, the scholar, was as well known to us, as children, as the man who sold licorice.

My father unfolded his dramas—the parent who said, "We'll get you if you don't pass my boy"; a prospective principal offering a bribe; tussles with a school board member insisting his prim spinster cousin be hired as seventh-grade teacher without qualifications. He loved his young, merry, pretty teachers who even though they had not studied all the "methods" held little children in their thrall, and was saddened that they *would* marry. He disliked dry old maids who used pointers and said, "How many sees it?" He spoke of his novel project for an "ungraded" room for retarded children, so they could enjoy achievement at their own level and not sit discouraged and hulking, in seats too small at the back of the room, overwhelmed by the difficulty of 2 times 4, or "Tom can run." Hungry children, he told us, could not learn, and he pioneered a morning-and-afternoon milk program in which the pupils gave their money to the teacher and no one knew who paid and who did not.

My father's people were mostly English, early arrivals on these shores. My grandfather, whose mother was a Sterling, had married Lophemia Kidder from Calais, Maine, and sold a carriage-making business in Pennsylvania to follow the lure of rich black Iowa land. He settled in a pretty curve of the Cedar River at Rochester, a small, hopeful village expecting prosperity when the railroad came through. But the life-giving railroad chose Cedar Rapids instead. The town remained tiny, sleepy, dwindling, its small rectangular brick or frame houses with centered doorways reminiscent of those earlier homes in Pennsylvania or Ohio that the pioneers had so hopefully left.

Father began to teach at seventeen and, not yet tall, had to lick the big boys who baited the teacher in winter when there was nothing else to do.

With money saved, he managed a year at the "Normal," state college for teachers. Again he taught, and scrimped again, to go another year to college. He was nearly thirty when he completed the normal-school course and, after a year at Riceville, was offered his first real position as superintendent at Emmetsburg, a village somewhat more sophisticated than anyone outside Iowa would expect.

My mother's early days had been passed mostly in Ohio, some of the time on her Grandfather Fluke's big farm. I have in my room today a contemporary drawing of the high, rectangular brick house, with four chimneys and stepped-down gable ends, built by my great-great-grandfather in memory of an earlier family house in Bedford County, Pennsylvania, where he was born.

My mother must have been a hungry child, as she remained of good appetite all her life. At ninety, she would ruefully conclude that she should not perhaps eat both pumpkin and hot mince pie, late, after an abundant Thanksgiving dinner, but asked to have one of them saved for her lunch next day. Her memories pictured for us, also fond of food, a farmhouse cold pantry where, in winter, a child could go and fondly count a dozen frozen pies—mince, apple, raisin— simply standing on the shelf, ready and waiting. She remembered a smokehouse with hams, and with sausages put down in lard; orchards laden with damsons, quinces, peaches, and cherries, and apple butter simmering spicily in huge iron kettles outdoors over a September flame.

Probably because of her own intense appreciation of food, my mother was an especially good cook. Poorly prepared dishes were, to her, almost a sin against generous nature. From her hand a plain boiled potato, mealy, freshly salted, lightly peppered, well buttered, hot, was a delight. On Sundays, though my mother had been to church with us, we came home to chicken with dumplings and golden gravy, Lady Baltimore cake and homemade ice cream; or juicy, deeply-browned pot roast, mashed potatoes feather light, open-faced apple pie, melting under a caramelized brown sugar and cinnamon.

I inherited my mother's hunger. I rise, keenly anticipating break-fast, and have always been greedy for the last drop of honey in the bowl, the last cookie on the plate. Food to me is one of the ardent pleasures of life. As Charles Lamb was suspicious of people who despised puns, so I tend to distrust people who do not look forward to their meals with anticipation and savor every bite.

My mother, spirited, fresh-faced, ever ambitious to see something of the world, had at eighteen sewed herself a wardrobe. In her second-best dark blue, with plaid cape, a small self-made plaid cap perched high on her golden-brown pompadour, she took herself bravely to the Normal. There she earned her living as assistant librarian. There she met my father, seven years her senior.

My parents seemed to have unbounded confidence in their own abilities, derived perhaps from their pioneering ancestors. They could turn their hands to almost any useful chore daily life demanded. So my mother sewed slipcovers, curtains, quilts, dresses, hats, and winter coats for her daughters. Years later, to my great astonishment, I was named one of the ten best-dressed coeds at the State University of Iowa. My major costume that winter had been a purple wool dress my mother had made from a two-year-old suit. On my head perched a turban devised from purple wool scraps, embroidered all over with yarn roses in lilac, soft blue and dusty pink. Wide choirboy collars of organdy in these pale flower tints varied the dailiness of my dress.

Mother did her own housework, except for sporadic aid from a washlady one day a week, even more sporadic cleaning help. These women varied, tall, short, lean, and fat, but they had one common quality—they had drunken husbands. I remember poor fat Mrs. Hubbard, crying over her washboard as she told how her husband, in liquor, came home and knocked her about; crying again, she told us she had taken cake to the jail, how sad to see him locked up there, all her fault. Dainty Mrs. Fisher cleaned and dusted our living room into disarray, every chair, every book set catty-cornered. "I like to make things look nice," she said, "sort of sprangle them around."

My mother still found time for serious reading and Sunday-afternoon drives beside my father, wearing her white wool suit and her black hat with a plume, her three well-dressed, frequently quarreling children wedged into the back of the buggy, behind the handsome bay Robert E. Lee. I was never sure in those days whether my father was prouder of his horse or of his children.

My active father worked in his vegetable garden an hour or so before breakfast in spring and summer. He loved long walks, strong swims in Minnesota lakes and Iowa rivers, with his old-fashioned breast stroke which he taught us all, along with fishing and rowing. He was an excellent shot (from boyhood days); so good that once, in his sixties, when offered a chance to shoot a little target practice with Bruce, he said, "Well, Bruce, my hand is getting pretty shaky," the 38-calibre pistol positively dancing in his hand as he took it; then he lifted it and—ping, ping, ping—he hit the tin can three times running. I'd forgotten to tell Bruce that the high-school rifle team he'd coached had won the national championship.

"I always wanted to be a lawyer" was the only complaint I ever heard him make about the slow, difficult process of his education.

He would have been a good one, too. He had a clear, almost too logical mind, a retentive memory, and a certain natural contentiousness about proving the other fellow wrong. He spoke well, with a dry wit. Late in his life my husband tried to persuade him never to drink raw milk, pointing out vividly the dangers of T.B. or undulant fever in drinking milk fresh from the cow. I heard my father, at eighty-two, say: "Well, Bruce, it may get me yet."

Bruce decided to let him die in his own hard-headed way, He did, at eighty-seven, of natural causes.

Almost every summer my father took a six-weeks course either at the State University of Iowa or at the University of Chicago and once even at Teachers College in New York, where he acquired a dislike for "methods" and a deeper belief in "humanities."

My mother, in Iowa City, walked a mile almost every morning to study advanced English and French, supplementing her two-year normal course with a B.A. Later, in her fifties, she gained a master's degree at Columbia, and she obtained a driver's license (after thirteen trials) at the age of seventy-three.

My parents believed it might be true that each person was born with a more or less fixed amount of brains (we didn't call it I.Q. then), but those brains were better if you burnished them. My mother often read early in bed—Shakespeare or the Bible—coming to her day's duties of cooking and dishwashing with her mind filled and her speech colored by their great poetry; my father did his thinking in the garden while he wielded a hoe around the cucumbers.

Deeply religious, my mother became a "convinced" Friend in her sixties, believing in the worth of each human soul—"that of God in every man" the Quakers say. But she never confused equality of soul with equality of attainment, considering that discriminating perception as to character, mind, and spirit is necessary in man's pursuit of excellence.

At home Mother could always suggest interesting games for children. Her clothes chest yielded a cape and a plumed hat for young Lochinvar; a lace-curtain-gowned Sleeping Beauty. On rainy days my sister Florence, perceptive companion then and now, made "autobiographies" with me, cutting from magazines glamorous pillared Southern mansions, dashing heroes, gentle Shetlands, ladies in high-bosomed gowns, to be described in the resulting picture books as "my ancestral home," "my parents," "my beloved pony, Star," and finally, end of the story, "my fiancé."

What wonder I have been a romantic all my life, casting an aura of perhaps fancied charm around the things I have, and see, and do— houses, friends, grandchildren like little peaches, like children in Renoir paintings, with thick lashes, dimpling apple cheeks, clear, wonderful eyes.

Our happiest home was in Iowa City. Here the old capitol building—Iowa City was state capital from 1846 to 1857—stood in the center of a university campus sloping gently down to the river. The slender, classical white building faced down new, ambitious Iowa Avenue, a "boulevard" centered by a mile of grass and shrubbery. We lived at the far end, where in a loop of twelve or fourteen wide-lawned houses we had our own private gate bearing the name "Woodlawn." We felt grand—at one end the famous old capitol, at the other end, Us.

There we gave plays in the hayloft. My younger brother, Roger, allowed me to play baseball with his team, thus fostering a lifelong passion for that most dramatic game, each player chewing, hawking, spitting, artful as any ballet dancer, at every turn, alone with his skill, alone against his fate.

There my first bicycle enabled me to go swiftly alone to new streets and distant places. Bicycles were frequent then; my father often rode his to school, as did stately professors, their long white beards floating interestingly in the breeze.

How forget the blithe summer day when I put on with ceremony my new red and white dotted swiss dress, braked down our rutted road to Woodlawn gate, sped the paved length of Iowa Avenue to Reichardt's Candy Kitchen. With queenly air, alone and grand, I ordered a maple-nut sundae at ten cents—a moment unsurpassed by Friday night at Maxim's later. Some of this same joy in swiftness I still feel as I speed down the Queen's Highway at Hope Town in the Bahamas.

My parents enjoyed the faculty society. Especially if the president and his wife were coming to a dinner my sister and I handpainted place cards and bonbon dishes with autumn leaves or tulips. Immediately after noon two tall, gaunt Bohemian women, the Kaspar sisters, arrived with enormous pots and kettles, cooked and served the meal. Practically no one but the president of the university gave a dinner party without the Kaspar sisters.

Alfred North Whitehead says, "Education takes place between 12 and 20, but character is formed from the mother's training in the home." Nowadays, we often seem to suggest that human character as well as intelligence is shaped before birth, springs full-blown from such random genes as we happen to inherit from this ancestor or that. I suppose no woman, no mother, ever quite agrees to that, except perhaps in failure.

In his strange and fascinating autobiography *Ushant,* Conrad Aiken has a passage to which one returns:

"One denies the good, and dishonors it, ostensibly in the name of freedom; but really because one knows that the good and beautiful are good and beautiful exactly insofar as they are *binding.*"

This sense of the limitations imposed by any aspiration of ethics or aesthetics can scarcely be transmitted in words. But it can be felt in the channeling of a disciplined childhood, where certain aims are expected, and certain limitations are imposed on the means of achieving one's aims.

Goodness and badness were clearer then. Being good meant being kind, being fair, being honest, and trying. At our round dining-table school-in-living-together were even quoted such words as "The cheater cheats himself" or those of Sir Walter Scott on his deathbed, to his son, "Try to be a good man. It is the only thing that will comfort you when you come to lie where I am lying now." My mother was high-spirited, quick of tongue. My father was stubborn and slower. They disagreed about a number of things: how their children should be educated, whether money should be spent for the country club and pretty dresses or saved to pay off farm mortgages. But I am grateful to both my parents, for many things—most of all for a sense of interest in daily living, of riches at hand for all who will reach out and take them.

Growing up in small towns, Bruce and I felt ourselves a part of the main middle stream of American life and thought. Middle West, middle class, middle income—how dull the Midwest has been made to sound. To both of us, growing up, it seemed a vivid, amusing base from which to go anywhere, to do anything, to launch into any orbit.

Tall, verbally precocious, only sixteen, socially still terrified, I returned from our later home, Ottumwa, Wapello County, Iowa (Indian names), and plunged with zest rather more into the social than the intellectual life of the pleasant, coeducational university—unpacking my handmade, lace-trimmed batiste underwear, my lisle stockings, my high-button shoes and two of the most delicious dresses anyone ever set eyes upon.

One was dark green silk with a white corded-silk collar and a rose-red flower on the shoulder; another had a pale gray taffeta basque bodice with tiny buttons up the front, a full skirt of pale gray chiffon, inset with points of gray taffeta—the whole over a flame-colored petticoat. These were works of art from my dear mother, whose skills of hand and heart persisted through party dresses of lilac and daffodil for her redheaded granddaughter, then on to doll costumes for three new young redheads.

Later my mother rested afternoons under a jewel-toned quilt, sapphire, ruby red, amethyst, jade, pieced from scraps of our college party dresses. With the same marvelous sense of color she later inspired our little granddaughters to crochet small rag rugs in vibrant oranges, pinks, and scarlet.

Kind older sorority sisters provided blind dates to get me started at Iowa. There were lots of parties. Appearance was practically obligatory at "Varsity," a big all-college dance, admission $1, held every Saturday night in a bleak hall with an excited band playing "When You Wore a Tulip," "Apple Blossom Time in Normandy," "Pretty Baby." We called our escorts "Mr.," and it was a significant moment (and could be an exquisite pleasure) when a shy, formal lad would say, "Miss Blackmar, may I call you Beatrice?" I danced about, not very skillfully, tongue-tied but happy, because I was there and seen. One merry youth, a chatterbox himself, took a fancy to my shyness and taught me to dance. He also taught me a song, "Sweetheart of Sigma Chi," and began, eventually, to hope I would be his, thus enabling me to obtain a fragile hold on the most enviable status of being "a popular girl."

Everyone must have an unhappy love affair.

A handsome junior, a college Prince Charming, talked about as the most fabulous date on the campus, actually looked at me, a freshman of sixteen, tall, slightly pudgy, fresh-faced, and dimpled. It never occurred to me that he was not the prince of Cinderella's tale; I certainly was the Sleeping Beauty.

The new beau had handsome, deep-blue eyes, fair, curly hair, and an engaging smile. By the time our slight romance had progressed to prolonged tête-à-têtes, I was so ensorcelled I did not realize we had little to talk about. We parted on a moonlit June weekend—he for a summer job in Kansas, and I for home to wait for his letters, which were affectionate in June, dwindling in July; by August he had a girl in Kansas. Next fall he fell, partially, in love with a pretty freshman and we never had another date.

The experience was painful but I learned that "the other girls' " estimate of a man need not necessarily be mine. I was freed to make my own judgments. I remember clearly the beginning of adulthood. I was propped up on my lumpy college bed, knitting a scarlet sweater. I had just refused an invitation to Varsity from a boy who did not especially interest me. If I preferred to read H. G. Wells rather than go dancing I could do so. I did not have to be what others expected. I could be the kind of person I myself wanted to be.

Hope is itself a species of happiness.
—SAMUEL JOHNSON

5 ❧

First There Is the Dream

In Des Moines' schools the demands made on us were not rigorous. It wasn't difficult to excel. But there were not many advantages in being near the head of your class when the pretty girls all fell for body-contact athletes.

Even though the bewitching girls did languish after gridiron heroes, I early felt that professionalized school athletics took more out of you than you got back, as I watched my muscled brothers nurse broken ankles and torn ligaments. I pointed out to them that both Euripides and Emperor Alexander contemned professional athletes. They only snorted, "You think you know too much!" Being ready to swing on anyone, despite my slight heft, who tried me too far barely saved me from the implication of being a sissy.

My dream of Broadway and New York started, I suppose, by discovering in our family's Dickens, Scott, Dumas, Opening-of-the-Chestnut-Burr type of library a huge leather-bound *Complete Shakespeare,* with an introduction by William Winter, Broadway's reigning critic in the nineties. It was too heavy, of course, for my scrawny ten-year-old arm, but, draped over it like an underfed dragonfly, I systematically devoured the volume opened on the drafty parlor floor and forgot where I was in the ensuing enchantment. Old-fashioned steel engravings showed Mrs. Siddons as Lady Macbeth, complete with bloody dagger. Garrick, Macready, Edwin Booth gazed back at me in all their costumed magnificence.

My father, when he discovered my absurdly passionate interest, lamented I would never see Booth's Hamlet, agreeing with William Winter it was "a part in which he has no living equal." Nor could any actress, ever, be as beautiful as Mary Anderson, whom my father had seen playing Juliet. Sadly, he shook his head. What I had irrevocably missed! I couldn't tell him I would see Sarah Bernhardt, wooden leg and all. And John Barrymore playing Hamlet longer than Irving did in London. Richard Burton's much later Hamlet was merely an interesting one—but Jane Cowl and Katharine Cornell were quite lovely Juliets. Ethel Barrymore was, well, Ethel Barrymore—as Juliet or Rose Bernd.

It wasn't until I was a full eleven and—turning my back on my father's socialism—already a businessman (buy cheap, sell dear, as carrier of a paper route) that I actually entered a theatre. I saw a real play for the first time. It sealed my doom.

Nor was it Hamlet that turned the trick. By that time I had, of course, read Hamlet several times—I hadn't gotten it all the first time round. The drama that made me willing slave to the theatre's Aladdin's lamp was called—and this title I am never likely to forget—*Sure Shot Sam*.

My elder brother, Earl, though not a devotee of the arts, ushered me into my first theatre, the Grand, where road shows broke the jump between Chicago and Omaha. From courtly Mr. Ernest, the only circulation manager I was ever to know who daily wore the high, wing-tip collar of capitalism, my brother had received a precious pair of Annie Oakleys. Two little boys in their best knickers were deferentially seated by a deliciously perfumed usher in the middle of the sixth row center—still my favorite spot from which to see a show. The lively music I located finally, by peering, was coming from nearly under the footlights. There was a sudden dimming of lights, the slow swishing rise of the curtain—as entrancing as the frou-frou of a beautiful woman coming toward you—and the play began.

My brother was treating me to this exotic evening because of my invaluable help with his heavy Sunday paper route, which took him, even with me along, until late noontime to deliver. Together we rose in the often ten-degree-below-zero cold of a typical Iowa winter. At 2 A.M. we went forth to make sure the good, unshivering people of Des Moines could laugh at Happy Hooligan, Buster Brown, and the Katzenjammer Kids. It wasn't easy to get such a willing helper as I at fifteen cents an hour—when the snow was twelve to twenty inches deep. My brother was showing his gratitude—according to Rochefoucauld "a lively expectation of favors to come"—by allowing me to tag along to the theatre.

I wish I could see *Sure Shot Sam* now—but I'd like to be eleven again. Since this is a more sophisticated day, maybe nine would be better. At the climactic moment, Sure Shot Sam, arriving from behind a convenient rock near the wings—he seemed to fairly spring from the ground—raised his trusty rifle and with one deadly bullet blew to smithereens the coiled rattlesnake about to sink its poisoned fangs into Sam's best friend, spread-eagled by heartless villains on the blazing desert sands. I think I got a piece of that blasted snake in my eye—at least for a moment I couldn't see very clearly as I wiped it in relief. The theatre that caught me that evening never let me go. I knew if I were ever allowed on my own to slip behind the proscenium arch—that keyhole to paradise—I would never ask for more.

Through an overstuffed school friend, Hubert, whose father was a baker happily employed in the Hotel Savery just across the alley from the stage door of the Grand, I could see plays free, I found. In exchange for an occasional pie or cake, the hungry doorman would slip us backstage through his magic portal. While he chomped on pie, we assuaged our own kind of hunger, deftly dodging harried stagehands. Occasionally, we were let stand in the wings, pressing hard and breathless against the flats as the Thespians entered and exited. The admiration in our bedazzled teen-age eyes must have satiated even an actor's ego. As we looked up into Kitty Gordon's aloof, made-up face that moment before going on, I could have leaned around and daringly kissed her famous back. What would she have done? It was bared, as advertised, all the mysterious way down to there—like a later Nita Naldi's—long before women had backs, and decades before *Playboy* was to sell bosoms by the pound. Julia Sanderson and Donald Brian waltzed out from the wings just the way I hoped to waltz the first time I stepped onto a ballroom floor to astonish my friends, without, of course, any previous practice. I mingled with the smelly mob of beggars surrounding Otis Skinner in *Kismet.* I suffered in the very crypt with Julia Marlowe dying in happy agony across the still warm corpse of Sothern's befuddled Romeo. I thought *Officer 666* the funniest comedy ever written. I believed William Faversham the most polished actor—what a way he had with a negligent pair of gloves!—Cyril Maude the most deft. David Warfield hardly acted at all.

It isn't surprising that I decided to go to far-off, beckoning New York at the earliest opportunity. I would write plays. Perhaps I would become a dramatic critic, like Winter. To get to New York was, of course, the problem, not the mere writing of plays.

Being around newspaper offices as a paper carrier, I saw reporters drifting in and out on their vagrant way to and from somewhere. One needn't, I realized, be hopelessly anchored to any city or town. The whole world was yours, just for the venturing. Couldn't I become a newspaperman, too—when the need arose—until I made my mark as playwright?

Hope, Lord Bacon said, makes a good breakfast but an ill supper. In my youth I didn't dine out much but I ate a big breakfast. I have always allowed myself, every day, ten, sometimes fifteen minutes of concentrated daydreaming. Like those remarkable remedies advertised in old-fashioned almanacs, daydreaming is good for almost anything that ails you. Its tonic effect on the spirit brings the flush of youth to the cheek. It restores the natural sparkle to the eye. That draggy feeling disappears. In fifteen minutes I've made fortunes in the Street. I've written half a dozen best sellers in ten. You walk, in your daydream, up to your most fearsome enemy and give him a couple of good smacks—he wilts. In five minutes I have conquered the most beautiful women in the world. They were grateful. I have advised

Presidents as to national policy. Astonishingly, for I've not always had the greatest respect for the intelligence of such Chief Executives as I've known, they have listened and immediately acted on my good advice. In daydreams. Presidents are certainly not very open-minded to suggestions in real life, or editorial writers and political columnists would have long since cleaned up every presidential problem. Come to think of it, writing political columns may be a kind of real-life day-dreaming I've somehow neglected.

To supplement my legitimate-theatre fare, scantier than I wished, I early formed the habit of going to every movie in town. Returning home from my west-side newspaper route I had to pass the Lyric, the Bijou, and the Strand. My mother simply gave up expecting me home for supper until she saw me walk into our humble home from whatever fairyland I'd just been visiting.

Through the movies, which were often preceded by a Burton Holmes travelogue to strange, wonderful places like Bangkok, the Blue Nile, Hong Kong, I moved into a world of unlimited splendor—as if I weren't even living in Des Moines at all. I walked the streets of cities I one day planned to see. I saw how people acted in hovels and castles. With the stars I ate in fine restaurants with fantastically intricate implements, in a dazzling world of fashion. I fell in love successively with Clara Kimball Young, Lillian Gish, and Elsie Ferguson, who had me completely bewitched until Norma Talmadge came along. My eyes swam with tearful laughter at the elemental distress of Charlie Chaplin.

Three high-school friends, as different as may be, introduced me to the magic of poetry, music, and the strange world of *fin de siècle* literature. I found, as Camus expressed it, "I could not live without beauty though that made me weak in the face of certain people."

A more unlikely troubadour than Warren Bassett would be hard to find, unless Yogi Berra suddenly befuddled umpires by spouting Swinburne at them from his squat behind the plate. Heavy-set, slightly bandy-legged, with a brow-obscuring shock of black hair, Warren worshiped poetry and brought into my life Housman, Dowson, Verlaine. He pined over pale, delicate, pre-Raphaelite females only, though in cornfed Iowa they were in short supply. Since his outer shell belied the truly sensitive poetic nature within, he understandably worshiped from afar. This is an ideal vantage point from which to write love lyrics. No one whose love is requited ever, I suspect, writes poetry of passion. Lovemaking, its own poetry, requires no further exposition.

Laurence Carter, slight, somewhat fey, looking like a lost leprechaun on a mystifying mission from nowhere, a boy seemingly born to escape attention, first made me aware, in high school, of music. Through him, the door to a world of music opened slightly. Laurence, at an early age, had gone on from Beethoven and Berlioz to Schönberg, Stravinsky, and even Ives.

From Harold Andrews I learned that all who did not recognize genius, especially ours, were Philistines—worthy only of contempt. Most of the populace, he assured me, were Philistines, and I was inclined to agree, since it suited my purpose. Oscar Wilde I heard of for the first time and of Wilde's wit Harold had mastered a fair working copy, handy whenever it was necessary for him to resist actual toil. Good-looking as F. Scott Fitzgerald, Harold eased over life's gritty moments—as he charmed all the girls—in a manner I could but envy. Until I met George Kaufman, Heywood Broun, George Jean Nathan, Ogden Nash, Walter Elliot, Harold seemed to me quite the wittiest young man in the world, Warren the most poetic, Laurence the shyest. The nicest too, and, being so, he died young. Somehow the friendships of one's boyhood have a kind of joyous discovery the more cautious friendships of adult years lack.

Under the prodding of my father and my teachers and through the diverse interests of my three far-ranging friends, I gradually learned a little about writers like Hawthorne; Mark Twain, who seemed to me the best; Cooper, the most exciting; O. Henry, whom I still like; Prescott; Stevenson; Bierce, who shivered my mind with his cold wit; Kipling. Finally, even Anatole France, Stendhal, Turgenev and Tolstoi were brought to my attention. Eventually, most of the vast treasure ships of literature moved slowly into view and like a ruthless pirate I raided them all for their golden treasure.

But I have never really lost my taste for thrillers like *Trent's Last Case, Rebecca, The Bellamy Trial,* and the lusty adventure tales of

John Buchan. The sadism, brutality, and crude sex of modern thrillers I can stand but don't much care for, but a good story that makes one momentarily forget the house is afire, the pig is loose, and the baby has wandered into the street again—a story, I fear, my father might call trash—holds me fast.

The most interesting thing about my East Des Moines High School days was my editing the monthly school magazine, *The Quill,* and the senior yearbook. The latter was, for me, unique. Halfway out of knickers, I was wholly in love—passionately, permanently, but very privately with blonde Gretchen Koenigsberger. Her black patent-leather, sixteen-button, white-canvas-topped shoes, almost but not quite obscuring the delectable swell of her calves, wildly stirred my heart. Gretchen was light years ahead of me, in 1915-1916, in swishy, sophisticated gaiety, and the boy's-size Norfolk jacket I was thriftily wearing, contrasting oddly with my new long pants of some wonderfully iridescent material, was, let's face it, no hussar's cape— my wrists dangled too far out of the sleeves; so I had just sufficient glimmerings as to my chances with that *princesse lointaine* never to declare my love—strictly daydreaming again. Besides, Gretchen, the only child of an affluent harnessmaker, was being ardently beaued by men seriously intent on marriage, which, to me, was only another word in the dictionary. One of the few I'd never cared to look up. But I could, and did, publish seventeen separate and stunning snap-shots of the delectable Gretchen in the *Quill Year Book,* as if it had been my private diary. It is as clinching an argument, I suppose, as anything could be against the right of any editor to print whatever he pleases when freedom of the press palpably becomes mere license.

When I graduated from East Des Moines High in 1916, at the age of seventeen, my father, anticipating Yale's Kingman Brewster in his today's dictum that the too young should work after high school rather than go to college at once, decided I should make a little money to-ward my tuition. For I would have to finance my college education at Grinnell, Iowa, where my older brother had paved the way.

It was decided I'd take over the job my brother Ralph had held for a year at the General Film Exchange, receiving $15 a week as poster boy.

In this job I learned how foolish it is to waste one's precious time dawdling over chores. The desire to do routine tasks quickly, so as to leave more time for daydreaming, made me a clean-desk man for life.

On late Tuesday morning when Stambaugh, the film exchange manager, stuck an inquiring head into my cubicle, he found I had finished the week's work—distributing glossy photographs and posters of Anna Q. Nilsson and Mae Marsh to the movie houses by railway express throughout Iowa so the public would know what was coming Saturday night. Indicating some incredulity, even alarm—he didn't want the posters and photographs scattered as if by an Iowa tornado —he murmured something about haste makes waste.

"Everything," I assured him in the resolute tones of an Alger hero in the making, "is all right."

Stambaugh left, slightly puzzled, but found next Tuesday the job all done an hour earlier. I admitted I couldn't better that time.

Perhaps he had been wondering whether the booker, the person just above me on the office totem pole, really needed a full week for supervising the distributing of film. In a trial heat I found it could be done in two days. So Stambaugh merged the two jobs, raised me to $25 a week and sent the booker on the road to sell films.

Since Stambaugh's sole occupation, it seemed to me—besides peering through his secretary's pink georgette crepe blouse at what must surely be expected to be there—was to sit in his office wearing each day a new version of cerise-yellow-blue-striped silk shirt, he decided that I could do his job, too. He upped my salary to $35 a week, called me assistant manager and let me express the posters, book film, and wear a $12 silk shirt more soprano than his that I had hastily purchased from Younker's to honor my new position. He joined the booker on the road drumming up business, silk shirt and all, the better to impress exhibitors who might think him direct from Hollywood.

A reorganization unexpectedly ordered from New York sent

Stambaugh to Minneapolis and ordered me to transfer the Des Moines office to Omaha. In recognition of my phenomenal rise, New York telegraphically suggested I take over Kansas City as manager.

When I went to Omaha, I ate, at company expense, in a restaurant for the first time. I can well remember the haze obscuring my sight of a doublefold menu filled with a strange variety of dishes, some in French, while a doubtless sneering waiter hovered contemptuously at my elbow. I scanned blurring type; "Hash" came clear. Hash and apple pie. I lived on both for several days. Then, taking a chance, I made the startling discovery one day that filet mignon was steak.

Though I now had my first complete long-pants suit, the eyebrows of the Omaha manager, a solid businessman of fifty, shot to Barrymore heights at my unexpected youth. True, I had barely turned eighteen and was just getting over acne. He wondered whether he shouldn't warn the New York office. Airily I completed my job of transferring necessary records and then informed him I was resigning to start college in the fall, cutting short my career in the mushrooming movie business, where, with any luck, I might have married the boss's daughter and risen to the top. Wearing the most gaudy of my newly acquired silk shirts, I swiveled my eyes toward Grinnell.

As I entered college, World War I had just reached the United States and young men, over twenty-one, were being drafted. My brother Earl had instantly volunteered and been turned down for officers' training. Eight years of playing varsity tackle—it was then considered sissy not to play straight through the entire game—had given him not one but two trick knees. Occasionally they cripplingly slipped out—not a recommendation for a combat officer. Even the draft board wouldn't take him. My other football-playing brother, turned down by the air corps for some slight respiratory defect, had, however, been promptly called up.

Not twenty-one until the middle of 1919, my mind more on art, aesthetics, intellectual pursuits, and girls than on the war, I looked, in 1917, unlikely ever to be drafted. For it was taken for granted that, once the Yanks landed in Europe, they would put an end to the nonsense overseas. George M. Cohan's "Over There" had already warned the Germans what to expect.

When I left for Grinnell it was with my mind solely on journalism, and Broadway playwriting once I'd graduated. My silk shirts, I felt, should get some sort of campus recognition. In this I was speedily disappointed; everybody there had silk shirts, more lurid, if possible, than mine. Silk shirts were, in fact, already a bit passé.

An earnest student working his way through Grinnell enjoyed a submerged though respected status. There was always the possibility he might amount to something, as would Harry Hopkins, just graduated, and Joe Welch, an especially bright and revered friend of Earl's who was to become Joe McCarthy's doughty David. In return for an attic room—happily one with a double bed ample for my sprawling six feet—I fired the furnace and shoveled off snow-covered walks for the affluent widow Peterson. For Stokes Drugstore, at sixty cents an hour, I learned, as man-of-all-work, to drive the car my family could not afford; became something of an expert repairman of Victrolas; and, incidentally, learned more about music in the course of playing and selling records.

But principally at Grinnell I fell in love with a freshman English teacher some years my senior. Good-looking—perhaps a little too plump—this worldly Vassar graduate seemed to know more about poetry, painting, and people than I ever expected to learn. She was putting in time in Grinnell's academic world while her fiancé served in revolutionary Russia with a valiant YMCA. Our affair had all the tempestuousness of grand opera, where the music sounds better than the words. Elinor's engagement ring gradually slipped off her finger or, at most, by May, loosely dangled there. I'm sure I benefited from this lively, impassioned experience. Baudelaire says, "Be always drunken. On love, on wine, or on virtue. But be always drunken."

Women only get fat when they are unhappy so my inspiring inamorata ended her first academic year eighteen pounds slimmer. I had begun thin as a rail so I only gained pounds of experience. I made an important discovery—that Vassar is not as far from Grinnell as it had seemed. Confidence can come to an awkward young man realizing for the first time that he, ill-equipped, somehow may interest a sophisticated older woman. Maybe the episode made me happy, too, but at 140 pounds, and six feet one, I barely weighed enough to be accepted by the Navy as a cadet for naval flying—with a waiver for underweight. For even in the latter days of our college romance my errant mind had already turned to what seemed an even more romantic interest.

Suddenly, still in my freshman year, my spirit flamed with the desire to be an aviator. Maybe, at bottom, I had something of any normal boy's desire to defend his country, particularly if it could be done heroically, with me in the center of the daydream. At a display of aerial pyrotechnics in Chicago, a pair of French aces in Spads tore the sky to ribbons. Guynemer, René Fonck, even the deadly Richthofen, came heroically alive. The Army Air Corps, overloaded with applications from young boys aspiring to risk their necks, had closed recruiting. But Naval Aviation, seemingly unheard of in Iowa—and I had yet to see the ocean—still took applications, even from boys as young as I, nineteen. I passed all physical examinations with ease. Duly I was enrolled as a Naval Aviation cadet, subject to immediate call. Astonished myself, I felt so delighted my pride wasn't hurt at others' even greater amazement.

Sworn in, and departing for ground school in Minneapolis' Dunwoody Institute, I wasn't unduly full of military ardor. I did want to fly. I would have liked to be a hero—preferably at no cost of pain. I wished I were better looking for the hero's role. I had chosen single combat training.

What my mother thought, as we said goodbye, I don't know. She was not one for tears. Now that I think of it, I don't believe I ever saw her weep. She wasn't smiling. Perhaps she thought I needn't have gone. She already had one boy in service. If this was her thought, she said nothing. My father pressed my hand hard, and, a surprise, kissed me on the mouth.

In the huge Minneapolis Naval Receiving Center, someone tossed me a pair of floppy pants, canvas leggings, an ill-fitting shirt, and a gob's hat I didn't know how to shape or wear. The military's idea being that idle hands make for the devil's work, I was immediately put to the task of cleaning the head. The flower of America's youth!

End of daydream.

Truth is the hardest missile one can be pelted with.
—GEORGE ELIOT

6 🐦

Learning by Teaching

After two years of self-romanticizing at the University of Iowa, with plenty of boys to smile at, and good marks altogether too easy to win, I was suddenly plunged into harder work than I had known, or imagined. And there a single word, the word *chimney*—or *chimley* in its local variation—perhaps changed the course of my life. At least it turned me into a journalist.

My father, doubtless feeling that his own spine had been stiffened by his early struggles, had decreed that both my sister and I should stay out of college after two years there, and teach school. My time had now arrived and, rebellious, resenting this hard interference with my pleasure, I was plunged into the most valuable, probably because it was the most difficult, experience of my life.

I was to teach in a one-room school, heated by a stove, with outdoor toilets, in a hilly, back-country district seven miles from Ottumwa. My classes included first-to-eighth-grade boys and girls from six to fifteen, there to learn reading, writing, arithmetic, history, geography, music. I served also as playground supervisor and janitor, keeping the room warm with a wood fire in the big black stove.

The farmer with the best house in the district usually took in the teacher. Among his large cheerful family I lived, paying $20 a month for board out of my salary of $50. My room looked neat, with iron bedstead and golden-oak dresser. And private, in September, with its own bowl and pitcher facilities. But, as chill November came, in that unheated room with water icy from the night, washing shrank to an uncomfortable minimum. Perhaps the boys at Groton, like Thomas Carlyle, have more stamina about breaking ice in the wash basin. I rather envied members of the family their more sociable morning splutterings over a tin basin in the kitchen, with warm water from the roaring range and the cozy roller towel nearby.

We breakfasted in the same warm kitchen on fried ham and eggs, frequently with pancakes on the side. My merry, handsome landlady, with bright blue eyes and the prettiest arms I have ever seen, strong, firm, yet tapering to slender capable wrists and hands, who seemed to surmount the drudgery of farm life with fun and inner gaiety, would be preparing my lunch: frequently a cold fried egg between thick slabs of homemade bread, cookies, cake, or a piece of pie as dessert. Fried or mashed potatoes with gravy, fried chicken or pork, hot biscuits made our suppers. Putting on rubbers or overshoes as the day required, my paper sack of lunch clutched in my hand, I would set out on the two-mile walk to school, over a rough, rutted road and a couple of barbed-wire fences, across a rolling, stubby cornfield, and then to the chill schoolroom. For the first few weeks sheer fright at the task I had undertaken walked with me most of the way.

The last weeks of summer had slipped pleasantly by—tennis on the YWCA court, my usual reading diet of romances, endless letters to absent friends detailing my father's cruelty in the course he required. I gave little thought to my future career. Teaching seemed to me something anyone could do. And, if I had ever known, I had mercifully forgotten the infinite variety, for good or ill, of the human young.

The first morning came. And as I stood there looking into those seventeen pairs of eyes, curious, measuring, challenging, with that implacability of childhood which will take every inch of advantage if an adult wavers, my confidence ran out of my toes. I was totally unprepared for a coherent morning's program, let alone the days and weeks to follow. In that awful moment the realization came that no one could help me but myself, that I alone was responsible for this frightening group of children, ranging from three little pig-tailed girls of six to the biggest boy, freckled, lanky, fifteen, taller than I. Some were illiterate, some apathetic or resentful, some perhaps all too clever for me. I must keep them orderly and learning, and unless I controlled them they would overwhelm me.

In a frozen calm, my hands clammy, I stared severely at those staring unresponsive faces. I welcomed them. I told them I was happy to be there. We would have a good year together. I wrote my name on the blackboard. Still they stared at me with eyes like oysters.

Suddenly I remembered my first college English class—write an essay about yourself. Pencils and paper were handed round. Each child was asked to set down a "get acquainted" piece. Since my scholars were not fluent writers I gained a few moments of quiet (the little ones were soothed with crayons) and saw that I must ask the children to help me. Willingly they told me how their classes had been arranged last year, how far they had gone in their books. I read aloud one of Hawthorne's tales. We dismissed early.

On that golden September afternoon I sat until twilight at my desk, smelling the child smells no schoolroom ever quite loses, exploring the few battered volumes of the school library, poring over ragged textbooks. I planned each fifteen minutes of next day's work. I read each lesson, solved, with some difficulty, each problem in arithmetic, memorized every date. It is amazing how the capital and principal products of Bolivia can flee from one's mind, or the exact relationship of Kosciusko to American history.

After a few weeks, the terror with which I woke every morning began to fade. The little girls could read a page or two. The big boys, I found, liked to help with the chores for a little praise. At recess we all played pom-pom-pull-away.

However, I could hardly wait for the weekends at home, the long steaming bath, the toilet that flushed, the comfort of talking with my own people, eating accustomed, delicious food.

Moreover, my landlady of the merry eye developed a plan, involving a young widower on the neighboring farm and the new teacher. She threw us together at a box supper, where the children entertained by recitations. Each lady's supper for two, gaily wrapped, was auctioned to a gentleman, the proceeds to buy a phonograph for the school. The young widower, briefed, bought my box. Later, he often dropped in of an evening, wearing matching jacket and trousers, a white shirt and a necktie. He was rather shorter than I. He offered to drive me home to our own house in Ottumwa on a coming Friday in his one-seated buggy. Paralyzed with shyness, embarrassed by his intentions, I could find no kindly meeting ground of conversation. Unwilling to offend my landlady, reluctant to endure another evening in his society, I soon felt I must flee this and other problems.

It was saddening to me that even the brightest child would not have any education after the eighth grade. There was no high school nearer than Ottumwa, a walk of seven miles a day. Emlyn Williams in his excellent autobiography, *George*, tells of walking ten miles, back and forth, for his schooling, but in this he had the proud approval of his family. In our neighborhood, most families were too poor to pay for board and room in town. They said the children had had enough education and were needed at home to learn farming or to help in the house.

I remember a jolting ride into town on the hard board seat of a farm wagon one chilly Friday through November's dusk with the German father of my ablest pupil, Charlie. I tried to persuade him that, somehow, Charlie must go on to high school. Charlie was an unusually intelligent boy, I told the taciturn, embarrassed man. But there was no money to spare.

"We need him—we need him on the farm" was all the father would say.

In Ottumwa, my sister and I had often passed on our own light-hearted way to school a large red brick building with a dreary fenced-in yard—the orphanage. There, we knew with passing pity, children without homes lived and played. When they were old enough to be helpful, children from this orphanage (sometimes at nine or ten, usually by twelve) were boarded out in farm homes to work for their keep. I had two such floating, homeless waifs in my school. Dark, secretive little Orville, with the winning smile, was a fluent, confirmed liar, life having already taught him at that early age to settle for the immediately placating reply, rather than to wait for the long-deferred rewards of integrity. And I shall never forget the sullen face of gray-eyed, pretty Irene, "helping out" in the family of a slovenly farmer with an ailing wife and five small, sandy-haired children. On wash days or when a baby was fussy, Irene stayed at home. She missed as many classes as she attended.

But it was the word *chimney* which defeated me. My pupils pronounced it *chimley*. I pointed out to them that it was spelled with an *n*—and that the *n* sound was n-n-n—chim*n*ey. They were polite but incredulous. Their parents and their acquaintances pronounced it *chimley*. *Chimley* it continued to be to them. I had thought to spark eager minds. I was not prepared for the dead weight of the familiar. The word became a symbol of all that I was not accomplishing.

Radio and TV have probably taught the children of my pupils to say *chimney*. And I am sure that Charlie's son can now go to high school on a bus, and on to college if he deserves it. Instead of in a brick orphanage, Irene, pretty and rebellious, might nowadays have lived in a series of foster homes—good, bad, or indifferent—perhaps becoming a Marilyn Monroe. Our care for neglected children has not improved greatly. Even lots of money, without continuity, love, patience, and individual concern, is not enough.

The problems overwhelmed me. But my father was right. Teaching was my greatest teacher. I look back with gratitude for its rigors, its lessons in self-reliance, sheer knowledge gained—more penetrating than any realistic novel could bring. But in the Christmas holidays I found another job and a willing substitute for my country post.

At college I had thought of journalism mainly because it seemed romantic, with connotations of Nelly Bly and travel in far places. I had even dreamed of being a writer, and my mother, an unfulfilled writer herself, approved my desire. I became a reporter on the Ottumwa *Courier,* at $6 a week. Home, delicious food, hot baths were once more, and more appreciatedly, mine.

Like most reporters, I began with obituaries, covering the school board, and rewriting stories cribbed from other papers. Soon a chance came for a feature story.

A lonely, awkward girl from an isolated farm had answered a marriage-bureau advertisement. She was to meet her future husband in Ottumwa and be married there. When she found that he was seriously deformed, which he had not happened to mention in his letters, she fled for help to the YWCA, since she had not even return railroad fare.

Her courageous but pitiful effort to break away from a hopeless life was moving. My human-interest story carried my by-line, right-hand column, front page. Some small checks answered her need—enough to buy a new dress (which her fiancé had promised her) and give her a little pocket money; and she had the offer of a job, as well as a great deal of advice from me—the big-city journalist—about better ways of finding a husband.

I had arrived. I was a journalist. I had also begun to learn something valuable, borne out in all my future reporting and editing—the unpatternedness of ordinary human existence. Each individual has a story and these stories are rarely dull, often are of incredible range and variety. The number of possible sins, sorrows, joys, and failures, the unexpected joinings of these, the dissimilar ways in which such problems are met provide sources of drama which even Shakespeare barely explored.

Soon I received an offer to go to the Des Moines *Capital*—at a salary of $25 a week! The United States had entered the war, and already many of my college friends were in uniform. Men on Des Moines papers were leaving for the army, and some girls were being tried out as reporters. My family allowed me to go, but it was arranged that I must live with my Great Uncle Ed, casting his spell as fashionable pastor of the First Methodist Church in Des Moines.

In my months of newspaper work in that capital city I not only reported the state legislature and dressed up as a Salvation Army lassie collecting dimes, but also covered every kind of trial—rape, murder, and incest. My conventional uncle would say, "In my day, no lady would be seen in such places." But my wonderful Great Aunt Addie, stern, rigid, intelligent, and warm, who sewed fine buttonholes evenings without ever leaning against the back of her chair, and scolded me if I slumped or sprawled, gave me quiet support. Six mornings a week she got up early to cook a hot breakfast before I left the house at 6:45 for my long streetcar ride downtown, to report at the city room at 7:30.

I was nineteen. I cannot see now that exposure to the raw side of life did me any harm. Sin and violence came as no surprise to one who had read Balzac and Tolstoi. My parents had taught me early that there were some bad people in the world—more to be pitied than blamed because their sins were mostly due to poverty, ignorance, or faulty upbringing. They had said that of course such sins must be disapproved, or punished, to show that society did not endorse such conduct, but that most people were good or tried to be good, like the people I mostly saw around me. This simple philosophy carried me through these days with little shock at what I saw.

I simply did not believe the tales of the lurid-minded girl reporter who insisted that all the rich bankers in town kept girls in Chicago and that most of the people along fashionable Grand Avenue regularly had orgies on Saturday nights. Vice, by economic classes, left me skeptical then as now.

Perhaps because I was young and fresh-faced, everyone spoke politely to me. Policemen rarely cursed in my presence. When they did, it was easily ignored.

And when a suddenly-rich movie magnate I was interviewing said unexpectedly, "How would you like to go to Minneapolis with me this weekend?" I did not flounce out of his office but simply replied, "No, I don't think so." His clumsy approach seemed to me ridiculous, moderately offensive—what a greedy man would do thinking he could reach out to take a person as he might take a luscious red apple. Of course, I dreamed of love, with which such a crass approach had nothing to do. Still, as yet, I had little sense of the subtlety and excitement of a gradually developing man-woman relationship, the continuing adventure which the interplay of two diverse personalities makes possible, offering constantly new views, enriched by sudden illuminations of humor or understanding. The dialogue of two minds and spirits, forever meeting yet never merged, has its own poetry;

even the great literature of love leaves riches yet unwritten. Probably even very young women have always known, with a secret, slight smile while they say it, the limitedness of young Rupert Brooke's poetic line "When love has changed to kindliness—," perhaps previewing the riper, deeply flavored fruits beyond.

By the time I returned to college in the fall I was, in my own eyes, an experienced journalist. I was allowed to report for the *Daily Iowan,* even write a few feature stories, and the next June I became its editor for the summer session.

Whoever will breed a boy to be good for anything when he becomes a man must by no means spoil him when he is young.

— MONTAIGNE

7

The Boy Grew Older

Being adored at nineteen by a sophisticated older woman lavishly insisting you're far more wonderful than even you could dream is poor preparation for the U.S. Navy. In the first few weeks of basic training my inflated soul was sent to the cleaners and returned as a wispy, shriveled rag. This mangling experience began with a warrant officer charged with keeping us out of mischief while our ground-school schedule was set up. He issued a routine order for our idle squad to polish a vast copper tank in the kitchen.

I pointed out that prior cadets had left it gleaming like a Kohinoor—and waited for him to make a more sensible suggestion. The humorless oaf briskly gave me two hours' extra duty.

While I pounded the unyielding pavement with bayoneted rifle over my shoulder, I had time to realize that practically all the cadets, like my brothers, were well-set-up college athletes trained to team play. Many had had a year or two of ROTC drill; I, not expecting to join the armed forces, had loftily ducked such training.

Called next day for an individual sizing-up interview, I couldn't

51

even properly stand at attention, I realized. And, when I attempted an about-face on dismissal, I found three of my four feet in the wrong places. A friendly cadet tried to show me the manual of arms; in my untutored hands the rifle seemed just a caveman's club. I found myself wrenched from my unit and thrown into the awkward squad.

Tall, I was immediately shoved into the front rank, where my fumbling of a Springfield seemed to infuriate the demonic drilling officer as a personal affront.

On the right of me was a gangling Tennessee mountain boy, to my eyes outlandishly clumsy. Why was I there beside him? While he was doing an about-face, his large foot tripped him up. Mine didn't behave well either. But I'd get the hang of it soon, whereas he was obviously doomed forever to louthood.

"Hupp, two, three, four" rose to an obscene roar. Dirty sweat stung my eyes. Hot khaki chafed my unaccustomed skin. We were prodded like cattle around the dusty drill ground. The drill and discipline martinet with eyes like two dried prunes goaded us on. I thought of throwing my Springfield at him. The first day's ordeal continued for hours. My arms trembled with the unaccustomed weight of the rifle held high as he excoriated us. The second day was worse. Muscles were sore, confusion multiplied. Each awkward squad cadet narrowly missed my head in his wild maneuvers. Mine were more controlled, I felt sure.

What did all this have to do with flying, anyway? A sickening foretaste of failure choked my throat. Given a little time (and my natural superiority, I thought) I could do all these foolish things the Navy cherished.

But time was what I didn't have. Every two weeks a new flight of twenty-five men, having completed this basic training, went relentlessly up as a unit. As a tight unit, it moved through ground school and on to flying school until, finally, the lowly cadet became an honored aviator, an ensign, and, by congressional fiat, even a gentleman.

But if for any reason you missed your first possible flight at ground school—there were a hundred cadets straining to make the unit of twenty-five—you got only one more chance, two weeks later. You must achieve that second unit of twenty-five—against a hundred

Beatrice never ate indoors when she could eat outside—
her family went along. Sesaly at left.   STEINMETZ

A publicity shot. Bruce and Beatrice with young reigning star
Shirley Temple, hoping to make the magazine—perhaps she did.

Beatrice, photographed by Wilhela Cushman below a portrait painted by Dietz Edzard in 1938. He called her "A Sunday Afternoon."

Beatrice before a Senate committee urging passage of a bill to finance the war against venereal disease.

equally desperate holdovers or new competitors. If you failed that second test, your career as aviation cadet abruptly ended. Three out of four inevitably became "washouts." Those in the awkward squad didn't seem to have a chance.

The needling drillmaster wouldn't, at first, even let me fix a bayonet on my piece. He intimated my bayonet might accidentally slit Tennessee's jugular. My disdain as I watched those sweating ROTC lads at Grinnell had led me directly to this; all my bright dreams of glory were dying on the ignominious drill ground.

At evening chow, with a wisecracking grin, I congratulated my luckier buddies. To Daly's mellow sax after supper I sang "Smiles," without, I hoped, revealing I'd never smile again. And when Hughes, our provisional unit's temporary leader, snappier on the parade ground with a column of men than in the classroom with a column of figures, sidled up to me one evening for help in simple mathematics, I would have traded my ease in the classroom for his command over marching men.

Perhaps it was Hughes who slipped in a good word for me. Maybe my red-faced determination to conquer that slippery rifle if it was the last thing I did impressed someone somewhere. Suddenly I found myself actually assigned to the next official unit, with Hughes designated the dashing student leader.

I was already learning, I fear, the Navy's hard-bitten "—— you, Jack. Hurray for me!" so I didn't give so much as a sympathetic glance to Tennessee left behind.

In our now official unit I found myself bunking alongside Marcus Aurelius Goodrich. From Texas his feet had strayed to more unlikely places. A grizzled, crewcut fuzz covered his lean, hard head, on which you could have cracked a hickory nut without any impression, so inured had he become to criticism as he made his own way. A one-time gob on a destroyer he had, by competitive exams, qualified for officer and had chosen naval aviation as his special branch. Nightly, during chow, he spun tales to prove that more salt water had run between his toes than his mamma-coddled colleagues were likely ever to see. Cadets listened open-mouthed, but at each tale's end the flight, in sheer, desperate protection of their damaged sophistication, would chant, "Oh, what a goddamned lie!" Mark, laughing louder than his detractors, would simply start another yarn as in any navy fo'c's'le since men took to the sea.

Just as the final note of taps sounded over our exhausted bodies, Mark, having perhaps jumped ship right after evening chow, would dash in from the outer world, naked under greatcoat, clothes in a tight roll under his arm, whispering lurid tales of just managing to escape by the window as a suspicious husband loomed at the bedroom door. No one was ever quite certain he hadn't simply undressed in the head to stage an act for our astonishment. He himself would be asleep and snoring while we bewildered cadets, unbelieving but not quite sure, were left to toss all night—despite massive doses of saltpeter—hungrily wondering.

Mark wanted to become a writer. Not just an ordinary writer; a writer of consequence. Like Melville, for choice. But, since he had barely completed grade school, he foresaw difficulties, welcoming me with open arms when he perceived I, too, liked to read. Eventually he produced the minor masterpiece he dreamed of writing, *Delilah,* a tale of men on a somewhat fabulous destroyer.

Double-timing for a brisk mile every dawn over the hard, frosty ground, doing pushups until our shoulders creaked, going through the manual of arms upside down and backward, we rejoiced by now in just being alive. I could at last play mumblety-peg with a bayonet. The hard drill cured me of walking looking down at my feet, and today I loosen even my tie in public with a feeling of guilt at such casualness. For, before we were even allowed to learn to fly, we were compelled to become starched officers of the line.

We learned how, blindfolded and with gloves on, to take a machine gun apart and put it together. We tore engines down and got them roaring again, skeptical as to what good these abilities might do in the air—since one could reach neither gun nor engine while flying. I was still fighting the Navy. But I was wrong. One should know the instruments of one's craft. Lindbergh, Al Williams, Jimmy Doolittle, perfectionists all, kept in the air, I noticed later, when many less meticulous boys were falling to death. No one has ever written so

imaginatively about flying as Saint-Exupéry, but he was said to have
been a menace, even to himself, in the air.

During the rigors of ground school, beautiful Red Cross canteen
girls—how beautiful they did seem in those days—cheered our
flagging spirits. The day our flight was finally set to be shipped out at
noon from Minneapolis to Miami for actual flight training, it was
Mark's wild inspiration that we owed these darlings of our dreams a
personal goodbye though we had been strictly forbidden by our portly
commandant to leave ship and ordered, furthermore, to report to our
cadet commander every hour on the hour for a check to see that we
didn't. Mark and I jumped ship right after morning chow, girl bound.

At noon, morale at topmast, we jauntily returned from our
romantic side trip to find our entire flight lined up, company front,
before headquarters, awaiting our instant decapitation—we had been
AWOL all morning. Every officer on deck silently watched our
cocky pace toward them. This time Mark, the old salt, had gone
too far. He just had time, as he swiftly took in the lay of the land,
to whisper hoarsely, "Say nothing but 'Aye, aye, sir.'" With a
military precision I, despite my quaking heart, never again approached, we snappily reported our presence aboard to the purple-
faced commanding officer.

Like a Captain Bligh about to order us hung up by thumbs our
commandant grilled us with malignant eyes for a moment. Incompre-
hensibly to me, he then barked furious orders to fall in, the flight to
leave. The cadence of our boots resounded triumphantly as we
marched toward the train. Not until our Miami-bound sleeper had
safely pulled out did Mark reveal his secret weapon. As an old hand
he knew that all the complicated paperwork transferring the unit to
flying school had long since been done. Records of minor mis-
demeanors against servicemen were not customarily transferable from
one naval station for action by another. Officially, our idiotic lark
had never happened; only we and the discomfited commandant would
ever remember—I suppose, alas, even the beautiful Red Cross girls
forgot, in time.

We might still be pilots.

Mark and I separated in flying school. The next time I saw him he was assistant drama editor of the New York *Tribune*. In the midst of clangorous Times Square, he immediately began explaining to me the why-for of a ragged hole in his battered fedora—showing me the perforated felt. Some varlet had shot at him, he explained, missing by inches. Mark hadn't changed.

In a gin mill hard by the old Empire Theatre, we caught up on the latest details of his gaudily embroidered career. He had just married the first of his wives, of whom the beautiful Olivia de Havilland was, briefly, number three. He had yet to write *Delilah,* a book that truly can be read with profit.

When we had reached Dinner Key, the naval air station, I found Miami a sleepy Southern town with one main street, one old wooden hotel approached through a palm-lined avenue. On far-off Miami Beach across a rickety causeway stood one lone house. The mattresses in our rundown barracks crawled with bedbugs. At reveille, half the cadets stopped bothering to rise and shine. From their bunks they sang out their names at roll call through the open window into the soft morning air—defying all discipline.

An armistice had just been signed. Flying slacked off. We were so far removed from the world no one knew from day to day just what would happen, though there was the usual flow of latrine rumors. Hearing they were still flying at Key West, I asked to be transferred; it was then that Mark and I separated.

At Key West—where they still believed the war might be resumed —I learned to fly in a hurry. One learned quickly or was washed out.

On our first hop mild-mannered Lieutenant Allen deliberately put us through whatever hair-raising stunts he happened to know. Some cadets decided the war was really over—and hurried back to college. The Navy seemed glad to see them go. We few remaining were theoretically given a maximum of ten hours' instruction before solo but were pressed to solo more quickly. Shakily getting the hang of flying after three hours and forty minutes, I was qualified to solo after seven hours and thirty-four minutes and suddenly found myself in a vast dome of sky all alone with all kinds of questions still unanswered, but with no one along to address my quavering queries to. I have never felt so alone with God; when I finally landed from soloing for the first time I took a moment to thank whatever powers there be.

In those early days most flying cadets had some close calls. With the armistice signed, the planes—elementary crates by modern standards—dangerously lacked mechanical care and were falling apart on the beach. A faulty throttle connection once broke in the air when, flying not far above the water, I was headed toward a railroad trestle connecting two keys. Stuck at half throttle, the plane hadn't enough power to climb nor had it height to turn without catching a wing on the water and crashing. So I chanced a hot landing and set that plane down faster than a practiced seducer zipping down Sophia Loren's blouse, sizzling to a stop just short of heaven. Most of the pontoon's bottom scraped off, but wobbling, still upright though half awash, the plane floated. Far down the tunnel of the years I can still hear my sigh of relief. On the desk before me now, though I've long quit smoking, lies a crude ashtray I hammered out from one of the damaged pontoon's copper screw plates. It reminds me I'm living, like most early flyers, on borrowed time, and that, in flying, as in life, any landing you can walk away from is a good landing. If you've seen *Those Magnificent Men in Their Flying Machines* you have the picture.

Later, at Pensacola, we practiced with machine guns, shooting at a towed target, a banner streaming one hundred yards behind the towing plane. The gun, mounted on a ring, swung on a universal joint.

I was sent up in a biplane with no control stick in the rear cockpit, piloted by Ensign Iwig, whom I had never before seen. He looked all right to my admiring cadet's eye, dark, compact, somewhat taciturn, as befitted an old hand at the controls. I didn't know he'd just come out of the hospital that morning after a bad bout of flu.

At twenty-five hundred feet in a tight Immelmann, Ensign Iwig fainted.

Helplessly, in the rear cockpit I watched the plane stall. Iwig's hands limply, slowly, slipped off the controls. His head leisurely lolled to one side. Luckily for me, his rubbery body didn't slump forward. Falling forward he would have jammed the controls into a straight power dive, precisely what had recently happened to Dobie Dyer, a boy in my flight, and one of the nicest and handsomest cadets in the group. When we'd seen Dyer inexplicably dive straight at the water from two thousand feet, at two hundred miles an hour, we'd thought him foolhardy. When he remained locked in the dive at increasing speed at one thousand feet we wanted to shout to him not to be a damn show-off fool. When he hadn't pulled out at five hundred we knew the worst; he crashed—the water, at that speed, hard as concrete.

Iwig's out-of-control plane went inevitably from the tight Immelmann to a stall and on into a wide, flat spin, spiraling slowly as it dived erratically toward the ocean. In those days pilots had no parachutes—one stuck perforce with the plane, riding it down. All I could do was firmly grasp my machine-gun grip, so, when we hit, the tremendous impact wouldn't swing the barrel around on its universal joint to break open my skull.

The dark ocean rushed steadily upward as the plane spun out its final moments. Everything seemed delightfully slow. I was in no hurry. Three of four cadets had been killed in a similar twenty-five-hundred-foot fall a week before, after two practice planes crashed in midair and locked. I said goodbye, and good luck, in my mind, to the few people I held very dear. Then we hit.

My head was just sticking out of the water, I found, after a moment of shock. My hand, with its death grip, still clutched the handle of that lethal machine gun. Gingerly, I wriggled free of entangling straps and twisted wires, moving legs and arms to see if I was truly all there. Surprised, I was.

"How," I asked the half-submerged helmet in front of me, "are you?"

A muffled reply from Ensign Iwig, now fully conscious, "All right, God damn it!"

It began to seem funny, and emerging with some difficulty from the wrecked fuselage we both laughed, waiting for the big crash boat plowing the waves at breakneck speed to pick us up alive or dead.

A heap of broken soggy matchsticks the plane looked in the snapshot someone took of the fantastic wreckage, giving me a copy so I wouldn't forget.

Then, since nothing seemed discoverably wrong, I was ordered up to solo immediately to make sure I hadn't lost my nerve.

The long leather skirts of our flying jackets, cinched at the waist, flaring and flapping about our knees, caused another accident, part of learning to fly in those chancy days. I had been piloting one of the Navy's largest flying boats, a twin-engine H-16, carrying a crew of five including two pilots. Putting the plane down far offshore on the rough turquoise ocean after my stint at the controls, I climbed onto the wide deck to stretch my legs before shifting to the bomber's forward cockpit while the other cadet took over. The tail of my flaring leather jacket was suddenly sucked by the slipstream into the idling propeller, pulling my behind into the whirling blades. The scar of a great gash deeply through the right gluteal muscle remains today.

For an instant I lay, felled flat on the deck, too stunned to move. This was just as well. If I'd carelessly lifted my head, it would have been bashed to bits by the prop unconcernedly whirling just a few inches above where I lay. (Years later, in a little Missouri town, I ran into a chief petty officer who showed me a scar on his upper arm nicked by the blade when he quickly thrust his hand between two whirling propellers to hold my groggy head down.) Woozily taking in the situation, I inched myself forward, slithered carefully into the bomber's bow cockpit while the relief pilot roared us off the water and raced for the base hospital before I bled to death.

Rain finally drove indoors two doctors who were playing tennis. The damage was considerable and the eight-inch-long, three-inch-deep wound dirty. It was decided not to sew the cut up. Too infected. They would keep it bathed in Dakin's solution, World War I's feeble but sole defense against gangrene.

I owe my life, I think, to a pretty, red-haired nurse with a delicate face, gentle hands, and infinite patience. Asking to be assigned to the care solely of me, she changed my bandages day and night. One morning she seemed strangely still. From my face-down position I skewed round. She was crying.

"It won't heal," she answered my look.

I had grown callous, I had watched friends die, without too much emotion. If one's number was up, it was up, I believed, with the fatalism of youth. The fact that this nurse was crying because of a stranger, me, struck a human note I'd almost forgotten.

"Don't worry, Miss Wagner," I said (gruffly, I suppose), "it will heal."

But it was months before I recovered. In official archives I am permanently 20 percent disabled; I long since stopped arguing with the Navy.

My real wound was that my human feelings had been numbed by long disuse. Owing to nurse Sara Mae Wagner, I got back some part of my ordinary, decent sympathy—maybe enough for a working world. She herself was very spare of words, I noticed, when I thanked her and limped out on my own power—the second boy she'd refused to let die by sheer personal slavery at her job. She'd already turned her heart to helping someone else.

I had learned to fly. Every man should be able to do something all by himself—something that gives him a sense of mastery. Fly, sing, write, bake a good loaf of bread, handle a Bowie knife, tap dance, find a new star, carve in ivory, shoot straight, know how to make someone who loves him happy. Man needs to solo.

Achieving my aviator's wings, I became an ensign of the reserve. The official Navy, even though uninterested in flying, was on the lookout for officer material. I could go on to Annapolis, as a commissioned officer if I liked, though I would have to take the full four-year course before really joining that exclusive club which runs our Navy.

Curiously enough, I was tempted. It was adventurous. It would give me time to write, I thought—find out if I could, while having something to write about. I would be serving my country, too, and I've always believed, very simply, that every man should be ready to lay down his life in its cause.

But the Navy's conviction that the man with half a stripe over you automatically has more knowledge than you—at least has the final say-so—is hard for a sensible civilian to accept, even one with a sense of humor. Perhaps especially for me, not being humble by nature. As an admiral, maybe I could be happy in such a comical situation. But to be an admiral took, among other things, almost an entire life. I felt I couldn't spare that much time.

Moreover, our World War I Navy took a dim view of the possibilities of naval aviation, since few military commanders prepare themselves to fight any war but the preceding one. We consoled our rejected selves with the handsomest uniform of any service, making the rake of our caps of primary importance, since we were all show and no blow. It wasn't really until World War II, when the Japs casually, almost leisurely, bombed to the bottom, off Singapore, the air-unprotected *Prince of Wales* and *Repulse,* that every chair-borne admiral was blown sky high, where he could clearly see the need of airpower if his Navy wanted to stay in being.

So I decided to go on inactive duty, and return to civilian life, where people, though tough, admitted something besides seniority determined one's rank.

Since I never fired a shot at an enemy in defense of my country, I chiefly remember World War I for its personal discipline.

I had begun to realize that intellectual superiority, fancied or real, must defer at times to appreciation of and cooperation with one's fellow men as well as to muscle in an animal world where the flesh is just as important as spirit. I can now cheerfully observe a male trapeze artist or even a necessitous, floundering advertising salesman with something of the same regard I had for Einstein shuffling along the streets of Princeton in sneakers and wild hair. I learned, too, I hope, that one becomes a man when he learns to accept full responsibility for all his actions. I learned that danger is something to be avoided, if possible, but something to be dealt with when it must be faced. Faced, its terrors dissipate. Guy Chapman, in his great book, *A Passionate Prodigality,* beautifully reveals the powerlessness of danger to intimidate the spirit of England's heroic young, fighting in the trenches in World War I.

By the time I returned to Des Moines, Warren, who had been wooing susceptible maidens on Chicago's North Shore, his lieutenant's uniform oddly becoming to his dark, ferocious looks, had, with the signing of the Armistice, hurriedly gone back to the University of

Iowa. In the fall term he hoped we could start a humor magazine for which he already had a name, *Frivol*. There seemed nothing to take me back to Grinnell—my freshman class had moved ahead or been split up by the war, Elinor was sensibly marrying her YMCA fiancé. The Ivy League no longer beckoned me since my boyish hero worship of the handsome Princeton lad who soloed me had dimmed with time.

At home my distinctive forest-green naval aviator's uniform stood out far too conspicuously. Its gold bars, stripes, and wings embarrassed one who knew how little he merited any notice at all.

I rushed into Frankel's and bought the worst-looking suit I ever owned—a belt-in-the-back mistake of the sort clothing manufacturers forced on returning servicemen desperate like me to fade into civilian obscurity.

My mind turned to the fall and to the University of Iowa, though I had no happy intimation that there I would meet Beatrice Blackmar, and that sunlight would come into my life for the rest of time.

*If you marry for love, you will have some very happy
days, and probably some very uneasy ones; if you
marry for money, you will have no happy days and
probably no easy ones.*

—ANONYMOUS

8 ✒

Love at Second Sight

I remember clearly my first meeting with Bruce. It was arranged by
me.

My witty, warm, and attractive roommate, Ophelia, now wife of
the famous pollster Dr. George Horace Gallup, and I had double-dated
at a college play. We sat side by side, a boy at each end. This plan
we followed frequently. In case our escorts did not fascinate us,
which sometimes happened, we could exchange small private jokes,
humorous glances and giggles, betraying nothing to the lads at our
left and right except that we were having a delightful, amusing
evening, which we were.

The tall young man, beanpole thin, moved on the stage with an air
of casual, almost negligent assurance. His voice was pleasing but low,
causing his listeners to lean forward in rapt attention, then as now,
breathless to hear sentences frequently witty, sometimes astounding,
or merely "I think I'll go take a nap." But more, this bit player in
Her Husband's Wife spoke as though he knew what the play was about.

Its wit was witty to him, its humor, humorous. His few speeches were not recited words; they had meaning.

I pinched Ophelia, sibilated sideways, "Looks interesting." She gave me that quizzical, sharing glance which has bound, these many years, her countless friends to her side.

Life at the State University of Iowa in those days was gay. For about a third of the students, the feminine share, it was also intensely earnest. We had our life's profession to prepare for.

Although the name Human Engineering Laboratory had not yet been invented, this might have been a fair definition of each coed's efforts. We might not have enrolled in a psychology course, but our concern was psychology, applied.

Our proper study was MAN. The grave hazard was whether one would win through, at the end of four years, to that sought-after diploma, opening the door to a working life arduous but fruitful and rewarding.

Our curriculum was far more difficult than that of our male colleagues. The materials for our research, the specimens for our microscopes were not to be found in the library—at least not on the shelves—nor, except occasionally, in the laboratory. Our scientific investigations were complicated by the fact that we could not go after our butterflies, so to speak, with a net, or dig for our rocks, frankly, with a pickaxe.

Homework was intensive and time consuming. Dresses must be pressed, sheer collars and cuffs washed—their frequent ruffles and frills ironed to a crisp, breath-taking delicacy. Hair needed curling with an electric iron, or teasing (we called it ratting). Then it was pulled high in a Grecian knot, or in pompadour and French roll, achieving some smaller version of the recent Jackie Kennedy bouffancy.

Our witchery lay not in blue-shadowed eyes, blackened lashes and encarmined lips. It lay in the femininity, the *difference* of our attire. In 1916 we had still worn long, full, many-gored skirts above our high-buttoned shoes, topped by most bewitching silk, chiffon, or organdy blouses, white or flower colored, hinting at lace-trimmed camisoles below. After the war, our skirts grew shorter, our general effect more dashing. We even stopped wearing hats to classes.

Our elementary exploration for our college major was often best carried on in pairs—the findings of one cool researcher supplementing those of the other. An understanding roommate was a great collaborator; Ophelia's judgments were instant and sound.

For we were engaged in an earnest study. We were interested in the future of the human race in an immediate, practical, personal sense. We wished to have a share in it, a handsome, healthy, and intelligent share. Like girls everywhere, we were looking for husbands, attractive, interesting, amusing, companionable, admiration-worthy husbands.

A state university in those days was a pretty comprehensive affair. Anyone with a high-school diploma could qualify. Well-to-do farmers, presidents of small-town banks, owners of shoe stores, doctors, prosperous butchers sent their offspring to the state university.

To do our own screening we must examine the candidates. That was the reason for the frills and furbelows, the need to be popular. It was necessary to be seen in the right places—Reichardt's for a sandwich after the movies; Whetstone's and a choc malted in the late afternoon; Varsity dances on Saturday night. How else could a girl be known? And, if not known, how could she know?

Two or three good friends should be counted on for the big formals —for their own fraternity parties, for an occasional canoeing picnic on the river. Different partners at Varsity dances, fresh faces at Whetstone's announced that one was not yet committed. Canny, often lovelier girls, willfully predatory, must be resisted with warm smiles and cold logic.

Doubtless our quest was not as defined as it appears now after forty years. We chiefly wished to have fun in the sun. Instinct taught us. Clever girls usually asserted to male companions that they never intended to marry, but would become (a) nurses, (b) famous writers, (c) missionaries, thus, of course, stimulating argument. "To speak of love is to make love," as Balzac said and every coed instinctively knew. We skirted the subject of marriage, impersonally, with lackluster interest—referring to it as a sort of imprisonment of the free spirit.

The Prince Charming legend still colored our romantic dreams, I suppose. He should be tall and fair—or dark—and impeccably courteous. No royal blood need run in his veins, but it might not come amiss if his father owned a prosperous watch factory, or had made a fortune in glue.

Even in midnight sessions, a ring of sorority girls in long, full white nightgowns required in the dark to answer with absolute truth (and occasionally doing so) any question asked them—even at those times a girl was considered by Ophy and me to be a little dull, a little timid, who insisted that He must be rich to be romantic. Was not becoming more fun than being?

Ophelia Miller was the daughter of the able editor and successful publisher of the Washington, Iowa, *Democrat*. Her mother, as a widow, later became a notable secretary of state in Iowa—the first woman to hold such office. Ophelia, like her parents, was intelligent, humorous, and literate. She also had hair like pale molasses taffy in color and sheen, but, unlike taffy, with a deep, natural wave; beautiful gray-blue eyes; a wide brow; and a creamy complexion. With music in her bones, when she danced she and rhythm were one.

We didn't need to tell each other. We knew. We both wanted husbands who would stir our minds, kindle our spirits with a sense of adventure, imbue our souls with respect, as well as fill our hearts with love. Perhaps even then we had some glimpses of a possible life enriched not only by love but by communication—of ever-renewed, ever-fresh thought—of ideas, sudden laughter, insight into unperceived truth.

At the moment of the historic college play my list of beaux was not entirely satisfactory. There was the tall, handsome football player, with magnificent back and shoulders—doubtless solid as a rock blocking on the football field, but somewhat solid also in his courting techniques. He had reached the ominous point of saying, together with goodnight, on a dark porch, "You're different from other girls"— at which point all my elusive tactics were called into play.

Then there was my dancing companion. Gay, frivolous, sunny-natured, the sort of lad described by more intellectual, certainly less mobile youths (with maybe a tinge of envy) as having "his brains in his feet," he danced superbly. What false moves does our social system make, to have the joy of dancing uncomprehended, even regarded with suspicion by many of the nicest men? Why should such a natural enhancement, not only of courtship but of all social life, be regarded as a sort of premarriage purgatory? A gift of mine to a third generation has been to teach my older grandson to waltz and foxtrot at the age of seven, then his younger brother and sisters. They have rhythm. In a few years happy girls at Oberlin or Stanford parties will unknowingly bless me. Yeats says,

> For the good are always the merry,
> Save by an evil chance,
> And the merry love the fiddle,
> And the merry love to dance. . . .

Good dancers were valued, of course, as were lads with hefty allowances. In those days we were continuously, actively, outrageously hungry. School meals were tasteless and monotonous. An invitation suggesting Sunday evening at the Jefferson Hotel, where hot roast beef could be followed by a meringue glacé, was almost automatically accepted.

When I saw Bruce on the stage of the Iowa theatre, I did not swoon. Nothing so impetuous for a girl who was seriously considering her future career. My interest was simply directed to a new field of study. I had, so to speak, closed Psychology, Volume 1, and was about to open Volume 2.

Next day I began collecting basic information. Bruce Gould—then known as C. Bruce Gould—having completed a year at Grinnell and a year in Naval Aviation, was one of three friends who had descended upon SUI determined to make their mark by establishing a college humor magazine. They expected to pale the Harvard *Lampoon* to a blushing pink, make the Yale *Record* grit its teeth, be even more sophisticated, if possible, than the brilliant Cornell *Widow*, then tops. Laughing, confident, literary, on a college campus where to be literary was a little odd, they were reported to be rebels— possibly even radicals. They scoffed at the fraternity system, the stodginess of the *Daily Iowan*. Somehow they had persuaded Sigma Delta Chi, the honorary journalism fraternity, not only to back their efforts but to appoint them to the three leading posts as editor, business manager, and circulation manager. Later I learned that, since no profits for the venture were anticipated (except by the shrewd three), it was included in the charter that whatever financial sum could be squeezed out above expenses should go to pay salaries to the hard-working staff.

As a journalistic student and a member of women's Theta Sigma Phi, my research was made easy. A sisterly interest in Sigma Delta Chi's new project sufficed. On the day the first issue was to go on sale, many Theta Sigma Phis volunteered, as did I, to help sell copies of *Frivol*.

Naturally, on the appointed day, my dress required care. It was violet cotton printed with tiny flowers, its airy white organdy vestee caught with violet ribbons. A conspicuous and valuable spot had been given me to set up my newsstand—the library steps. Many students of both sexes would pass my way, be validly drawn into conversation. Twenty-five copies of *Frivol* were assigned me to sell. So I was justified in buttonholing all the more attractive young men as they went by, to peddle my wares. Pleasant chats resulted—more chatting than selling. Almost forgetting my newsstand duties, I was about to stroll over to Whetstone's for a refreshing chocolate malted offered by a likely young man when my major objective of the morning appeared, tall, humorous, but with something observant, aware, deeply personal in his blue gaze.

He is still deeply personal. He is the joy of old ladies. If he sits beside them at a party, he does not ask the usual questions about their grandchildren or where they will spend the summer. Within fifteen minutes he has them telling him about their love affairs, past and present. Whenever I go to a dinner party with strangers, always one, often two, of the women beside him at dinner come to me after-ward saying, "I have had the most delightful (interesting) (fascinating) (amusing) talk with your husband." Why? He is personal. He is interested in people and cuts through most conventional approaches. He treats a stranger as a good nut whose kernel will repay cracking, not as a necessary fifteen-minute duty of politeness.

The still-unknown young man on that day scolded me for selling so few *Frivols*.

"You're a pretty girl—you're not trying. I'll be back in an hour to check up."

The checkup was a chat, then a stroll back to the journalism office. "I suppose I shall see you at Iowawa?" I queried. Progress could be reported in my notes.

As he left me, I noted that his hair was sandy, reddish. I had always admired red hair and had once said to my roommate, "I shall marry a man who will give me red-haired children." However, I attached no special significance to the sandy hair at that time. I was curious only. This young man was humorous, literate, had obvious strength of character. He was not, of course, my dream prince. I was still pretty conventional about my dream prince. But he was challenging.

It is possible, if one is discerning, to read the life of a man of fifty in his face. Success (success in living, in aims fulfilled, not necessarily by worldly measure) shows in a kind of completedness. The realized personality stamps his own features, just as irresolution, bewilderment, disappointment mark the faces of those for whom life has not unlocked its best secrets. Men of character get better looking as they grow older—provided they keep their figures. A high, straight forehead, a strong nose overshadowing a young face, later suggest intellect and command. Mouths, well used, become both resolute and humorous. Intelligence lights the eye more luminously at fifty than at twenty-one, when the face is lighted also by youth's glow.

My husband is better looking now than he was at twenty-one, with a nose too big for his face, hands too big for his sleeves, and a skin still showing marks of the days when two Hershey bars and an early movie substituted for supper.

"I suppose I shall see you at Iowawa" had dropped from my lips at our parting—in no sense to be construed, except by a cad, as an invitation—merely a temperate statement of probable fact.

Iowawa was the big do of the following Saturday night. A huge benefit, all the student body taking part, it hoped to raise funds for the projected Student Union building.

My jobs were two. In the early evening, from a booth, I would sell coffee and doughnuts, donated by faculty wives and kind matrons of the town. Later, I was to be a ten-cents-a-dance girl, luring dimes into the coffers of the Union by my slight terpsichorean skill.

After a certain amount of frittered and wasted time serving customers who were merely hungry, Bruce appeared with three or four Kappa Sigma brothers. I sold them all doughnuts. He lingered. We chatted. He suggested we walk about a bit and see the fun. Soon he proposed that, since it was such a nice night, we might take a breath of fresh air. We did. As I remember, it was moonlight. We walked down the hill of the campus to the bridge over the Iowa River.

I never went back.

I deserted my post.

Iowawa gained no dime-a-dance profits from me.

I spent an entire evening, fascinated, interested, and compelled. I have been fascinated and compelled ever since.

The boy who had planned to take me home, my amiable dancing friend, who had been saving his dimes for the evening, telephoned immediately after 12:30, the hour we must be in our rooms. "I just wanted to see if you got home safely," he said coldly. "I couldn't find you."

"We must have missed each other. I didn't see you anywhere either," I said, with a modicum of truth.

When I woke up next morning I didn't think I was in love. I was challenged. I was curious. This man was so different. He quoted Baudelaire and Swinburne, admired Aubrey Beardsley. I had been brought up on the Victorian novelists. He read Anatole France and Shaw. I, Jane Austen. He did not ask me to dance. I thought his clothes were terrible. I seem to remember a tweed suit with purple and orange flecks—but perhaps I exaggerate with the years. I did not like his scoffing friends. He accused me of being proper, conformist, unimaginative.

But we saw each other often, under circumstances difficult then, often difficult forty years later. He hated schedules and loved the free feeling of a wholly uncommitted day or week ahead. He still does. His invitations tended to be last minute. I sometimes took a certain pleasure in saying I was already engaged.

He could ask me to Sunday-morning breakfast at the coffee shop—and be half an hour late because he had failed to set an alarm. I would not be there. This tended to cause friction. Some of that friction persists today. He carefully prepared a philosophy paper on Euripides, and, on the day he was supposed to present it, slept through the eight-o'clock class. When the professor threatened to flunk him in the course, Bruce said he was sorry if he had inconvenienced him but he didn't mind being flunked because he had got all the good out of reading Euripides and preparing the paper and that was more important than the credit. He felt sure the professor had had no difficulty in extemporaneously taking over the class. I did not think that was funny. I thought it rude to the professor. He thought it rude, too, but he also thought it was funny.

At the same time he opened my eyes to new ideas, new thoughts, new writers. He was so amusing that whenever I grew angry a funny remark would make me laugh. He knew my weakness for food. He always kept me well fed with the very best. It took two years of courtship before I could admit I was wholly in love, and another year before we could be married.

> *Heaven from all creatures hides the book of fate.*
> —POPE

9

All Roads Lead to Rome—
Even the Detours

In O. Henry's *Roads of Destiny* the hero travels each of three separate forks in the highway, in each case winding up at the same end, killed by the same bullet from the same pistol. If I'd taken the low road to Annapolis or the high road to Princeton, instead of jogging pedestrianly down the middle road to the State University of Iowa, I might still have met Beatrice, wooed her on Broadway, and gone on to edit the *Journal*. But the frightening chance of somehow missing Bibi along the way terrifies me, even as a supposition.

I arrived at Iowa nearly broke—perhaps $200 jingled in my pocket. The government gradually got around to doling out scholarship money to disabled veterans, but it was quietly done. After supporting myself halfway through my three years at Iowa, I learned I might legitimately have received $75 a month all along for my patriotic disabilities, which included a back injury that was to plague me for many years. My actual service to my country merited nothing but gratitude from me for a valuable experience.

So I foraged for myself at Iowa in the way struggling college students since the founding of Bologna have always scrounged for a living, in low ways while elevating their minds. Besides washing dishes at the university's hospital next to a retarded female teenager for my scraggly meals, I picked up odd muscle jobs at so much an hour to pay room rent, buy books, and meet incidental expenses. This was, admittedly, something of a comedown from the officer and gentleman I had been made, at least temporarily, by act of Congress. One or two fraternities looked me over—rather distantly, I thought, and I couldn't fault them. Their tacit rejection saved me humiliation. I couldn't have afforded one at the time, even if they'd found me acceptable.

Warren, Harold (who had joined us), and I had little difficulty establishing *Frivol* all by ourselves. No one else would touch it. Everyone was sure *Frivol* would fail.

The university's official censor and student publication adviser, a knowledgeable professor of Greek, Dr. Charles Heald Weller, had, as an undergraduate, ambitiously published a college humorous magazine. This had resulted in such financial disaster, he felt sure we too would fail. The university's refusal of its official backing threw *Frivol*'s ownership and responsibility entirely on us three. If we went broke, we would have to quit college to pay off the printing and engraving debts we had incurred.

But by bribing Sigma Delta Chi with the promise of 10 percent of the profits, if any—and no responsibility for debts—we gained that journalistic fraternity's official backing. The university thereupon gave us permission to publish *Frivol,* on campus, as our private enterprise.

We had scanned a dozen or more college humor magazines. Cornell's *Widow* seemed best, Charles Baskerville outstanding as its sophisticated cartoonist. Princeton's *Tiger* was not so good as it had been before Scott Fitzgerald left the campus. We were blithely sure we could produce, at Iowa, a better humor magazine than any Ivy League confection. Whether the mentally lethargic, average (as we conceived him) SUI undergraduate would have the wit to support our spectacular magazine we could not be certain.

Because Warren had only two more years at Iowa, he should be editor at first, we decided. I would be editor the second year, Warren modestly demoting himself to associate. Harold could be editor the third year—with Warren gone—if, by that time, Harold had gained the sense of responsibility which he demonstrably didn't have at the moment. For the first year I would be *Frivol*'s associate editor and advertising manager. And, since no one seemed to want the job of circulation manager, I took on that.

Iowa's bedazzled undergraduates must have thought they were buying, along with copies of *Frivol,* a half interest in the pretty Theta Sigma Phis who helped sell it. One way or another, we disposed of seventeen hundred copies, at twenty-five cents a copy—most college humor magazines sold for ten—which more than paid our printing costs. And since as advertising manager I had managed to sell quite a few pages at $250 a page—though one or two merchants seemed to think the rate was pretty high—we were in.

Printing *Frivol* proved as profitable as counterfeiting. Surprisingly, it was legal. Rapidly we revised upward our opinion of the Iowa campus intellect. Most editors start with too low an opinion of their readers, often smarter than the editors. But this was a new thought to me. It would be a new thought to many editors today, I guess— feeling superior is such a pleasant emotion, and one literary people particularly like to indulge in.

Changing overnight from campus freaks to campus celebrities, joyfully quitting our menial jobs, we redoubled our extracurricular activities and multiplied our enjoyment of life's golden moments.

Most of our *Frivol* wit, strictly imitative of those professional iconoclasts Nathan and Mencken, wouldn't seem funny, even to me perhaps, today. Now pretty well outmoded, Mencken and Nathan were my generation's angry young men.

Both felt the way to fame lay in savaging opponents. Laying about with broadswords, both had sound cultural standards and good taste in the arts. Carrying high the banner earlier in the century hoisted by James Gibbons Huneker, they salutarily influenced American litera- ture and art—and young men who aspired to both. Nathan, a polished and sophisticated refugee from the Illinois heartland, touted Shaw, O'Neill, O'Casey in a theatre commercially smothered by the Shuberts.

Mencken, a Baltimore journalist of substance, extolled Dreiser, Cabell, Sinclair Lewis with complete disregard for the life, limb, or reputation of any who held differing views. Morons he dubbed the collective booboisie. Could this country have culturally matured without both? Burned up by America's complacency, like charred casks they helped age the national spirit.

The pair indelibly marked Warren, Harold, and me with their lively prejudices. Avid readers of *Smart Set* and *Vanity Fair,* we brashly adapted for our own much of what they wrote—if it was easily enough imitated. Swinging through the bewildering jungle of culture as sedulous apes, we thanked Robert Louis Stevenson for advising young writers to copy their betters.

Collegians and their rolled-stockinged flappers suddenly became "flaming youth." *Judge,* the magazine, and John Held, Jr., its cartoonist, set the flapper's pace. Fitzgerald had just written *This Side of Paradise.* Short skirts and high jinks, the male hip flask and the uncorseted hip ruled supreme. *Frivol,* on the crest of the wave, continued a howling financial success. Movie houses flashed on their screens, during intermissions, jokes from the leading campus magazines. Collegiate wit, for a moment, had status. When *Frivol* was quoted we applauded like fathers whose baby has just been adjudged winner at the county fair. Here are some college efforts which made the grade:

(From *Our Contemporaries*)
HE: My clutch is awful weak.
SHE: So I've noticed.
—Cornell *Widow*

STUDENT (translating): The—er—er—er—
PROF: Don't laugh, gentlemen, to err is human.
—Yale *Record*

The little pig was weeping,
For his father had been slain;
But a porcupine, consoling, said,
"Oh, porcupine in vain."
—Harvard *Lampoon*

(From *Frivol*)
Father, is it difficult to be an honest man?
No, my son, but it's expensive.

EDGAR LEE MASTERS
A garrulous bellhop
Paging the Jukes family.

How do you like Harper?
Well, I don't know him well enough to pass any disagreeable comment
on him.

MODERN MAXIMS
Beauty is only skin deep. If it were deeper, no one would be interested.
A rolling stone never gets a greenback.
Familiarity breeds attempt.
The modern man wants a good girl and wants her bad.
He who hesitates is bossed.
When you see a boob holding the attention of an audience of wise men,
he is talking about his affairs with women.

SHE: Do you believe in original sin?
HE: Oh, why be original?

Youthful humor's single-minded purpose was met, but our desire
to upset the status quo and infuriate the elders was not. Authorities
at Iowa infuriated us by never losing their cool; the Midwest has
always possessed common sense and generally followed it.

Warren, as editor, suddenly found himself a Big Man on the
Campus, and, hence, not as bad-looking as he thought. Girls no longer
shied away. Unwilling to go back to obscurity, he prevailed on me
to let him continue as editor his final year. By this time we had raised
the price of *Frivol* to thirty-five cents so we'd have more money to treat
our girls. I was to take over when I became a senior, so both Warren
and I could finish in style. Harold assented. But after Warren graduated, Harold pled to be editor. It would give him status and impress
his family. Moved by his earnest entreaties, I agreed. Besides, I was
then president of the University Players, trying to learn to act, to find
out what made audiences respond, and tinkering with playwriting.
Campus honors, I thought, might as well be shared around.

During my two summer vacations before graduation from Iowa I worked for a Midwest Chautauqua company. The first season I superintended one tent. The second summer, having done well, I ran the entire Chautauqua as circuit manager. My hardest work, it sometimes seemed, was to keep the husky, high-school crew boys out of the dressing rooms of the skirt-twirling, provocative college dancing girls masquerading as Highland lassies. With some understandable sympathy for them I found it a thankless task. Though I was paid $100 a week, my biggest reward was learning, first hand, how many wonderful cooks flourish throughout our well-fed country. As circuit manager I spent a day in ninety-one villages of under one thousand population in Iowa, Illinois, and lower Wisconsin, supervising and renewing contracts, only incidentally protecting the girls' morals. When I arrived I would inquire of the stationmaster, or taxi man, who were acknowledged the two best cooks in town. They always knew. It was Millie Bakersfield and Lottie Brohrmann. Either, I found, by simply ringing her doorbell, was glad to feed me, as a kind of visiting celebrity, at her own table. So for three months I ate as if dining at Lapérouse and La Petite Auberge but at seventy-five cents per *déjeuner* and fifty cents for a *petit déjeuner* of two eggs, crisp bacon, sweet oatmeal, coffee with rich cream, with four or five kinds of jam to choose from for my hot biscuits. I'm sure there were half a dozen other cooks in each town as good as Millie and Lottie but I only asked for two. So I realized, early on, how unfounded was the prevailing belief that American women knew nothing about cooking, a bit of knowledge I valued even more when we edited the *Journal,* and had these women for critical readers.

Just before I left college, one of our journalism professors—owlish, sophisticated Bill Maulsby, lately from Tufts—had given my ego an unnecessary boost. Without consent, he had leafed through a bulging notebook of casual thoughts I, as a knee-pants Chekhov, had carelessly left open at my desk. Half-humorously he offered to stake me in New York, like a promoter backing a prize-ring hopeful, to $2,500 a year for as long as necessary in exchange for 10 percent of my future earnings once I got on my feet. Not being a Cassius Clay, I feared he'd never get his money back—and thanked him.

One of my Kappa Sigma brothers, Marquis Childs, looking like

Scott Fitzgerald and no less of a playboy, did not yet promise the brilliant political columnist he became. And I, at least, failed to foresee in rather practical, able Ted Gallup the man who would shed new light on democracy by his brilliant method of measuring men's minds, confounding pundits who wanted to say public opinion was what they desired it to be. Ophy saw more clearly.

Beatrice and Warren had been working in Des Moines as reporters during my senior year at Iowa, she on the *Tribune,* he on the *Register,* both owned by the Cowleses. I did a lot of commuting that year between Iowa City and Des Moines—in order to visit my mother. She must have become tired of hearing me say hello and goodbye, without then seeing much of me in between, because I was hovering around Beatrice every minute she could spare. When, after graduation, I received an offer from the *Tribune* to work as police reporter at $22.50 a week I signed on for the summer with the dream still strong of getting to New York somehow.

I had, despite some understandable jeers from Warren and Harold, composed a splendid letter to Frank Crowninshield, editor of my then favorite magazine, *Vanity Fair.* Crownie's magazine was subsequently to be reabsorbed into *Vogue*'s womb, a life cycle fortunately peculiarly limited to periodicals. It was then dying of anemia, and needed a hurried transfusion of good red blood from the Middle West, I suggested, standing ready for the sacrifice. I didn't detail the deficiencies of *Vanity Fair.* (This omission was probably a mistake. Most editors realize, all too well, that their magazine's potential far exceeds performance.) I did tell Crownie, at some length and with the full backing of my own say-so, what a remarkably cultured fellow I was, still unknown to the wide world, languishing in Des Moines. He would be lucky, I indicated, if he made me his managing editor before it was too late.

All I received in reply from *Vanity Fair* was a polite, somewhat aloof—and I thought stilted—epistle from the managing editor I offered to supplant. It rejected, in toto, my generous offer of rescue. I later got to know Crownie, a most amusing and generous man; mercifully he did not recall my letter.

In the middle of summer, Beatrice suddenly learned she'd been awarded a Lydia Roberts Fellowship at the Journalism School of Columbia University. The thought of setting out for New York, even without a job, became even more desirable. Fired by our enthusiasm, Harlan Miller, a friend from high-school days, decided he, too, would join us.

What was there to lose? He hadn't yet met his delightful Doris.

Warren and Harold had, however, found local girls who charmed them; both subsequently married their Loreleis. So they sagely decided to remain in Des Moines, as reporters and men-about-town. They would let us test the cold bath they saw us headed for in New York.

> *. . . Better to live rich, than to die rich.*
> —SAMUEL JOHNSON

10 🐛

New York, Here We Come—
Ready or Not

In the fall of 1922, three scantily equipped but ebullient travelers, Bruce, Harlan, and I, steamed down the magnificent Hudson from Albany on the day boat, into New York's old 121st Street dock. This entrance to the city, backed by Harlem and slums, had been chosen because it was near where I was to live. Transportation for myself and my trunk would be cheaper.

My possessions were few, my suit was old, but my courage and spirit were new minted. Not one single soul in the city did I know except my merry traveling companions and the Columbia University professor, distinguished Dean Pegram, who, after visiting Iowa, had accepted me for a fellowship at Columbia's School of Journalism. I did have one treasured letter of introduction—to a famous journalist (who else would count?), Bruce Bliven, then managing editor of the New York *Globe,* who years before had gone to school to my father in Emmetsburg, Iowa.

I also had a room waiting for me on 121st Street, near the university —a room engaged by letter on the single glowing recommendation that the daughter of my landlady was an acquaintance, a friend even, of Heywood Broun. What a shining fact, this nearness to literary-journalist circles, to the famous Round Table of the Algonquin, known country-wide to aspiring writers through cartoons and columnists. My friend Lillian Prentiss had lived in this same room the year before while studying art, and had told me that $15 a week was the minimum on which one could hope to live in the expensive metropolis. Blithely assuming, on no previous evidence, that my tastes could be minimal, I had scraped together about this essential sum, and railroad fare, to supplement a fellowship which assured my tuition for a year. My father, caught now in the Iowa farm depression of the early twenties (his savings all invested in the rich black Iowa land he loved), could not help me at all. Moreover, he thought New York distant and uncharted for a girl alone and journalism a rakish and uncertain profession, and he saw no reason why I should not settle down, honorably, as a teacher at home. My mother, her color high, her blue eyes bright as she thought of the new and distant horizons to be explored, gave me all moral support, and backed it as usual with her dressmaking art.

Bruce, resisting an offer to become advertising manager of a furniture store in Des Moines on a salary which might even make marriage possible, had decided this was the time to try his fate as a playwright in New York. (He envisioned of course a few intermediate steps— perhaps a brief period as distinguished dramatic critic or columnist.) The third of our trio was red-headed, quizzical, engaging Harlan, already a well-tried journalist on the Des Moines *Register*—a man of the world, too, since he had been abroad as a stripling in World War I with our Air Force, had fallen in love with an older woman in France, had worked under Herbert Hoover in Polish Relief in his ancestral homeland, when Hershey bars and cigarettes were black-market currency, and had actually spent a little time in New York collecting a few reporter acquaintances. A voracious reader, he had it in mind, like most reporters of that day, to write, someday, the Great American Novel.

In budgets as limited as ours, railway fare to New York was a costly item, not to be squandered on a swift rush over our fascinating country, extra-fare-express. Spending as many nights as possible en route with relatives or college friends, for purposes of economy as well as pleasure, riding day coaches in daylight hours, we managed to work in dinner and a theatre in Chicago, visiting with classmates in Cleveland, a boat trip on Lake Michigan and Lake Erie to Buffalo, and a day at Niagara Falls, where, conspicuous as a trio among honeymooners, I was christened by my amused escorts "Beatrice the Beautiful Bigamist." Then, from Albany, we floated down the majestic Hudson on a palatial gingerbread-with-white-icing steamer into the city we were hoping to conquer.

The apartment house, my home, was dingy and rundown, and my room was small. I hardly noticed. As I unpacked my wardrobe trunk, I scarcely observed that my one window, on a narrow court-yard, admitted all the clatter and odors from a restaurant three stories below, so aware was I of the warm greeting from my landlady's red-haired daughter, Eva Nöe, commercial artist and member of Heywood Broun's famous circle. It was not that I expected to *meet* Heywood Broun, at least not yet—not until I was a successful journalist. Now, to sleep under the same roof with someone who knew him was a privilege. From my trunk I took a violet tea set— a graduating present—and a Sterno stove, as I expected to serve tea often to interesting friends and did, in my crowded room, arranged as a sitting room with its studio couch. I unpacked a violet vase, a graduating gift from Ophelia (teaching school now among the snow-drifts of northern North Dakota) to be used often for a single rose, or one of those limp bunches of violets thriftily sold on subway steps just before they wilted for good. Even journalism students could often spare a quarter—and Bruce sometimes remembered how I loved violets and lilacs. My typewriter was set up, my dresses put away. Several were old, but there was a favorite brown velvet, its worn sleeves replaced by new ones of gold lace. My winter coat, that cruelest item in a limited budget, too, was old, and must remain hidden, and I cold, as late in the fall as possible. But there were two new dresses, a navy blue wool of elegant simplicity and beautiful cut, and a magnificent formal of turquoise silk, its long full skirt trimmed only with a casual, lovely vine of handsome silk flowers, in shades of mauve and violet. (Even now, after some years of close acquaintance with the fashion salons of New York, Madrid, Rome, Paris, I feel that my mother, intellectual as she was, had the talent and taste to be a designer for Vionnet or Lanvin, had she grown up in a different milieu.) With this creation I wore, no matter how chilly the evening, a lustrous mauve silk shawl and soon was to wave airily, kindness of Bruce, a pale mauve feather fan.

Our first expedition, the day after arrival, was of course to the Algonquin for lunch, where we were granted an insignificant post by that courteous, memorable headwaiter, George, and could devour with our eyes, one by one, the celebrities of the Round Table. F.P.A., no cartoon but there in the flesh, so ugly he could only be a humorist, piquant Dorothy Parker presumably spouting wisecracks, owlish Alexander Woollcott unmistakable. At last we were in the main current. Like an Englishman who, from the back of the throng, had glimpsed a hand waving from a carriage, a smile frosted by glass, and has seen the Queen, we felt honored.

No thought of expense was ever allowed to deter us from important occasions like this one and as a trio we were unanimous. Better bread and cheese, much of the time, or a can of sardines if necessary, and then the great splurge at least once in the most famous places. "Never daunton youth," said John Buchan's sturdy Scot grandmother. We never allowed our poverty to daunton us. Dairy lunches might be our mainstay, but we had one meal at the Ritz, then and later, in any city we visited.

My chief object at the Journalism School was to enter a famed short-story class under Dr. Walter B. Pitkin, admission being granted only after one had submitted a short story acceptable to him. I was fortunate to be allowed to join the small group of eight under this brilliant teacher. Growing up, I had read Mary Roberts Rinehart's subdeb stories in the *Saturday Evening Post,* laughed with P. G. Wodehouse's Bertie and Jeeves, and appreciated the way in which Alice Duer Miller's smooth wit glossed over her shaky, implausible plots. Never one to fancy that great or even moderately memorable literature would flow from my pen, I still believed that the skills of light, amusing storytelling could be learned. This I was determined to try.

My courses, therefore, were arranged to leave at least three mornings a week free for my typewriter. Afternoons I could give to other kinds of education—a memorable series of lectures on American literature by Carl Van Doren, a course in sociology under Dr. William Pepperell Montagu, of Barnard. Under the spell of the rights of women and the Lucy Stone League (why should a wife drown her personality by taking her husband's name in marriage?) I wrote my term paper, I cringe to tell, on the somewhat debatable theme "The Right of Unmarried Women to Have Children."

With work at Columbia well organized, I had much time for adventure with my friends. Few young women are lucky enough to descend on a strange city with one beau; accident and geography had given me two. Many of our explorations—of theatres, ferryboats —we were very young, we were very merry—Chinatown, Greenwich Village restaurants, Fifth Avenue double-decker buses—were conducted as a threesome. Harlan was a gallant and amusing companion and, with a keen, rather roving eye for feminine beauty, often made up a foursome with a girl of his own. To us it was a fabled city; to go to the Biltmore and actually sit under the well-known clock, famous in fiction, gave us a sense, almost like a miracle really, of being transported from prosaic Iowa streets to the glamorous world frequented by Scott Fitzgerald's gilded youth. Bruce, then as now fairly allergic to walking, preferred absolute quiescence or more active sports like squash or tennis. Harlan and I roved the city. We familiarized ourselves soon with the backbone of Manhattan by walking the length of its spine. Starting early, we breakfasted at my clattering cafeteria on the corner of 121st Street—already cherished by me in my fruitless effort to live on $15 a week. There two big hot, crumbly, raisined bran muffins with butter and coffee with cream could be had mornings for ten cents. There, when I was regrettably unescorted, and funds were low, I could manage a filling supper for fifteen cents—a glass of milk, a dish of cole slaw, and a baked potato—shamelessly pointing out the largest potato on the hot tray,

Daisy Fellowes, one of *Vogue*'s "beautiful people," introduced Bruce and later Beatrice to a dazzling world of fashion, art, and leisured life.

Nancy Astor, when young; tart-tongued, warmhearted, family friend, she threatened Bruce with marriage should Beatrice leave him a widower.

Mrs. Franklin D. Roosevelt, in her Washington Square apartment after the President's death, serves tea and discusses her future.

The *Journal*'s modern houses rated a show at the Museum of Modern Art, but Vice President Henry Wallace seemed more interested in Beatrice's hat.

and often looking wistfully and successfully at a second pat of butter
as well.

Bravely bemuffined, and fortified further by an egg for the arduous
day ahead, Harlan and I walked through the sunny September fresh-
ness of Central Park, idling briefly on a bench near the reservoir.
The Plaza for lunch had been our thought, but we were early, so we
strode gaily on, our eyes on ghost crab stems for every stately turreted
mansion of a Vanderbilt, every renowned, dazzling shop along upper
Fifth Avenue, down to the old rust-red Waldorf squatting block-
square on Thirty-fourth Street and glittering with social history. In
its dark, impressive dining room Harlan grandly commanded a
window table overlooking the avenue, where we dawdled and rested,
our eyes raking the passing throng for a Fannie Hurst or a Percy
Hammond, over a magnificent and filling lunch, ending with what
else but crêpes suzette—Harlan must have received his first pay
check. Portlier, we sauntered down Fifth Avenue to pink-brick Henry
Jamesian Washington Square. Gathering strength as we grew hungry
again we crossed to the dingy Bowery, peered into the dim hallways
of Chinatown, then to City Hall and Park Row, center of our journalistic aspirations because the New York *World* faced the young
Woolworth tower there, the New York *Tribune* and *Sun* hard by,
down to the canyon of lower Broadway, lovely Trinity Church on our
right, the mysterious, faintly wicked financial heart of the world
pulsing on our left—on down to the salt smells of the Battery with
its valiant tugs and steamers from afar, and to Fraunces Tavern for
strong hot tea. Weary, we subwayed home to join Bruce at our
favorite cafeteria for supper, then I regretfully went to bed, a little
fearful lest I miss something the boys might see or do later.

Before presenting my solitary precious letter of introduction to
Bruce Bliven, I looked closely at my wardrobe, took myself to the
millinery supply shops in the Thirties, with the kind advice
of Eva Nöe, herself not unaccustomed to the improvised costume
gallantly worn. There I purchased four bunches of artificial violets
and a buckram shape, created a small purple toque, similar (in idea)
to one I had seen in an elegant Fifth Avenue window. With my battered coat negligently over my arm (fortunately the day was not

chilly), in my best navy-blue dress and my new hat, I set forth to call on Mr. Bliven at his *Globe* office. When he invited me to lunch, I naturally instantly said yes, realizing that my two comrades would appreciate the importance to us all of strengthening this slight line of communication with the great world of the press, even though it meant that they were left expecting me for lunch at the Algonquin, to hear the results of this potent interview. A hasty telephone call transmitted by a secretary said only that I would see them at 2:30. Lunching in a dim, second-floor restaurant, off Vesey Street, obviously a storied newspaper hangout, where my host was hailed with waves, called-out greetings, and a certain curiosity by journalistic cronies, I felt that I was in the center of things at last. Dazed by this intimacy with the very heart of the world I longed to enter, I made my bemused way, by subway, to the Algonquin, where Bruce, with a certain hostility, was waiting. But, when he learned that I had been invited for Sunday tea to meet Mrs. Bliven, he felt that my tactical treachery was justified by this slightly opened door. Later, Bruce Bliven, who had also thrown over his customary lunch cronies, told me his friends had evinced some curiosity about his sudden companion. "Just a little girl from Emmetsburg, Iowa," he told them airily. "H'm," they were reported to have doubted, "looked more like Paris to me." Such kind words gave me confidence in my amateur millinery efforts, far more, I am sure, than they deserved.

I believe we saw every important play in New York that winter, usually from seats in the second balcony, whenever possible buying tickets at Le Blang's in the basement of Gray's drugstore, where tickets could be snatched at cut rates just before curtain time (then, as now, the best shows were not always the most popular). Sometimes we even had press passes. Harlan was a reporter by then, and another Iowan, Paul Frederickson, studying at the School of Journalism and working nights at the United Press, had joined our fun-seeking group. Since Bruce, with thriftily saved *Frivol* money, was not yet broke, he saw no pressing need for a job at once. Newspapermen make wonderful beaux. Not only do they often get free tickets to plays and concerts, even opera—and, if so, the best seats—they are sometimes asked to cover night-club openings, or occasionally charity balls at the Ritz or Plaza. Paul was the best dancer I had yet met. He, my beautiful blue formal gown, and I had many a delicious evening staking out a traffic-free corner for our spectacular waltz pivots in some of the handsomest ballrooms in New York.

To the ill-concealed astonishment, not only of myself but of all my friends, the first short story completed under Dr. Pitkin's perceptive counsel sold immediately to *Pictorial Review*—and for $500. Instantly, I invested almost half of this sum in a beautiful winter coat—black, with a lush silver-fox collar—at Bonwit Teller, then on Thirty-ninth Street. Lesser sums went for entertaining in one or two recherché restaurants friends who had so lavishly entertained me. The moiety remaining fitted handily into my budget, since my intention of living on $15 a week had not been wholly successful.

Bruce Bliven and his warm, friendly wife, Rosie, who lived on wind-whipped Riverside Drive near 116th Street, became friends. And one day Rosie asked me if I wouldn't like to bring that tall young man in to tea—the one she had often seen with me near the university (Bruce and Harlan were living on 110th Street), the one who carried a stick and wore such an odd-looking hat. Bruce, anticipating his career as a playwright, had invested in a rather sweeping hat of black velours—much the sort of thing impresario Morris Gest might have worn. Through the Blivens, we met writers and journalists. I was even invited by my landlady's daughter, Eva, to her tiny studio on Thirty-eighth Street near Sixth Avenue, where she entertained Broun, F.P.A., Neysa McMein, and one or two Wall Streeters who admired wit and the literary set. There I sat on her studio couch, silent as a mushroom, tongue-tied but radiating awe and admiration. It was some years before I could speak an intelligible word to any of these glittering creatures; many of them later proved kind. But epicene, waspishly funny Woollcott, with his elaborate, ill-natured, off-center humor, silenced me to the end of our acquaintance. I liked him a little better on the printed page.

In the midst of this exciting spring, I still found time to complete a second short story, and just after I returned to Ottumwa for the summer it sold to the *Ladies' Home Journal*. This second sale, and the fact that my fellowship was renewed for another year, left no doubt that New York was to be my field of adventure, at least for the time. With my tuition provided for, and almost $500 in hand, I said farewell to Iowa and entrained for Philadelphia, where I had been invited to meet the *Journal*'s editor, Barton Currie. Little did I dream, as I walked under that splendid columned portico on Independence Square and entered the marble hall, how often my feet would climb those steps in the future. But I had known when I saw Bruce, waiting to meet me at the station there, his tall figure nonchalant, relaxed, but his eyes, a deeper blue, seeking mine—then I had known I was fully committed, at last. We were married that fall.

And from this point on, since I am a lazy writer, more interested in swimming, sailing, reading Trollope, playing with my grandchildren, and making fish chowder, than in my pen, his will be the burden of this, our joint tale. As has been the custom in our married life, he will do most of the work and I will claim half of the credit, if any.

Naturally, however, since men and women are different, and ours has been one long happy argument, it will be necessary from time to time for me to intervene—to interpolate, "I don't agree" or "Not at all, it was this way" or even "Don't be silly!"—to jog his memory when, fascinated by his recollections of early New York journalistic life and playwriting adventures, he forgets to mention such stunning events as the birth of our first child, our red-headed daughter, Sesaly. Occasionally, too, in order to do justice to the truth, elusive to him but evident to me, I may find it needful to sit down and write an entire chapter, beginning, doubtless, "Now let me tell you my side of the story."

Heaven is not a mythical place, it can be found . . .
in the heart of a man who has found the work he
loves and the woman he loves.

—HELEN ROWLAND

11

You Meet So Many Interesting People

Elated by the sale of her second story to the *Ladies' Home Journal,*
Beatrice instantly thought of herself as one of New York's promising
young writers. Thriftily, she decided to economize by taking an expensive apartment. (All her life she has somehow justified her greatest
extravagances as long-run moneysavers, though her feminine logic
sometimes escapes me.) If she had to pay $100 a month rent for an
apartment instead of the modest $28 her tiny room near Columbia
cost, surely, she pointed out to me, she could easily make up the
difference by the greater cheapness of getting her own and better
meals at home. Restaurants charged $1.50, or $3 for two, for even a
halfway decent dinner; she could cook a meal for less than half the
price. Convinced by her indisputable logic, she sallied forth—conscience clear—in search of an expensive place to live.

On Gramercy Park, with Honoré Willsie Morrow, then editor of
Pictorial Review (with whom Beatrice had had a memorable tea),
living just catty-cornered, she found an apartment she instantly had
to have. When I looked at it with her, it seemed apparent to us
both that we should be married at once and live there happily ever

after. The big living room was on the fourth floor of a fine old brownstone mansion. Across verdant, iron-girded Gramercy Park, open only to us and other key holders, its three windows gazed cheerfully down on the entrance awning of the one club in New York I longed someday to join, the Players. On our apartment roof glistened a glass bubble, once an artist's studio, now a bedroom. At dark the Metropolitan tower rose tall and sparkling as a Christmas tree, winking across the low intervening roofs.

We were married in the Madison Avenue Presbyterian Church, with a minister friend of Beatrice's family officiating to let those back home know it was a real wedding. We couldn't afford to go home and be married. And Bibi's parents, to whom every $500 was important then, couldn't afford to come East. Beatrice's red-haired college friend, Ann Lichty, and red-headed Harlan backed us up. Better behaved than usual on this humbling occasion, I was only a few minutes late for the ceremony.

The fact that the glamorous apartment was unfurnished, and we had no furniture or money to buy any, did not daunt us. Nor did the fact that the kitchen, where the economical meals were to be prepared, was outfitted merely with a small table on which squatted a one-burner electric plate dispel Beatrice's romantic, money-saving dream.

I slapped together some makeshift bookcases—our greatest need because, my head suddenly addled by delirious bargains in a going-out-of-business bookshop, I'd squandered my last cent there. Many of these books I still possess—paying far more, doubtless, in portage charges, as I lug them from here to there, than their original cost. But books have a spiritual value. One absorbs something from their very presence. Beatrice, when she thinks I pile up too many, assures me one can't master a book by osmosis, by merely having it under one's bed.

Deciding to acquire some necessary secondhand furniture, we idled through the dingy shops along Third Avenue, picking up chairs and an occasional table as if they were asphodels to perfume our garden of dreams. So naïve were we, we even bought a secondhand bed, with the natural result. Our ignorant attempts at hasty fumigation nearly asphyxiated an innocent actor conning his lines in the back apartment. We found that bath towels cost an astonishing amount of money. So did blankets. Tableware, even from the five and ten, mounted to unexpected figures. And, after an attempt to simmer a homey, old-fashioned pot roast on the electric plate, and the dampening discovery that the romantic crystal bubble on the roof, while giving us Manhattan's starlit heavens at night, sprang leaks in a rainstorm, we finally decided to economize further. We took an even more expensive and glamorous but fully-furnished apartment nearby (also with a key to Gramercy Park)—thus saving all the money we had just discovered we would have to spend on furniture if we weren't to live like gypsies on the floor. Our harassed landlady seemed unwontedly eager to tear up our lease.

Our new abode was in charming, tree-shaded East Nineteenth Street, between Irving Place and Third Avenue (O. Henry had once lived around the corner), called the "Block Beautiful" because it was. In the old, well-maintained mansions, with flowery window boxes, brightly painted doorways and gleaming fanlights, lived piquant Dorothy Gish and handsome James Rennie. John Barrymore and Michael Strange had quarreled just down the street. Across the way red-bearded Ernest Boyd, distinguished author and critic, pontificated. And in our own building upcoming radio commentator John Vandercook shared his personal views with us since, by airshaft connecting our tiny kitchens, he lived just whispering distance above. New York's brilliant, englamoured literary and theatrical life seemed to throb at our very door.

My newspaper pay, $35 a week, was upped to $40 on my marriage by Edmund Bartnett, the *Sun*'s humane city editor. My salary, it is true, just barely covered the rent—$150 a month—but Beatrice confidently expected to sell more short stories for eating money. Thus we peered serenely into the dark future.

Somewhat to her surprise, however, Beatrice found the responsibility of keeping a small apartment in order, preparing two meals a day for a hungry husband not content with snacks, while commuting half an hour by subway to Columbia University for her second year at the School of Journalism, took more time than she had anticipated. The short-story output dwindled.

But I had persuaded Burton Rascoe, editor of the New York *Tribune*'s saucy book supplement, and his corruscating, acidulous, kind-hearted assistant, Isabel Paterson, to let me do book reviews at $12 a column. Each evening, Beatrice in her cupboard-like kitchenette, about four by five, whipped up an economical meat loaf or a long-lasting casserole for the tin oven which sat on our, by now, two-burner gas stove. There might be, also, salad and Fairy Gingerbread—as it was then called in the Boston Cookbook, bible to brides, torn of leaf but with us yet. After dinner I wrote savage, opinionated book reviews as though the future of belles-lettres depended on my judgment about an opus often better not written at all except that it helped keep Beatrice and me alive. Each Sunday we would rush for the *Tribune* book section and measure whether the iron-fisted makeup editor had cut my stretched-out opinions to $8, $12, or down to a mere $2.

Isabel Paterson generously doled out weekly books for review. I shall always cherish her, though she alienated many an aspiring littérateur with her waspish wit. Screwing up her antic, monkey's face, strangely beautiful because of the intelligence of her lively eyes, she would let go her shafts, each tip poisoned. Once she asked me why novelist Donald Douglas was not speaking.

"I should think," I ventured, "because you called him a fool—in print."

Her eyebrows shot up, incredulous. "But he is!"

"To have it pointed out in public," I countered, "seems to anger people. Some people even resent its being said privately—the really thin-skinned ones, that is."

Perhaps my fondness for this brilliant, strangely lovely witch stems, in part, from her abrupt remark one day, apropos of nothing it seemed. As I was loading up with an armful of dubious books for review, she said sharply: "You're bound for success!"

When one is earning $40 a week, and struggling to keep two chins above water, a stunning observation like this cannot be ignored.

"What makes you think so?" All New York seemed pointedly ignoring this possibility.

"I can tell," she said, all sibyl, expertly rolling a cigarette from a bag of Bull Durham and clicking a kitchen match alight with her thumbnail. She didn't like her Delphic pronouncements questioned. I went out on air.

"How does she know?"—my mind drifted off into one of the most satisfactory daydreams I'd had in months.

Beatrice did sell two or three short stories that year. The cash plugged up unforeseen holes in our fanciful budget and enabled her to buy a new $25 hat. I even fulfilled an ambition—fired in me as soon as the magazine was launched—to sell an article, in its first year, to *The American Mercury.* "Wells of Correct Thought" brought in $150. We celebrated by a lavish dinner at the old Brevoort. Now I felt I'd really achieved that dream of far-off Iowa—being admitted to membership in the intelligentsia by my twin gods Mencken and Nathan. And when Nathan followed up Mencken's surprising acceptance of the piece by asking if I'd be on tap to revise manuscripts which might have intrinsic merit but weren't in *American Mercury* style, I got really intoxicated. But the news, marvelous as it was, was difficult to translate into dollars.

In my first months in New York I had somehow failed to convince Carr V. Van Anda, brilliant managing editor of the *New York Times,* that he should hire me to review plays. He had listened nearly an hour while I made my pitch. I finally left, courteously trying to shield him from the knowledge he'd live to regret the turndown. Nor did the famous producer Winthrop Ames seem as anxious for my services as, in my opinion, he should have been. He suggested I might try being advance man for a road show—thus to leave the New York I had barely reached. Such early kindnesses to an eager nobody by important men I, later, tried to repay by being accessible to aspiring youngsters, especially those without solid silver introductions.

I had managed to get a job at all only because of Harlan's machinations. With money running out in our first year in New York, I had fallen in with Harlan's generous, quixotic idea that I explore with him the Athens of America, Boston, where he was being transferred as United News' New England correspondent. His job paid $35 a week; he offered to halve this sum with me. I was to take over every other night. Thus, though we would each have only $17.50 weekly to

sustain life, we would have half our time free to write. Harlan, however, usually sauntered into our dingy Portland Street headquarters
just before each midnight news report was put on the national wire.
Complaining of loneliness, he was probably guarding me against
fatal error. His newspaper experience was far greater than mine and
his was the official responsibility. I, on my off days, stayed selfishly
closeted in our Harvard Street lodgings, in Cambridge, feverishly
writing a play, *The Woman You Marry,* designed to conquer Broadway. It only needed a good second act. In the immemorial fashion of
beginners, I was having some trouble devising one. The first act
merely gets the character into trouble. Any novice can do that.
Solving the plot takes skill.

Before we left Boston—Harlan going to the United Press in New
York—our salary had been raised to $60. Through no fault of mine,
I felt sure—though on a dull night we once did trap Amy Lowell into
denying she was about to wed a lesser poet, John Gould Fletcher.
After twenty minutes' sputtering, good for a column of copy, La
Lowell exploded: "I believe you're just making this all up," whereat
we hastily rang off.

Even more fanciful was Harlan's masterful letter of recommendation, one of the most imaginative bits of fictional characterization,
if not of actual mendacity, ever concocted by a journalist. Little
wonder I've preserved it. Under his letterhead as Manager, Boston
Bureau, United News, Harlan wrote:

. . . Mr. Gould is blessed to a high degree with the ability to meet personages in all walks of life on terms of ease and equality. In personality
he is exceedingly pleasant, and considerable acquaintance with him con-
vinces me that he is a young man of sound principles and high character.

His writing is lucid and concise, forceful and illuminating; and his
copy is accurate and straightforward. I feel no hesitancy in vouching for
his ability to acquit himself creditably in positions demanding newspaper
writing ability of high order.

What else could the New York *Sun* do but hire me, enabling me
to marry Beatrice as long as she didn't expect me to support her.

The *Sun* city desk, I think, soon realized I was a rank amateur,
but one of the qualities necessary for a member of the working press

is brash brass. Newspapermen lead a charmed life. You don't have
to believe with Horace Greeley in

> . . . . . the voice of the Press—on the startled ear breaking
> In giant-born prowess, like Palla of old;
> 'Twas the flash of Intelligence, gloriously waking
> A glow on the cheek of the noble and bold.

but it helps.

If you are a newspaperman even on a reporter's salary, Manhattan
is yours. No doors are barred, since it's not you on whom the door
would be slamming, but your powerful paper. You and your paper
are one. An indignant press woman, refused an interview, was heard
threatening a reluctant Senator, "You can't do this to the *New York
Times!*"

At the center of tomorrow's headlines, one watched Lindbergh
wobble off toward Paris and fame. With Queen Marie of Roumania,
that lively beauty, one did the town. Mayor Walker answered or
evaded impertinent questions, though you were palpably trying to
convict him of crimes for which he subsequently fled to Paris as the
Seabury investigation closed around him. One shared a table in
Texas Guinan's night-club speakeasy with Peaches Browning and a
noted beau, his baby-talk letters later published fully in the press.
Senators running for office listened flatteringly to your opinions. The
head of Keith-Albee surprisingly sought your view of Nazimova to
headline a curious one-acter. Helen Hayes received you in her
dressing room and Texas Guinan in her bedroom—her ceiling one
vast mirror. Peggy Hopkins Joyce told how she won her men. (It's
not as simple as you think.) One watched John Barrymore idly sort-
ing a collection of mail, by burning unopened bills at the Players'
open fire, as he told you his concept of Hamlet. Theodore Dreiser,
suddenly successful with *An American Tragedy,* and Mae West,
sentenced to jail for disorderly conduct in a play called *Sex,* which
subsequently brought her fame and fortune, met you warmly. Otto
Kahn, that Renaissance man, with his cultivated mind and mid-
European accent, showed treasures of art in his Fifth Avenue palace.
One discussed at the speakeasy bar of "21" what the world would
read next day at breakfast.

Members of the working press are usually literate, rarely uninteresting. Among my occasional companions were scathing George Kaufman before he scintillated in *The Man Who Came to Dinner* and *Once in a Lifetime;* quiet, sardonic Dick Lockridge, perhaps even then planning amusing Mr. and Mrs. North for *The New Yorker;* Russel (Buck) Crouse, as blandly funny then as in *Life with Father* or *The Sound of Music,* and as modest, famous, as unknown. Like many of our hard-drinking craft, he quit drinking, he told me, when, a young reporter in Kansas City, he found himself riding a streetcar one morning, a lily in his hand, without any clear idea where he got the lily. Jim Thurber was dreaming up Walter Mitty, his wit already pointed when the New York *Evening Post* thought him overpaid at $55 a week. Ernie Pyle, reporter extraordinary of the ordinary man, might never have grown famous if the ordinary man, as G.I., hadn't suddenly in 1941 become man-of-the-hour and Ernie his moving historian. It wasn't just the pleasure of knowing Stanley Walker, Laurence Stallings, Frank Sullivan, H. R. Knickerbocker, Nunnally Johnson, F.P.A., Bill Laurence, and others either famous or on the verge. The day-by-day routine newspaperman, whether he was later to become a Scotty Reston or to live and die Pat Clancy, had a special point of view, curiosity, a humorous, often antic verbalism, coming partly from his oblique, chancy acquaintance with the shoddy, the raffish, the great, and the merely notorious—all of whom he must weigh as well as report.

Everyone helps the new boy. Portly Joe Vila waddled across the *Sun*'s city room to try to make a sports writer of me. If he had, I would have disappointed him by trying to write like Heywood Broun; later Joe Palmer and Red Smith set even better models.

But I was more interested in tickets to plays, free for merely writing a review. Frank Munsey, Park Row's favorite ogre among newspaper publishers, as Adolph Ochs was its deity, was the *Sun*'s boss. Owing to the kind intervention of Bartnett, I never actually met Munsey, though I nearly met him under circumstances which would have terminated my newspaper career. I had been asked to cover the glamorous, bediamonded opening of one of those recurrent

Marion Davies movies William Randolph Hearst kept trying to foist on a resistant world. Miss Davies, an affectionate little Follies girl, touched the heart of every man who could afford such expensive emotion. She especially moved Mr. Hearst, whose string of papers staunchly supported his generous notion that Miss Davies was an actress. I definitively settled this question—not in Mr. Hearst's or Marion's favor—turning in my column story at midnight to the night city editor with a consciousness of duty well and pitilessly done. But when I scanned the *Sun*'s morning edition my review was nowhere in sight. Instead, there appeared half a column of slavish praise straight from one of Mr. Hearst's handouts. Bartnett quietly beckoned me over to his desk.

"Mr. Gould." They called even reporters Mr. in those days before Roosevelt's calculated palship ended such punctilio. "Mr. Gould, I killed your fine review, which I enjoyed reading very much. Mr. Munsey and Mr. Hearst lunch together often at the Ritz, where Mr. Munsey lives. They are very good friends."

Should I have quit? Was it not important that the public be told the truth about Marion Davies? They did seem to divine it since they stayed away from her movies as if her acting might mark their unborn children.

But this assault on the freedom of the press was outweighed by my obligation to keep a roof over us. Luxuries we often got free. A friend's dinner jacket snugly fitted me; he didn't seem to be using it much. Since night-club openings happened frequently in the Roaring Twenties, I merrily went out-on-the-town often with only subway fare in my pocket—and knowing in what pocket every last nickel was. For fun I continued third-string dramatic criticism for the stellar Woollcott, whose scrimshaw style and gingerbread sentimentalisms won a wide public denied acerbic Percy Hammond and deftly humorous Broun. Here was I, just as I had daydreamed back in Des Moines after seeing *Sure Shot Sam,* telling people on Broadway, as the great William Winter had, what actors, playwrights, and producers were superb and when, alas, they had somehow not measured up. I remember Sophie Tucker once writing me a humble letter promising me next time she'd do better. Impossibly, yet inevitably, my tenuous vision had become a fragile reality. I was a Dramatic Critic—third string, that is.

The second year of our marriage we moved into the top floor of a rundown but once-handsome four-story mansion on a more than usually slummy Greenwich Village street. Our enormous, pale-beige living room soared into the high dark-raftered roof. A studio window stretched entirely across the north with a window seat running the room's width below. The real fireplace took off the chill with crackling cannel coal. This coal, and blocks of ice as well, were brought up four full flights by a short, smelly, cheerful man from round the corner. All very Barefoot in the Park, and as much fun. A small stairway crept up to a dark wood balcony under the peak of the roof—our guest room for friends from near and far. The recess below sheltered a walnut refectory table from some ancient French monastery and six austere monks' chairs—our dining room. In front, each with a tall dormer window catching all the southern sun and high enough to miss much din of clamorous Morton Street below, were two small, gay, slant-ceilinged bedrooms, one pale yellow, one aquamarine. A full-sized bath and a good kitchen with skylight completed our ménage. Our chairs, chests, and tables were provincial French, simple and old, in pale tones of fruitwood or dark walnut, collected in France by our artist landlady.

Since we were living entirely in the future, betting on a horse still at the starting gate, buying all that beautiful furniture on time seemed ideal. Eventually—after the agony of scraping up payments always due at awkward moments—I reached the old-fashioned conclusion it's better to pay cash or do without.

[Beatrice enters a demurrer:
Bruce came to this conclusion after he could afford to pay cash. At that time, without credit, with no cash, we would have been forced to live without a dining table or chests for our clothes.
So I would recommend the same extravagance to

any bride today, even though poor (if there are any such in these days of working wives, unemployment insurance, severance pay). If you must, live with one slip—a good one—and two pairs of shoes. Squander, if you need, on a charming place to live, one attractive to you and your friends. Your silver and china may come from Woolworth's. That doesn't matter.

I remember, years later, having tea with Eleanor Roosevelt in her apartment in Washington Square, being served in the same blue-patterned cups with which, at ten cents each, I had begun my married life. And she was the President's wife! The French provincial furniture we, struggling, bought on time, still beautiful, still cherished, is worth ten times what we paid for it. If we had bought what we could afford, it would have long ago been thrown away.

Try never to show a poor face to the world; it dampens your spirits.]

At Morton Street we spent several happy years. In an old frame house nearby, one of the few remaining, lived Vilhjalmur Stefansson, a witty bachelor twenty years our senior, with a trained explorer's eye for tropical ladies, whom I sometimes called the Friendly Arctic. He originally intended, he confided, to write blank-verse plays, but after reading William Vaughn Moody he decided he couldn't surpass either him or Shakespeare. So he briskly went into the less competitive field of exploring—his chief ambition was to excel and become famous. He did become one of the world's greatest explorers and geographers and helped open the air age across the poles. As a sideline he popularized the life-sustaining diet of "beef and bourbon." Always, he kept his friends laughing with shrewd, surprising comments. His brilliant *Standardization of Error* still amuses.

Malcolm Ross and James M. Cain—before the famous postman had even rung once—eked out a Greenwich Village existence right next door. There one night at a party a voluble, engaging extrovert,

Briton Hadden, full of drink but even more intoxicated with a mad project, told of his precarious young magazine to supplant *The Literary Digest,* called *Time.*

While in our Morton Street eyrie I was suddenly, to my dismay, shifted to Wall Street by the *Sun.* They wanted, Bartnett said, the city-room point of view in their financial pages. I disliked leaving my amusing cub reporter friends, and I didn't expect to enjoy the Street. Money, to me, was still somewhat sordid, reminiscent of those fat men with dollar sign vests of my youth.

Wall Street newsmen, I found, hadn't always the poor-but-proud rectitude which chiefly prevails in the city room. My piece about Wall Street for *Editor and Publisher,* revealing that certain financial reporters, for something of value, touted stock that insiders were anxious to unload on the public, seemed irritating to certain of my new associates, though I pointed out that not all Wall Street reporters were corruptible, any more than all stockbrokers became Richard Whitneys. A thousand dollars, I was shocked to learn, could reward the right sentence at the right time, in the right gossip column.

Most working newspapermen were, in my experience, fantastically honest in a world ever ready to bribe them if they would be bought. In spite of many faults, ruthless prying into personal lives, arrogant interruptions of busy men, opinionated criticism, journalists go far toward keeping the world as honest as it is, though newspapers are not unmindful of their own interest.

I recall a reporter's telling me of Fire Commissioner Dorman's response when the *Sun* gave him an opportunity to read, in advance, a muckraking exposé of the Fire Department. Dorman declined to glance at the series.

"I'm sure," he admitted cheerfully, "my department sometimes neglects its duty. For instance, I suspect that *Sun* building of yours, built for a department store, has so many fire violations it would cost $200,000 to satisfy a really vigilant fire inspector it was fireproof."

When the *Sun's* managing editor learned of Dorman's candid reaction to the proposed critique the series was, not surprisingly, dropped.

We journalists frequently exceed our rights. Sometimes we step beyond common decency in the excitement of the chase. Or, motivated by pique, to which even high-minded reporters, alas, are humanly subject, we can and do sometimes ride the object of our private dislike pretty hard, mistaking it for our public duty. But outright venality and political subservience, fairly common in the non-English press, seldom successfully exist in the United States.

James Reston, certainly one of the clearest-eyed commentators today, recently said:

> Our capacity to criticize everybody and our imperviousness to criticism ourselves, are still unmatched. . . . I believe in my profession. . . .
> The reporter is an educator, and the press and television have more effect on public attitudes and assumptions in the nation than all the schools, universities and books in the land.

In Wall Street I lost my naïve ideas about wicked moneychangers. The ethics of some might be low, but the standards of the leaders, I found, were high and rigorously maintained. Had I remained in Wall Street longer, I might have legitimately made a little money for myself, as most Street reporters did. Barney Baruch said, "If you want to make money, go where it's being made." But the New York *Post,* newly purchased by Curtis-Martin, asked me to return to the city room as reporter, offering me $65 a week. Harlan was there—perhaps he had spoken to his editor about me.

In the *Post*'s city room ambitious unknowns seethed and churned. Herschel Brickell was daily book critic; I later succeeded him. Amusing, percipient John Mason Brown, now famous as writer and lecturer, followed, as dramatic critic, lank, acrid John Anderson. The *Post* became a lively, readable paper which, however, like all Curtis-Martin newspapers, steadily lost money. Later, after Cyrus Curtis' death, the papers either were sold or folded—having lost, Cary Bok, a Curtis grandson, once told me, some fifty million dollars made by Curtis' profitable magazines. Curtis like Munsey, both from Maine, both successful with magazines, never got the hang of running newspapers.

Out of a casual interview for the *Post* grew a lifetime friendship. I'd been sent up to interview Daisy Fellowes—I suppose because she was a famous international beauty (one of the ten best-dressed,

Vogue said) and had written a light, sophisticated, not very good book, *Cats in the Isle of Man*. And, as a Singer-sewing-machine heiress, she was probably of interest to the advertising department. Maybe my assignment was simply a "Business Office Must." I remember, at the time, it didn't seem very important to me as I subwayed up to the Ritz. Odd, because Daisy became one of the important women of my life.

Daisy always insisted I was the only man who ever fell asleep while she was talking directly to him. If so, apparently in this respect, at least, I was unique. She had more than a little reputation on three continents as a *femme fatale*; I'm sure no one else ever fell asleep facing her. Her pride piqued, I became, perhaps, someone to subdue. In any case, when I left her as a reporter she asked me to return as a friend.

Of course I hadn't really fallen asleep in Daisy's presence then, nor did I ever. It was simply that when interviewing someone I used, at times, to half close my eyes. Thus I could register on my memory what the person said. Perhaps she thought I fell asleep, but I doubt it. Her lively mind was given to humorous little conceits she wove fantastically into a cozy fabric of friendship. Because of her French *r*, for instance, she couldn't pronounce Bruce without sounding like a stuttering Sam. So she teasingly called me her prickly pear—thus by indirection reminding me I should always be nicer to women. I was, in those days, rather unnecessarily thorny and stiff of spine.

In *The Red and the Black,* Stendhal, speaking of upstart Julien Sorel, says: "A beautiful woman of fashion is the sight that most astonishes a clever man of country origin when he arrives amid the higher ranks of society."

When I first came to New York I was certainly a wide-eyed country boy. Fortunately for me, unlike Julien Sorel, I had early learned one can be friends with beautiful women without mixing sex into it more than just to be aware that your delightful companion is a girl and likes always to be treated as such.

Before marrying Reggie, a cousin of Winston Churchill and a most amiable boulevardier, Daisy, daughter of the Duc de Caz, had been the widow of the Prince de Broglie, killed in World War I, by whom she had two daughters. She had a fourth by Reggie, and one in between. Determined to live her own life as amusingly as possible, with enormous wealth, impeccable clothes and décor, she had selected Reggie, I'm sure, with as much care as she might have picked out just the proper umbrella to add the exactly right finishing touch to her always delectable costume; handy, too, for a rainy day.

Daisy was the only woman I was ever to know, rich or poor, who insisted on carrying her own silk sheets for sleeping car and hotel. Even in wartime London, later, she always had with her a softly voluminous mink throw for her couch. Into her Rolls she secretly smuggled a hot-water bottle in what seemed an innocent little cushion to tuck behind her straight little back. In short, she always made herself as toastily comfortable as a cat. Daisy was the only very rich person I ever knew, male or female, who seemed to know what money is for—to make living easy and attractive, for yourself and your friends, to preserve energy for enjoyment.

A friend who had lived long in France once asserted that Daisy was "the wickedest woman in Paris." If that was so, it was a side of her life she amused herself with when there seemed nothing more important to do. After all, she was widely curious, as interested in sitting with the woman magistrate all day in Jefferson Market Court as spending a cocktail hour at Elizabeth Marbury's theatrical salon on Beekman Place. She was not limited in her interests either to virtue or its opposite. She neither hid nor flaunted her private emotional life, her adventures in sex—more for conquest and adventure than for affection, it seemed—and I could scarcely have been unaware of them, since I saw her so much.

She wasn't too eager about them either, being willing to stand up a lover if there was a chance to sneak into a most exclusive speakeasy and see Legs Diamond plain. The world of fashion then seemed hopelessly fascinated by gangsters. Taking her once to a Harlem boîte for the sole reason that four minor gangsters had been rubbed out there the night before, I noticed an outsized diamond on her finger worth perhaps $200,000, I surmised. Sternly pocketing it, though she protested it was insured and if it was pinched it might enable her to buy a bigger yacht than her present 250-tonner, *Sister Anne*, I said:

"I don't care about you losing it. I just don't want you to lose a finger, too. We are not going among very polite people."

The possibility of mayhem seemed to make the expedition even more exciting. But the diamond remained safely in my pocket.

Daisy was the only thoroughly worldly person I had ever known, charmingly and wittily so, shrewd as to money, reveling in material splendor, polished like a stone by an unloved childhood, unloving parents, amused by social one-upmanship but giving her best in a few friendships.

To my vehement statement, once, that above all I wished to retain independence in living, in working, in creation—not, of course in marriage; that would defeat that fascinating dual arrangement—Daisy sagely questioned: "Can you afford it?"—thus showing the difference in our measures.

After I had known Daisy a bit she evinced curiosity regarding Beatrice, about whom, of course, I had spoken a great deal. She suggested Beatrice come to tea without me, which, for reasons of her own, Beatrice decided to do.

My friendship with Daisy had naturally irked Beatrice somewhat, though Bibi was determined to be fair about it. How could an intelligent wife, Bibi argued with herself, object to her husband's innocently opening the door into a totally different world? It might have been less of a strain if the witty, charming, worldly, sophisticated, fashionable dweller on that planet leading me by the hand hadn't been quite so beautiful. But we had come to New York to see, to do, to learn— why quibble because my cicerone was naughty as well as nice?

Dutifully, I had shared my enlightening experiences with Bibi, who, cooking our dinner or bathing our child, loved hearing about Daisy's fabulous clothes—her voluminous chinchilla wrap, which must have decimated the entire Andean rodent population—her dinner parties, her endlessly amusing idiosyncrasies, her barbed comments illuminating a world neither of us knew as yet. But when I told Bibi that Daisy, with Paris gowns, jewels undreamed of, crystal bowls floating whole acres of fresh gardenias in her salon at the Ritz, was really an unhappy woman because she had never been truly "loved for herself alone,"

Beatrice startled me by turning from her sizzling frying pan to give me a sizzling glance.

She pointed out to my masculine ignorance that most familiar tactic of a man-collecting woman—the poor little me who has never found true love. Put so bluntly, I did see Daisy's appeal had its funny side; perhaps my sorrow for Daisy's plight *was* unduly pitying.

But Beatrice agreed with me, I think, that the building of a slowly explored, affectionate friendship can be a lasting pleasure—and Daisy was a most engaging, many-faceted friend.

Beatrice was saved from jealousy, too, on another count, one on which both of us showed ourselves almost childishly naïve. It scarcely occurred to either me or Beatrice, then, that a woman of Daisy's advanced age (she claimed thirty-eight) could be sexually irresistible.

In any case, Beatrice, invited for tea, went, dressed in her best two-year-old navy-blue suit. Being a good reporter, she gave me a blow-by-blow account of that meeting, recalling every second of it— Daisy's lacquered dark head, her blue brocade hostess gown—doubtless by Schiaparelli—her doll-like poise, the mannered social greeting (so similar, as she told it, in its sculptured intonations to the phrase made famous in *My Fair Lady,* "How kind of you to [let me] come"). Daisy, Beatrice told me, was sitting for her portrait to Cecil Beaton when she arrived. Bibi was, it appeared, to have the pleasure of watching, cup of tea in hand, that amiable, dandified photographer-artist demonstrate how to flatter the rich or royal into posing. He was directing a stream of compliments toward Daisy to ensure the responsive gaze, the pleased half smile he needed for his picture.

"In Venice—that beautiful gown with roses at the Duc of ———'s ball . . . shall never forget your rising from the sea at Antibes—like Venus."

Beatrice heard all this with easily disguised pleasure. Occasionally, when her presence was recalled, a conversational bone was thrown her way: "You've been to Capri? No! Too bad. You must go—"

Beatrice, not unduly critical of persons merely because they were unlike her, but interested as she might be in a brilliantly colored denizen of an aquarium she was inspecting, endured all this with outward calm for a space, but, having been taught that guests should be included in the conversation, she felt her blood begin to simmer. After all, the fish in this aquarium was her hostess. Here Bibi was —from her point of view, at least—giving this beautiful woman as her gift her husband's society and friendship without a display of normal, wifely jealousy. But she certainly was not going to be patronized for her generosity.

Outwardly unruffled, she soon rose to go. Daisy, rising to say goodbye, slightly spilled her tea, to Beatrice's—she admitted to me, later —savage joy. At the door, however, as she shook hands, Beatrice looked Daisy firmly in the eye and said, with a significance no one could misinterpret: "Thank you, Mrs. Fellowes. I've had a most *amusing* afternoon."

Daisy, startled out of her complacence, returned Bibi's gaze, felt the barb in her comment and, not unwilling to laugh at her own discomfiture, was amused in turn. They shook hands warmly.

I wasn't at all surprised the next day when Daisy said to me: "Your Beatrice makes me realize how much I paint my face." And, later, "It was as though the sun came into the room."

On Daisy's last night in New York Beatrice and I had tickets for a play. Daisy asked me to dine with her at Jack and Charlie's, on Forty-eighth Street, and see her off. Beatrice said, "Go, and say goodbye to her properly. We can go to the play another night. But tell Daisy I would like to give her a farewell present—my husband's company on her last evening."

Experience is what makes you recognize a mistake when you make it again.

—EARL WILSON

12

Broadway Drama

In our apartment, whose balcony rail I adorned with the stained scarlet-and-gold capote my friend Juan Belmonte used in his last bullfight, we entertained journalistic and literary friends at tea. Ours was not a hard-drinking group though we lived among those people later to become known as "the lost generation." Perhaps life itself was too stimulating and absorbing for us to need the prod of liquor or the tranquillizing of drunkenness. We were almost all enthralled by some dream of work to be done which required our best.

Finding her short-story inspiration running dry—a not uncommon occurrence among beginners—Beatrice took a job on the New York *Sunday World*. Following Bruce Bliven's canny counseling, she presented to the managing editor several good feature ideas thought out ahead—sure way to catch a hard-pressed executive's attention. Her story of twenty diverse families living in one of New York's uptown apartment houses as unacquainted neighbors was spread across the entire front page of the *World*'s Sunday feature section, launching Beatrice as a metropolitan journalist. On the strength of it and several other cogently developed stories in a new vein she became woman's editor of the *Sunday World*. Across the hall from her crowded, shabby quarters, F.P.A. and Heywood Broun each had a tiny office. At desks adjacent to hers were Phil Stong, then writing *State Fair,* successful novel and enduring musical, and Louis Weitzenkorn—truly the ugliest man I have ever known but like Scarron, the poet, with beautiful women always in love with him. Likable, fantastically incorruptible, he and desk neighbor Paul Sifton were both to become not-too-well-known Broadway playwrights.

We had been living so hard, absorbing the many-faceted life of New York, we had not been able to embark on our long-time ambition to write plays. True, I had started that comedy *The Woman You Marry*. But, as I lived my adventurous way through a few years of matrimony as it is, I found my verbal ideas of women and marriage, mostly borrowed from Wilde, Shaw, and Sheridan, neither as funny nor as sound as they'd seemed to an all-knowing bachelor. Then, I knew all about women. I could concoct an epigram about them more easily than falling downstairs.

Comedy is corrupted by wit, says Macaulay.

The real object of the drama is the exhibition of human character . . . situations which develop character form the best plot.

No writers have injured the comedy of England so deeply as Congreve and Sheridan. Both were men of splendid wit and polished taste. Unhappily, they made their characters in their own likeness. . . . It was not from want of wit that Shakespeare adopted so different a manner . . . he knew that the purpose of playing is "to hold the mirror up to nature."

The Woman You Marry proved sterile.

Now, secure in two well-paying jobs, we had reached the time to test whether we could, in fact, write a producible play. With my new sophistication as part-time dramatic critic, I was becoming aware that many plays are written, most never produced. Even after staging, barely one play out of twenty succeeds. But, though betting on the races stirs in me only mild interest, gambling with life excites me. We resolved to try our luck—the odds, obviously, a hundred to one against success. But why die wondering?

The character of Ninon de L'Enclos—famous *fille de joie* in Louis XIV's time—had aroused our interest; maybe, I should say, my interest.

Beautiful and witty, she had many lovers, many of whom became her friends; her friends included the most distinguished men of her day —La Rochefoucauld, Condé, Corneille, St. Evremond; to young Voltaire she left a legacy to buy books. They admired her conversation, her intellect, her loyalty, as well as her charm. She was patently no lady. We decided to call our comedy *The First Gentleman of Her Time,* since Ninon's courage, wit, independence, and integrity seemed a masculine pattern of virtues at least in her time.

During the winter Beatrice researched in libraries, reading the diaries of St. Simon, the letters of Mme. de Sévigné, all she could find about the period, some in her sketchy college French. We rented for August a primitive cottage on Bailey Island, Maine, deciding we could scrimpingly live there for a month on two weeks' vacation pay. Rent and overhead of our New York apartment went on. My wife, a planner, insisted on writing regularly each crisp morning on our open porch looking out over the turbulent sea. An intelligent Simon Legree, she believes one cannot just trust to getting around to writing after dawdling over everything else the day offers. Each morning we resolutely inched our play forward. After lunch we would catch cunners off the weathered rocks for supper, play tennis, or on more balmy days plunge briefly into the icy surf. At the end of a second August thus spent, we returned to steaming New York with $19 and a completed play manuscript in our pockets. Recklessly, using our first pay checks, we squandered $110 having *The First Gentleman* as beautifully typed as she deserved. With fond confidence one moment and utter disbelief the next, I took it round to the leading agents of the day, American Play Company, founded by Elizabeth Marbury.

A call from American Play a few days later asked me to come in to see its head, John Rumsey. White-linen spatted, portly with Ritz garden restaurant eating, a man of the world who'd handled plays of all the theatre great, Rumsey balanced my whole future on the edge of his tongue as I awaited his verdict, rigid on my chair.

"Mr. Gould," he said—I could scarcely hear over my pounding blood—"Mr. Gould, I think you have a valuable property here."

Stunned to hear our Shavian, Ibsenistic, Congrevian (with slight overtones of Henry Arthur Jones) comedy referred to in such crass commercial terms, I was torn between delight and anger. His interest resided simply in the fact that the play might make money! Valuable property! All he could see was his 10 percent! Unimportant to him that the drama might be a masterpiece! It was years before I realized that both Shakespeare and Shaw were first-class businessmen, intent in squeezing the last dollar out of their genius—and doing so. But, though momentarily unhappy over Rumsey's sordid obsession with mere money, I took my racing heart speedily home to impart the five-star final news to Beatrice. We celebrated, as I recall, not with champagne, scarcely yet in our experience, but with another magnificent lunch at the Brevoort, breast of guinea hen under glass, flaming crêpes suzette.

Day followed day—Broadway didn't immediately take fire—and we found ourselves continuing on the journalistic treadmill. We had drifted slowly down to earth when the next amazing news reached our ears—Ethel Barrymore was taking an option! Five hundred dollars—minus Rumsey's 10 percent. Ethel Barrymore was already old —to us a beldame in her forties—but still the most glamorous member of that storied Barrymore dynasty. With John and Lionel, she was undisputed Queen of what George S. Kaufman and Edna Ferber called the Royal Family. Rumsey nodded his sage head. "I told you, a valuable property."

Though Ethel Barrymore showed no immediate intention of producing the play as weeks and months followed, still, for us, the die was cast. Taking the entire following summer off, again in Maine, we wrote *Man's Estate*.

In October, 1927, our daughter was born—you see, Beatrice, I did remember (when prodded!)—a happy and healthy child. We had spent months looking up names in our family trees. Finally we found one among Beatrice's illiterate ancestors back in the sixteenth century when, I suppose, they spelled Cecily Sesaly. Sesaly was the red-haired child I'd promised Beatrice when we first spoke of marriage.

We built her a small porch (or screened-in-box) on the roof projection sloping out from one of the south dormer windows. Here she took her airings twice a day, sleeping in the sun in her little basket, or later playing with her toys and watching raw life in grimy Morton Street below.

While we were delighting in our new and miraculous toy, there came a day tattooed on my memory. Beatrice had, as usual, bathed her child—directing at her that stream of conversational trivia which Sesaly seemed to be attending with wide-eyed understanding as she gazed up at her babbling mamma—had given her a ten-o'clock feeding, put her out in her sunny little box for the morning sleep, and departed for her office at the New York *World.* At this time I was working much at home, doing a daily book column for the *Post,* so Beatrice felt freer to leave her child with our housekeeper helper.

In the early afternoon, the telephone rang.

"Is this Mr. Gould? This is Katharine Cornell."

Perhaps some friend was being antic, but the unforgettable voice was magical even over the phone. I uttered a strangled "Yes."

"Guthrie" (her husband, Guthrie McClintic, a successful young producer had just had great success with Maxwell Anderson's *Saturday's Children*) "Guthrie telephoned me from Seattle. He wants to do your play *Man's Estate.* He will be in touch with you personally when he returns."

I think I mumbled, "Thank you." I am not sure. I hope I did—my brain was a whirling kaleidoscope.

Pacing up and down the length of our apartment, envisoning opening-night glories with that volatile imagination of the addicted daydreamer, I could already hear the thunderous applause, read ecstatic reviews. I decided to wait until Beatrice came home and meet her at the door with the astounding news and our lovely daughter, who, with the play, comprised our two formidable creations to date.

The telephone rang.

The American Play Company's Richard J. Madden, gradually taking over from John Rumsey, was speaking. "Can you go up and see Jed Harris right away?" he asked. "He wants to produce your play *Man's Estate.*"

Jed Harris at that moment perched on the pinnacle of a stunningly successful career. Every play he had produced had been a smash hit.

All made theatrical history—*Broadway, Coquette, The Royal Family*.
Legendary before thirty, a multimillionaire, with the touch of Midas,
yet fanatically devoted to excellence, he was called the Boy Genius;
and thought of himself in slightly larger terms.

On advice of the American Play Company—with all-knowing
Woollcott, too, assuring us we couldn't go wrong with Jed Harris—
we accepted the Boy Wonder's offer. Guthrie McClintic's career, while
outstanding, indeed amazing, was not meteoric like Jed's. That evening
we spent a goodly share of our expected $500 advance celebrating
with friends, dancing in night spots and Harlem clubs—then risky
but not dangerous—following this by a scrambled-eggs-and-sausage
breakfast at Childs in time to start another day's work without last
night's sleep. After years of scrimping, soaring dreams, and discouraging drudgery, it seemed we had finally found rainbow's end. We had
reckoned without a true knowledge of Jed Harris.

Jed, a small, slight man with a dark, saturnine face, was, in spite
of his narrow head and long jaw, rather good-looking when he was
shaven (about half the time). And, when he wished to charm (less
often), he could call birds out of the air. When he chose to be
winning he was hypnotic, weaving a spell of flattery which was intuitive
as to one's hidden vanities and dreams. His happy victim moved,
shining with success, in an airy castle built by Jed's flattering verbiage.

"Do you know the French Riviera? You must take a villa at Antibes
to celebrate your first hit."

"You have a baby? A fortunate child—with such gifted parents!"

"We will all go to London in June for the English production."

For several days Jed overwhelmed us with compliments which,
in our dazed condition, seemed to us less like flattery than the bare
truth. Contracts were signed and the play immediately cast with what
looked like a dream collection of stars.

But swiftly Jed could revert to vituperation, choosing again with
uncanny perception his opponent's most sensitive points to wound
with rapier words. So beguiling was Jed's blue-bearded, long-jawed
smile when he was in flattering mood, one realized only too late his
smile was that of Peter Pan's crocodile.

Gradually it became apparent, even to us, that Jed had bought the play as a vehicle for the plain, almost ugly, brilliant young actress Ruth Gordon, who had starred in *Saturday's Children,* and with whom Jed was beginning to fall in love. For her, he wanted the entire play rewritten, he slowly made plain, the ending completely changed, so that the young woman (Ruth Gordon) became the dominant, heroic figure.

Theoretically, by Dramatist Guild contract, an author has complete say about every detail of his precious manuscript. Not a word can be changed without his permission. Practically, however, the producer exerts almost total leverage. With Jed's record of infallible success—Broadway at his feet—this was especially so, while Beatrice and I were Hansel and Gretel babes-in-the-wood. Our only similarity to Jed was that we were all under thirty. Lulled by cunning flattery, beguiled by his glittering fame, we eagerly took time off from our jobs —city rooms are generous that way—to try to make the constant revisions Jed required. Rehearsals, held usually late in the day and often running far into the night, can be agony to one whose metabolism is not on the nighthawk side. Beatrice, a fresh-as-a-daisy-morning girl, with a child to care for, adjusted gallantly but it was grueling uphill work. When Jed did not like new lines we had written, he would cry, in mortal anguish, perhaps at 2 A.M.: "Give me a new line—quick! My God! You slow-witted Nordics!"

Those who displeased him were lacerated. An elderly, adequate but not brilliant actor from the musical world playing the father's part—Jed was hopefully casting against type—was finally whiplashed into bumbling confusion. Gradually we learned, and saw, why Jed Harris was to become a thoroughly disliked man on Broadway—only Ruth Gordon, who, with her own strength and confidence was fascinating him, momentarily escaped his cruelty.

I recall the story of an old actor rehearsing in a play put on by a well-known producer. For days the producer had been slashing his psyche to mincemeat. The old actor had difficulty remembering his few lines. His acting skills, from long misuse, had become stereotyped. Too rigid for fresh ways, he would, it seemed likely, be fired before the opening. Dress rehearsal night it was raining, a cold and miserable night to venture out. The old man carefully put on his rubbers against the chilling damp, then stepped forth into space from the window of his high hotel room.

When this story was told to Jed, there was a thoughtful moment before he said anything—long enough, perhaps, for his racing mind to accompany the old actor down that long, lethal drop.

"Did he bounce?" he asked finally, his crocodile smile widening.

Jed perhaps felt hurts so much the only way he found to protect himself was to act as if he was inhuman. I found it impossible to hate Jed—mostly he irritated me, or roused my pity.

Our Broadway opening was scheduled for the fall of 1928, preceded by June tryouts. At the first, in Long Branch, the father-actor, miserable and confused, fortified himself with drink. Remembering his triumph in Gilbert and Sullivan operettas, he did everything except a pratfall to get a laugh. Our play, already distorted by Jed's changes, which seemed motivated by passion rather than art, ballooned out of shape like bubble gum. The audience laughed in the wrong places. What was supposed to be funny sounded glum. Beatrice and I, cowering in the back row, could finally bear it no longer. We crept out of the theatre to walk up and down before a chain shoestore near by— I can still remember with anguish almost every $3.95 shoe in that bright-lit window. The world's drama trembled in the balance as I heard myself saying:

"If this is what audiences are like, I—I—I won't write for the theatre!"

Such a transfer of guilt, as he threatens the theatre with loss of his genius, has saved many a playwright's reason. It takes considerable experience to teach him that a coughing, hard-of-hearing, program-rustling public can be spellbound only by life distilled in poetry— with, of course, a little assist from actor and director.

Friends who had come down from New York for the opening were reassuring. The assistant director murmured confident words. During the second week, in Atlantic City, the play seemed to pull together, audience response improved. Much work on the manuscript would admittedly be needed during the summer. Suddenly Jed seemed cheerful. He resumed his ebullience; soon we would be more rich and famous, possibly both, than we originally thought. The day before the show closed for the summer he sailed luxuriously for Europe. It was not until the boat was well out at sea that his manager, Mr. Whitaker, invited me to his office. Jed was dropping our play overboard. He couldn't afford a failure—or a half success—and the play hadn't worked out for Ruth Gordon. His option would be allowed to expire. We could peddle the manuscript (even with the improvements Jed had so generously suggested) elsewhere.

Word of failure runs along Broadway like fire through dry grass. We had lunched at the Algonquin, and acquaintances there, Beatrice felt, looked at us uneasily. With her intuition, she refused to go with me to Jed's office. She had some shopping to do at Stern's. She would wait for me at the Sixth Avenue entrance. She knew my news when she saw me. Even Richard J. Madden, that imperturbable friend of beat-down dramatists, was somewhat discouraged by the blow.

We had planned to return to Maine and start work on another play. Beatrice had given up her *World* job for the summer, deluded by promised riches. Luckily, I still had my book-reviewing column, which I could handle wherever I was. Villas on the Riviera crumbled. The London season vanished in a fog. Once again the problem was how to write and still eat. Beatrice, I think, got some happiness from the knowledge she needn't ever see Jed Harris again.

Maine was lovely, but the blow, after supreme confidence on every side, proved nearly deadening. Slowly we regrouped our forces. Icy water, reviving sun, pungent scent of pine needles helped us to breathe again. Salt air and bracing water remind you that your ancestors survived much more difficult times, while building a nation. At last we began another play—its subject suggested by our experiences in the theatre with Jed Harris.

Jed—his real name Jedediah Horowitz, born somewhere near Newark—might have ruled Broadway as his private kingdom for a generation if, along with his brilliance, he'd been capable of love. No producer rivaled his impudent talent in that period of the twenties when Broadway was at its best—perhaps the best in the world. But a wicked old fairy had, at birth, done something to Jed—he lacked heart.

Most plays don't earn even the money spent to get them to Broadway. Half-a-dozen plays each year do succeed fantastically; everyone connected gets famous and rich—usually not the same ones who became famous the season before. But many die out of town, as had *Man's Estate,* whose title Jed had changed to *King's X.* Maybe he'd always had his fingers crossed.

When we returned, restored, in the fall, we learned that Dick Madden had not lost faith in our play—not Jed's version, but our original one. Guthrie McClintic, justifiably piqued, would not reconsider. But someone at the Theatre Guild had "asked for further copies." Our spirits began to rise. Meantime, Ethel Barrymore renewed her option again on *The First Gentleman,* requesting a fresh copy. (Before each renewal that lovely lady lost her copy—did she paper a room with them?) With Barrymore's $500, less 10 percent, in our hands, and a loan from my father-in-law, we made a first payment on the New Jersey farm where we now live. Harry Blackmar, having retired from his school superintendent's position, had been almost wiped out financially by the Iowa land depression, which had dealt so disastrously with Ted Gallup's father and a thousand others. He needed a place to rest and recover his spirits. My mother-in-law, with that remarkable ability of women to meet adversity like an old friend, had taken her master's degree the preceding year at Teachers College, Columbia University. Offered a position by Hunter College in their extension courses, she began teaching night English classes for foreign-born students. Commuting from the Hopewell farm, spending two or three nights a week in town with us, she provided from her modest fees a tiny income while Harry restored his health, like Candide, working in his garden.

Hope and discouragement alternately marked that year. Our daughter took her first outings in a fuzzy, lettuce-green snow suit, its hood framing a rosy smiling face and rosy hair. But "No-definite-word" from the Theatre Guild stretched on longer than a delayed answer should. There were half-a-dozen Guild directors all with volatile personalities and all with a vote. We were fearful of upsetting a delicate balance by pressing for decision. Fearful, too, of learning what the decision might be.

On exhilarating weekends we explored our new farm (financially speaking, about one-fifth ours), with its fields, brown and bare, or

Never Underestimate the Power of a...Woman and a Man!

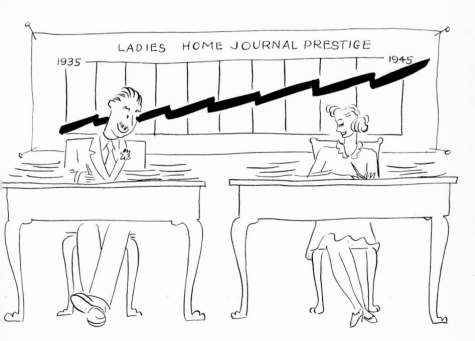

"Never Underestimate the Power of a Woman" cartoon illustrates Bruce's continuing belief that a woman, not afraid to speak up (and Beatrice never was), might be helpful in a magazine for women.

Famous pollster Dr. George H. Gallup discusses education with old Iowa classmate in the Goulds' New York apartment topping the RKO building.

Bruce and Beatrice outside the Curtis building in Philadelphia.   JOE DI PIETRO

green with winter wheat, its partly pre-Revolutionary house and its Constable meadow along winding Bedensbrook. We got acquainted with Princeton—young, good-looking, untidy students with tidier minds; campus hangouts, the Balt, Renwick's; the somnolent, Romantic Victorian library, open to all. By good luck I had been made dramatic critic for the *Wall Street News*. This gave me entrée to every theatre in New York and a modest salary to supplement the steady one from the *Post*. There I had changed from book critic to aviation editor, being a great believer in the future of flying.

While awaiting word from the Guild, we amused ourselves by thinking about our next play, thinking more than writing. It would be called *The Terrible Turk* and be about a theatrical producer named Turk, in some respects like Jed Harris.

In early spring of 1929 the Theatre Guild suddenly decided to make *Man's Estate,* in our original version, the last production of their subscription season. The Guild was then, like Jed Harris, at the top of its reputation, famed for imaginative productions, from Shaw and O'Neill to old Ben Jonson and young Sidney Howard. Merely to have a play chosen by them was deemed a great honor, especially for Hansel and Gretel. And then, after our scarifying experience—our torture with Jed—how pleasant we thought to deal with distinguished, brilliant gentlemen and ladies—cultivated Lawrence Langner, wealthy patent attorney in his spare time; suave banker Maurice Wertheim, patron of the arts; Theresa Helburn, Vassar-educated, vital, handsome; aesthetic, uncannily perceptive Philip Moeller, their chief director; homely Helen Westley, acerbic character actress; trail-breaking designer Lee Simonson. All personages famous along Broadway, London's Strand, even, indeed, as far as Vienna, Paris, and Rome through caricatures and interviews as well as imitated productions, they ran the Guild when New York's theatre was at its height. These luminaries, steeped in Shakespeare, Ibsen, Shaw, the poetic dramas of Wedekind and Strindberg, the ironic comedies of Schnitzler and Molnár, would prove far different, we were sure, from upstart Jedediah Horowitz, who had scrabbled his way to the top —by brilliance it is true, but also by taking what he wanted when he wanted it.

And what casts the Guild could command. Dudley Digges was to be father and direct the play, Elizabeth Patterson, the mother, with brilliant Osgood Perkins and Armina Marshall, Langner's wife, in support. Our young lovers would be radiantly lovely Margalo Gillmore and Earl Larimore. With peace and confidence in our hearts, we attended the first evening rehearsal—a mere reading of the script in the new and handsome Guild Theatre. After it, in the habit of the theatre, so grueling to sleepy-evening people like Beatrice, the Guild board met round a bare table on the bare stage. Overhead burned the usual lone rehearsal work light.

The session began with a low question from Maurice Wertheim beside Beatrice: "Did you think of your young hero as a special individual, or more or less as a type?"

"I think we thought of him as representing many of the dreams and the problems of his age," she replied unwarily.

"I was afraid so." He sighed gloomily, turned away.

"There have been a lot of bread-and-butter young-love plays lately. But Margalo and Earl may freshen this one up," someone said.

"Why can't Helen Westley play the mother?"

"She's too hard-boiled—this is a conventional, ordinary, whining woman—"

"I wouldn't dream of playing that part," stated Helen Westley in flat, convincing tones.

"If we could get Rouben Mamoulian to direct, he might pull it through," offered one.

"He's already refused. He can't see the play at all. The only one we can get is Dudley Digges. He'll be good for a folksy Middle West piece like this. Phil Moeller couldn't do it."

"Can Dudley direct and play the father?"

"Oh, it's a simple play to do—too simple, of course, really—and it's the end of the season." (We didn't understand then quite what that meant.)

"It's a good part for Armina," said Lawrence Langner, speaking of his wife.

"Heaven help us, don't be so personal—is that why you voted for the play? I thought there must be some reason!"

"For God's sake, if you're so brilliant why don't you come up with a better one?"

"Well, you turned down that Hungarian play that had real smash. Rouben would have directed that one, too."

"We've got to have some American plays—even if they're dreary."

"I suppose you've never made any mistakes! How about that play that you shrieked and yelled about and threatened you'd resign from the board if we took—and then it became a smash hit?"

We listened, appalled. These and other fragments remain etched on my memory. Explosive temperaments took over. The exchanges grew more intense, more quarrelsome, vituperative. The ladies and gentlemen of the Theatre Guild squabbled as briskly, as woundingly as a group of eight-year-olds—pointing out with apparent delight each other's faults and foibles.

They began with offhand innuendoes and casual, general insults during what can only be described as a warmup; our horrified ears soon quivered and recoiled as the heavier artillery took over. Old grudges, old failures, old "I told you so's" stuffed like rusty nails in muzzleloaders raked the bare table fore and aft until, the carnage complete, every director dripping with blood, the august Guild paused for breath.

Our macerated play lay on the table, dissected, disemboweled, all too evidently no masterpiece, simply a job of work to be gotten through, apparently as quarrelsomely as possible. Insipid, obvious, fried-potatoes young love, it was to them.

Except for an occasional almost absent-minded sideswipe we seemed to have been forgotten in the fratricidal strife. Beatrice was almost numb, every nerve end lacerated. I do recall, crazed by the general hysteria, rising to my feet as the only way to engage attention, and assailing the entire board as a group of slow-blooded, middle-aged has-beens who, having forgotten what love was, had no glimpse of the emotional truth and beauty of our play. My words might just as well have been a sweeping formal compliment. No one gave the slightest attention to my furious remarks, a mild diatribe, apparently, in their measure. For, by this time, the directors had found something they could all—except Helen Westley—denounce in concert: the hat that Miss Westley had just bought and was now wearing, a hat so meretricious in design, so horrifying as to shape and color, it was manifestly a disgrace to all the Guild's reputation and purpose. It should right now be ripped from her head and torn to shreds. I think maybe it was.

Having gained some experience since then, supported by reading a number of books on theatrical adventures (including one wildly amusing, *The Curtain Falls,* by Joseph Verner Reed), I realize that the theatre is almost inevitably explosive. Tension is the start of every enterprise. Success depends on fusing and harmonizing temperaments of star, actors, director, producer. Each must passionately believe that he (and he alone if crossed) has the *true* interpretation, the saving idea, the whole artistic vision—or failure threatens.

Beatrice rarely attended rehearsals after this one. Never overconfident about her own work, she suffers agony to hear it torn to bits —especially in the dark of night when her courage is at its lowest point after a day of expended energy. Criticism, then, whether brutal and personal like Jed's or more politely shredding the play rather than the author à la Theatre Guild, is too heavy a load. By herself, she would have far too much sense to enter the theatre at all except as a delighted customer out front.

But the play began to take shape. The leading lady, Margalo, indulged in several of the milder tantrums open to stars, walking off the stage—to be pursued flatteringly by the male author to a nearby telephone booth where she had rather effectively awaited recapture. But we thought there was something lackadaisical about the rehearsals. Part of the trouble might have been, as we were beginning to suspect, that *Man's Estate* wasn't a very good play. Conviction grew in the authors' minds that the Guild did not, perhaps, consider this the most brilliant play ever written, or even among the best the Guild had done; it might be they lacked a better to fill out their subscription season—for which tickets were already sold.

We had innocently assumed that the Guild unanimously loved our little masterpiece, saw in it all we had dreamed, longed to give it breath and movement on the stage. We later learned that the board bought plays if four of the six members approved, which was rare.

When they divided, three in favor, three against, they delayed their decision, hoping a better prospect might come along. But they must deliver their final play of the season. Naturally, a three-three decision, which ours quite probably was, provided rich opportunities among such verbal, uninhibited personalities for recrimination, vituperation, triumphant I-told-you-so's. We were dumb by-standers—their targets were each other; their weapon, our play. Not that they thought it bad. If so, they wouldn't have produced it—simply they wished it better than it was.

Opening night at the Biltmore Theatre came and our pretty, red-haired Sesaly of eighteen months, dressed in pale crisp dotted swiss, was there in the lap of our young Irish nursemaid, Val. Sesaly's cheerful chirpings in the back row (she may not have realized how much was at stake) finally drove the house manager to suggest she be taken out. (I think we visioned this as Sesaly's historic presence at the first of a series of theatrical triumphs, so stagestruck were her parents.) We were fortified by our best clothes. I now owned a dinner jacket; Beatrice wore her first made-to-order evening gown—pale apricot chiffon, very short pleated skirt and beglittered loose "shell" top, almost in the fashion of the sixties. We were fortified, too, by the presence of many friends, among them Harry and Bernardine Scherman, cherished then and now, giving a party after the show as we awaited the critics' verdict.

Reviews were mixed—some good, some bad. Our fall was not so great as we sometimes feared it would be, nor was our success so blazing.

In the *World,* Alison Smith said: "A tender rueful little piece which tells its story with a simplicity and a sympathy which marks it as one of the happiest events in the Guild's season."

Brooks Atkinson, *Times:* "Despite a sly and purring humor in some of the scenes, it is a little clipped and thin and as wanting in originality as a modern novel."

Richard Lockridge, *Sun:* "A very fine first play. Seldom have the old problems been presented more clearly in words better fitted to the ideas conveyed."

Burns Mantle, *News:* "It is stirring in its humanities and in its human weakness."

Gilbert Gabriel, *American:* "I must step out of the parade and wonder, was it worth the Guild's while?"

Percy Hammond, *Tribune:* "A delightful diversion, sometimes sluggish, but more often entrancing, and the romance in it is incessantly thrilling. A drama much more fruitful than the Broadway average, aided by the Guild's competence of production."

Bruce Gould, *Wall Street News:* "I can think of nothing more chastening for a dramatic critic than to submit a play of his own devising to judgment of his peers. The experience is designed, like a near escape from disaster, to make one resolve to live a better critical life. Henceforth, one determines to temper justice with mercy in the knowledge that sympathy no less than understanding is a juristic prerequisite."

Jed Harris, who dealt only with smash hits, could smugly feel he was right in not bringing *King's X* to town.

But the Theatre Guild production had two great assets for us. One, being honored, as neophytes, by the Guild at all. The second that, because of their subscription season, any Guild play was bound to run at least six weeks. Ours ran seven or eight—and in each of those weeks, we as authors netted something over $1,000 in revenue. Since neither of us had ever had more than $500, really $450 after subtracting the agent's 10 percent, in hand during our entire married life, this was wealth. We made some further payments on our farm, supervised some needed repairs, and Beatrice, I suspect, bought a new hat. The rest of the money we invested in Guaranty Trust stock, considered in that boom spring of 1929 to be slightly more conservative than gold bullion. I had asked advice. Tommy Gammack, in Wall Street after his *Sun* days with me, told me Tom Lamont was buying Guaranty for his mother. That seemed a good enough recommendation. I wondered, later, whether I shouldn't have asked Tommy if Mr. Lamont really loved his mother.

Beyond the money, we were encouraged that our first play had been optioned, and was still held, by Ethel Barrymore; that our second play had been bid for by three of the most prestigious producers on Broadway. With this record behind us, we thought of the theatre as our real future. Beatrice said she would help me write plays but would never, in future, attend rehearsals.

We went to Maine again that summer, recuperating from cumulative shocks—and beginning to write our play *The Terrible Turk*.

Jed left behind him many an embittered playwright who held him in distaste. Several wrote cruel memoirs about him. George Abbott, in his autobiography, paints the fairest portrait—not exactly flattering. Perhaps some actor may still be waiting to throw rocks on his coffin and sing, "Poor Jed is dead"—when the final curtain descends.

Kaufman's bitter, dismissing comment after reading, later, *The Terrible Turk*, was a few cold words: "You've made Jed a human being."

Choose in marriage a woman whom you would choose
as a friend if she were a man.

—JOSEPH JOUBERT

13 🌿

Then Came the Depression

Cheerful and confident, we returned from Maine late in September of 1929 to a new apartment, the two top floors of an old house at Bleecker and Eleventh. The rental was twice what we had been paying, with a three-year lease, but this seemed entirely reasonable in view of the fact that we were now established (well, almost established) Broadway playwrights. Moreover, we had three jobs going. Beatrice had given up being woman's editor on the *Sunday World,* but continued a tiny column. As dramatic critic for the *Wall Street News,* kindness of its editor, Stanley Phraner, I had three or four nights' work (and pleasure) a week for a comfortable salary. My aviation editor's job for the New York *Post* brought our basic income to about $200 a week. We had never been so consistently prosperous.

Our yeasty neighbors were young writers, illustrators, and journalists on the make. Three living-room windows overlooked a block's run of former high-fenced backlots turned into a pool-centered community garden where children played by day and adults communed at night. Several roofs, securely fenced, made a morning

124

nursery playground for the littler children. Sesaly climbed, built, and chugged about in sooty sunshine with the two- and three-year-olds of the Siftons, Mark Van Dorens, and others in our reasonably literate community.

Our cherished French furniture, still not wholly paid for, sat stark in our greater space of seven rooms. We eked it out with solid Victorian chests bought secondhand on Houston Street, together with some beds, chairs, and Rogers Brothers plated tableware from R. H. Macy which demanded cash, less 6 percent. Sterling was not yet in our cupboards. More furniture was on order when one Tuesday, late in October, I telephoned Beatrice right after the stock-market opening to say:

"If you can cancel that sofa we ordered for the living room, I believe I'd do it. There's been a bad break in Wall Street. It's a madhouse. I'm down here now for the story. Things may be tight for a while." Regretfully she agreed. After I'd called my Crash story in to the *Post*'s rewrite desk, as a little flyer I bought a few shares of General Motors at bottom prices—the old theory is that, after a bad fall, stocks rebound. Sure enough, the next trading day I did sell that stock for several hundred dollars' quick profit. Immediately, the market plunged again. That was about the last day, for several despair-filled years, such a transaction on the up side could have been profitably maneuvered. From then on the market was driven down, down, down by "Sell-'em-Ben-Smith" and other like-minded realists who, selling short, made killings on the down side. True believers still hoped for a miracle on the up side. Not until June 8, 1932, did that falling market touch final bottom.

Day after day, month after month, our nest egg, our all—that Guaranty Trust stock we had bought on the play's riches for $600 a share (and had seen climb to $1,200 during the summer)—sank to the price we'd paid, then continued its merciless shrinkage.

"It will come back," we told each other, echoing President Hoover. Ogden Mills, his austere Secretary of the Treasury, held out similar hopes. Could they both be wrong?

Tragic tales brushed us closely. One or two Wall Street figures I had known jumped from high windows to solve bankruptcy troubles.

Newspaper editors rationed disaster stories, so many per page. Our shocked intelligentsia began to look at Communism with a hopeful eye—some were briefly to become converts. Even Lincoln Steffens, the realist, had reported, after visiting Moscow, "I have been over into the future, and it works." Bibi and I took what comfort we could in not having bought our nest egg on margin. Our assets, shrinking like Alice, were at least all ours.

I was not so busy in the evenings, now. Fewer plays were produced. Established hits were closing. People did not seem to be going to the theatre much. A few night clubs still opened—we loved to dance; the floors weren't so crowded, either.

We enjoyed our expensive new apartment, our greater opportunity to spend time with each other—many broke or badly bent husbands were rediscovering loyal wives. Weekends we spent on the farm, taking pleasure in the tawny, shocked cornfields, the frozen brook, the wild bare trees against a pale winter sky.

In my spare time (there was more Time then than now) I had dashed off a book about flying, *Sky Larking*. It zoomed briefly to the best-seller list as an early description of the newly discovered continent of the air. I fear I celebrated in far too lyrical terms the beauties of dawn, clouds, sunset, city lights at night as seen from the cockpit. The jacket carried a flattering photograph of me, a real live author's profile, thoughtful pipe in mouth, looking exactly as a young writer in those days was supposed to look—wild mane, open shirt, uncouth and angry air is more the thing now. From this absurd photographic glamorization I gained much solid personal satisfaction at a bad moment, together with a few mash notes from susceptible young ladies who thought it wonderful a man could fly, enjoy beauty, write about it, and look fairly handsome to boot. I agreed with them and admired their frankness in expressing that honest opinion but, I'm ashamed to say, showed some of the mushier letters to Beatrice to hear her lovely laughter. I also signed a contract to write a novel, *Puritan*—mostly to get the $750 advance, though I did have a rather startling beginning. Since I had no appropriate story from then on, I never wrote more than the sixteen-page signature necessary to show to booksellers, but those pages were as breathtaking as the first

span of an unfinished bridge—I thought. It's always easier to start
than to end a story. If one hadn't to solve the plot, the world would
be full of successful writers.

In the following summer, with a piercing suddenness, the *Wall
Street News* suspended publication, quietly merging overnight with
the *Wall Street Journal,* then wobbling also, now prosperous and
distinguished. With its demise went a third of our income.

Interludes of luck, that spring, staved off disaster. Anthony H. G.
(Tony) Fokker, famous World War I designer and manufacturer of
airplanes, who had transferred his business from Holland to America,
approached me, I suppose on account of *Sky Larking,* to ghost his
autobiography, but signing my name with his.

Tony, Java Dutchman by birth, had started building airplanes early,
learning as he went, like all the early birds following hard on the
Wright brothers. Neither France, England, nor Russia would adopt
Tony's experimental plane. Just before World War I Germany did—
which was bad news for the Allies. Tony's quick-climbing, lightning-
fast Fokkers excelled in swift, aerial combat, especially deadly diving
out of the sun. For a time after he'd first invented the simple method
of shooting machine-gun bullets through the whirling propeller, Fokker
pilots—led by Boelcke—ruled the air on the Western Front. Allied
flyers like Fonck, Guynemer, Nungesser, Bishop, Rickenbacker—
not to mention Beatrice's brother-in-law, Ralph Snoke, an American
ace flying with the RAF—were given a hard time by Fokker's continuously improved planes, often better than our French, British, or
American ones.

Tony emerged from the war a multimillionaire at twenty-seven.
Now he was introducing his pacemaking Fokker trimotor to the
United States.

I had always shunned such "as-told-to" jobs. But the guarantee
of $5,000 seemed desirable in view of our suddenly shrunken in-
come, our expanding family, and our expensive overhead. We were
paying Valentine Kenny, our gay young Irish helper-nursemaid, $90
a month—high enough wages then. We were obligated for a heavy
apartment rent and large, sickeningly regular payments on our
Hopewell farm. So I took the $5,000.

While Beatrice spent most of the long, hot summer of 1930 on the farm with Sesaly, I managed by myself in our torrid, dusty New York apartment. Working with Tony on his book, I naturally lived on his cooling yacht as much as possible. He'd been spending one morning laboriously provisioning the boat before we cast off for a coastwise cruise with all the different kinds of food and drink his finicky guests might require.

"Don't ever have a yacht, Bruce," he groaned, as he puffed up the gangplank laden to the gunwales with some special foodstuffs. "Just have friends who have yachts."

I can't think of a better piece of advice to pass on to a young man facing life—and I've never owned anything larger than an Abaco dinghy, myself.

Flying Dutchman, briefly on our best-seller list, did well in England, Holland, France, Switzerland, and the Scandinavian countries, too.

We were expecting our second child in September. Weekends I spent on the farm with Beatrice, helping my father-in-law transplant near the ancient house small elms from "the draw," eating the luscious ripe red tomatoes and fresh green corn from Harry's garden, accustoming our nearly-three-year-old to the swimming hole in Bedensbrook used by neighborhood boys for generations. Since the house had no plumbing, electricity, or telephone, it was at its airy best in the summer months.

Our second child, a handsome, dark-haired boy, Douglas, was born in late September and died ten minutes later, after an exceedingly difficult, delayed birth. Everything went wrong—a 9½ pound infant, placenta praevia, breech presentation. The doctor, foreseeing difficulties, had tentatively suggested a Caesarean. Beatrice, proud of her health and her previous easy delivery, was against the idea. Because of this she mourned unduly, blaming herself for the death of her son.

In despair at the bedside, I watched Bibi's struggle with deep grief.

Finally, Sesaly, ruddy-cheeked, plump, and gay, dressed in her prettiest, was brought in from the farm to Beatrice's bedside, full of glee at seeing her mother.

"We have a lovely child," I said.

For years we could never speak of Douglas even to each other. To our sorrow, we had no more children.

In the fall, I finished Tony's book and he urged me to go abroad with him on a generous travel allowance to see about foreign publication and possibly get some new material for the European editions. In spite of our precarious finances, Beatrice persuaded me that two can live as cheaply as one—at least they can enjoy the living more. Tony, who liked her, agreed she might come too, ostensibly living thriftily on a share of my expense money. *Post* editors reluctantly gave me a leave of absence, extracting a solemn promise I'd return in not more than six weeks; their flattering insistence suggested I was desperately needed in the city room.

We sailed first class on the just-launched *Bremen*. Tony had gotten his millions so recently he wasn't chary of throwing them about, unlike the seasoned rich. Tony preferred the role of lavish host with pretty women about to help him enjoy his money. His extravagance developed in us a never-to-be-completely-satisfied taste for caviar and champagne and revealed to us that a truffle can mean as much to a bit of meat as a kiss to a maiden aunt.

In Berlin, in early '31, Tony renewed old friendships with pilots like Goering and Messerschmitt. One could hardly help learning that the Germans, with small secrecy, were training flyers in Russia, directly contrary to Armistice terms, and building forbidden naval planes in Peenemünde, near the Baltic, as they prepared for the next war. Very likely our military attachés, to whom I duly communicated this information, knew all about such violations, so helpful to Germany's aviation dominance early in World War II. In any case, our government took no overt action—nor did the British and French, who weakly hoped a revived Germany would content itself with gobbling up eastern Europe. Adolf Hitler was fast coming on, though to many ordinarily astute observers he seemed more like a mountebank than a menace. Neither Dorothy Thompson nor H. R. Knickerbocker, whom we met for the first time in Berlin, was disposed to take Hitler seriously. These were the years of the ostrich. Berlin, crowded with decadent night clubs, swarming with inflation-rich entrepreneurs, seemed less than menacing. But Hitler's growing influence did prevent

Tony's book from being brought out in Germany. Tony had been out-spoken: he was forever insisting, "The German is half soldier—he can be ordered to do anything." Publishing firms like Ullstein and Scherl were already feeling the weight of Hitler's repressive and soon-to-be-lethal hand. The Swiss edition, however, sold briskly in Germany.

It was at Knickerbocker's Christmas-night mulled-wine party in Berlin we first met Dorothy Thompson with Sinclair Lewis, just down from Stockholm after receiving the Nobel Prize and, naturally, center of the stage.

Edgar Maurer asked Beatrice, at his side, if she admired Theodore Dreiser, with whom Lewis had recently had a brisk, front-page tiff, and when she innocently replied that she did he impishly turned to Dorothy and said, "Mrs. Gould is crazy about Dreiser."

Dorothy's look was so ferocious as to intimidate us both. We did not realize then that she would soon become a warm, admired friend. Perhaps physical misery augmented her loyal anger. She had been complaining of not feeling well that evening but Lewis, happily launched on his amusing monologues—like many articulate authors he was an eager amateur ham—refused to go home as long as the audience and the drink held out. Dorothy, finally, went back to their hotel alone. Early in the morning, she went on, again alone, to the hospital for an emergency appendectomy whose warning symptoms she had futilely mentioned to an unhearing Lewis.

Paris, serene in its disciplined stone, under a mistily pink evening sky, looked astonishingly like the Paris known to us from books and paintings. Thus I learned again what a preparation for living wide reading is. We lunched, of course, at the Ritz to prove we could. We stayed, however, in the spacious, fading splendor of the old, inexpensive Grand. Now, probably, its brass beds and rose-strewn walls are once more "in." We tried the races with Tony, and bistros without him. We sauntered along the Seine, looking in bookstalls for first editions Anatole France might have overlooked. We rushed, I'm chagrined to recall, into the Café Marguery one evening, ordering its famous fillet of sole, to be ready at once as we were hurrying on next door to the Comédie Française—thus arousing the hostility of the entire staff. We behaved as foolishly, I fear, as young Americans do when first actually seeing, smelling, and tasting the wonders of this fabled city.

When, on impulse, I whistled up a taxi and ordered the driver to take us to 28 Rue de Tournelles, we enjoyed one of our most satisfying moments.

A bank seemed to occupy the premises. But, like good journalists, we went inside to inquire whether anything remained at that address of the once-famous town house of Ninon de L'Enclos, the setting of our play *The First Gentleman of Her Time,* and familiar to us from letters and diaries of the period.

"Oh, yes," was the smiling reply, "just come upstairs."

Through a corridor and a dusty door we walked into it, aged but intact, pale gold damask on the walls and chairs, gold damask curtains, Ninon's elegant, formal yellow drawing room just as we had pictured it in our minds. Its worn paint and old brocade whispered of ghostly, polished men and women who had walked there—Mme. de Maintenon, La Rochefoucauld, Ninon herself. Now Ninon seemed true. We wished Ethel Barrymore had exercised those options she kept buying.

We went, of course, to Neuilly—the name impossible for me to pronounce to a taxi driver—to visit Daisy in her white stone house, imaginative as all her houses were. The enormous living room had one glass wall, which sank to include a formal flower-bright garden; its polished dark floor was scattered with stage-green artificial grass rugs beside Englishy green-and-white chintz-covered sofas; near them stood a pair of handsome Regency cupboards from some Orléans ancestor. The library next door, floor intricately inlaid with signs of the Zodiac in contrasting woods, was furnished with formal, prim Louis XIII chairs and tables. Her dining table was one thick slab of green sea-foam glass beneath which rosy flowers were muted, as though under water; again a solid glass disappearing wall gave its view of the prim small orchard outside. In these rooms one met her aged, elegant ex-father-in-law, the Prince de Broglie, Bea Lillie, Somerset Maugham, and the young Duc de la Rochefoucauld, whose ancestor's celebrated maxim "There may be good but there are no pleasant marriages" seemed relevant to that society.

Because of my promise to the *Post,* I forewent the chance to go on with Junius Wood to Russia, whose violent Bolshevik regime he was reporting for the Chicago *Daily News.* Instead, very reluctantly turning our back on the Old World, we returned to deepening depression in the New.

Because of Tony's book, there had been little time for playwriting, which we usually did in our summer holiday. We determined to finish *The Terrible Turk* that winter of 1931.

Beatrice arose implacably each morning at five. She prepared coffee and toast and brought them to my bedside. Shocked awake, propped up side by side against fat pillows, we slaved steadily each morning from five-thirty to eight. Then I must hastily dress, catch the subway, and be at the New York *Post* by nine. Somehow the play was finished.

It was the morning after St. Patrick's Day, 1931, in the depth of the Depression that I telephoned Beatrice suggesting she meet me for lunch at a favorite French restaurant, Charles, Tenth Street and Sixth Avenue. She was as surprised as she was delighted by this unwonted extravagance, since much of my $5,000 advance from Tony had gone and we were living strictly on "Short Street," as Queen Mary used to say of her straitened life before marriage. When I saw Bibi's lovely, illumined face as I entered Charles, as usual a bit late, my heart sank. After a magnificent lunch, concluding with French pancakes and apricot jam, I idly remarked:

"You have always wanted me to give up newspaper work and become a writer. I am now a writer."

"Good!" she exclaimed.

"The *Post* has just fired me!"

"Good!" she repeated, with what seemed like equal enthusiasm. "Tell me."

I had written a story for an early edition of the *Post* about the annual St. Patrick's Day parade. Since this was a routine event, there was not too much news in it. To give background to my story, I consulted the Encyclopaedia Britannica and found to my surprise that this august publication did not list Patrick as an official saint. He was just another Irish myth. The Britannica's skeptical position seemed

to me good for a couple of spoofing paragraphs to the general effect
that the encyclopaedia was a notorious British publication originated
by Sassenachs to down the Irish. Expatiating on that feeble joke had
the effect of getting me to the end of a column—and, as it turned out,
to the end of my newspaper career.

Someone in Sears, Roebuck, then publishing the Britannica, felt
aggrieved by my light tone. What I had written was an obvious in-
justice to a balanced, fair, accurate encyclopedia. Jack Martin, then
in charge of the *Post* (he had become a great newspaper publisher
overnight when widower Cyrus H. K. Curtis married Martin's mother-
in-law), lent a receptive ear to Sears, Roebuck's complaint. By
Martin's orders I, and all who had to do with the offending story—
which meant the night city editor, William G. King, and the night
copy man, Ernie Pyle, of later renown—were fired. I was not permitted
to take all the blame. Three heads must roll. Perhaps this was a convenient way to cut down the payroll in increasingly stringent times.

With Beatrice's usual refusal to be daunted, we had an apricot
brandy to celebrate my unsought freedom.

"You've been in newspaper work long enough," she maintained.
"You've had all the fun and the experiences. Do something else.
Write!"

Our regular income was now down to the $25 a week Beatrice
earned from her *World* column. Our duplex apartment cost $175 a
month, and the barest kind of living meant $100 or $200 more.
We still had our Guaranty Trust stock, its worth dwindling, and a play
manuscript which was widely praised but not produced. The New
Jersey farm mortgage required monthly payments. Sesaly, nearly
three, ate well and drank a lot of milk.

"Let's," Beatrice said practically, over the brandy, "think."

"I have thought," I said. "I have an excellent, simple plan to meet
this dire emergency. Like all newspapermen I have been certain I
could write short stories if I only had the time. I now have the time.
So I guess I'll write a short story for the *Saturday Evening Post.* Don't
you agree that's the logical thing to do?"

"I'll help," she said, "if you need me."

"I figure," I said, "if I can make a living writing short stories in the depths of this Depression, I could certainly make a living writing short stories when good times inevitably return."

"Start tomorrow," Beatrice said.

Beatrice has never lacked courage. Trivial mishaps irritate her— like my failure to mail a letter or my being two hours late for dinner. But she rises like a zooming Spitfire to danger.

I was never a great reporter. This was fortunate for me, perhaps a bit tough on my employers. The one thing I wanted to do was playwriting. Had I been a great reporter, or even a very competent one —both of which take some doing—I might have been so diverted from the theatre I'd never have returned to it. It is dangerous to be too good a carpenter if what you really want to become is Chief Justice of the United States. The world will pay well for first-class cabinetwork and your chance of becoming Chief Justice will seem, to everyone but yourself, fantastic. A little incompetence in ordinary affairs may greatly accelerate the climb up your favorite ladder.

Next morning as I sat down to write a short story for the *Saturday Evening Post,* to concoct a tale which would shock those *Post* editors into an awareness of a new writer, which would bring in a check we'd be needing more and more desperately every day, that story idea didn't just leap to mind. Thoughts raced around inside my cranium like rats escaping a terrier. Finally, I got one firmly by the neck and shook it into submission. I'd write a story about the absurd French opera hat I'd bought when I'd been temporarily flush enough to purchase a suit of tails after our Guild opening. The plot was based on how long the hat's interior mechanism would last before finally collapsing, the hero's pretensions more or less with it. I called it "The Hat of a Thousand Plops," a light tale to comment on the scene, to amuse, to make people momentarily forget their worries. After a month, with Beatrice's helping hand giving it a last, final pat of approval, I mailed my first completed story hopefully to the faraway *Post*, and wondered where I'd ever get another plot.

Before we could begin to worry about its reception, back came a slim *Post* envelope. A check for $500 would be arriving next Wednesday, they said, adding the thrilling suggestion I send them more stories of what, in magazine circles, is called "young love."

The *Post* liked "The Hat of a Thousand Plops" very much. It said so right there in the letter. I don't know how many times I read it. My brash confidence wasn't perhaps as brash as I claimed. I could hardly bear to part with the check, but our starving bank account growled for its bone.

The New York *World,* once a great newspaper, had faded sadly after the death of the first vigorous, talented Joseph Pulitzer. His sons, except for Joseph, Jr., of St. Louis, more interested in yachts, Palm Beach, and Paris than metropolitan journalism, had inherited a job too big for them to handle.

Joe Pulitzer, standing in the old *World* Tower, once pointed out to Edward Steichen a tall man looming high in the street below at the back of a crowd watching while baseball scores came up on a bulletin board. The man was perhaps six foot one—maybe two.

"He's only," said Pulitzer, pointing him out to Steichen, "a *little* taller than everybody else. That's about all the difference there really is between a great man and an ordinary one. Remember that."

True, of course, but, as Mercutio said of his wound—not so deep as a well nor so wide as a church door—it suffices. Old Joe Pulitzer's disintegrating *World* died of the difference between him and his sons.

Perhaps progenitors should be prohibited from leaving inferior offspring their valued creations—newspapers, theatres, magazines, great banks—unless the offspring can prove to an impartial jury, not to a purblind parent, competence to carry on. No one expected Thackeray or Shakespeare to have a son capable of picking up his pen. Charlemagne failed to pass on his kingship to his firstborn. The most ardent Rooseveltian is, happily, not now looking forward to a son of Roosevelt in the White House—and even the magic name of Kennedy may not make it too easy for John John to succeed the martyred clansman.

To the deep mourning of newspapermen everywhere the great old *World* tottered and fell. In October, of 1931, some of its features, along with its name, were absorbed by the *Telegram,* which became the *World Telegram*—F.P.A. and Walter Lippmann going to the *Tribune.* But the real *World* died with the merger. So many able journalists were thrown out of work in the middle of the Depression the loss of Beatrice's weekly woman's column seemed trivial. But though small it had provided our only regular paycheck.

Paper, pencil, and imagination were henceforth the only weapons between us and a genuine, bared-teeth, howling wolf at the door. Optimists, we had visioned our pre-Crash prosperity as bound to last, blithely assuming obligations on that hope. Our rent was falling in arrears. We were behind with Sesaly's tuition at the City and Country School.

Luckily that year, I sold five short stories in a row to the *Saturday Evening Post,* which had raised my price to a thousand dollars a story. Curtis had $20 million cash in the bank. It was weathering the Depression all right, though the size of the *Post* had been more than halved by a precipitate decrease in advertising. From running a dozen stories an issue, it cut down to four—at half the pay—making it triply hard for a newcomer to crash its gates.

Around the same time a young producer, Eddie Blatt (who'd had at least one pre-Crash success in the theatre, *Subway Express*), decided to put on *The Terrible Turk.* We later learned he had so little financial backing he had had to borrow from Leland Hayward the $500 option money he paid us.

Our spirits held. We did not lose hope that *The Terrible Turk* would somehow be produced, and be successful, despite Eddie Blatt's drawn-out difficulty in financing it. Angels for plays had vanished from Broadway.

We had a proud moment. George Jean Nathan, the most respected, or at least the most feared dramatic critic of his time, wrote handsomely of *The Terrible Turk* in a *Vanity Fair* preview of the oncoming 1932 season. Since he seldom mentioned unproduced scripts, our natural inclination to believe the play was brilliant, witty, and moving, was multi-magnified. Hopes ballooned that his comment might influence possible backers. He said:

Its central character, observed with a nimble wit, is recorded with a waggish skill and is humorously lithographic. Properly cast and played, it should be good for a steady dose of chuckles. . . . The character of Lew Turk, a New York theatrical producer—(I am told by those acquainted with the Broadway world that there is one who more or less

resembles the authors' invention). . . . The man's extraordinary feeling
for the theatre and his real genius, together with his mountebankery and
posturing . . . are adroitly orchestrated by the playwrights into an un-
commonly lifelike figure . . . making the audience feel the man's fundamental sure and certain virtues. . . . In the character of this Turk the
playwrights have surpassed anything they have previously confected for
the theatre, a character alive in its bitter humor and sure in its every
little stroke. . . . That it smells of Broadway, and richly, is nothing against
its real quality. It is replete with dozens of sharp little reflections of
actuality and its mouth, in its utterances, is true to its inner integrity. . . .
all are scored expertly into dramatically honest counterpoint.

At two o'clock one morning, Beatrice, coming out of the depth of
early sleep, answered the telephone and heard Jed Harris' low, con-
fidential voice whispering through the black night: "Beatrice, you
have done what no playwright has ever done before—written a play
about a genius"—meaning, of course, himself, Jed. He asked us to
come in and talk to him about his (Jed Harris') producing the play.
He thought it would be amusing and talkaboutable for him to produce
a play critical of himself.

Skeptically, we went to his office. With the planned insolence which
was his nature, he received us sitting in a barber's chair having that
prognathous jaw shaved. (We later learned he had received Moss Hart
for the first time in his bathroom, shaving naked.)

He flattered us, as he had before, but the old spell failed. Because
we were not at once ecstatic over the brilliant originality of his plan,
he scolded us molasses-slow Nordics crossly, pettish as a child. He
hadn't changed. He wasn't satisfied that we had, in George Kaufman's
phrase, "made Jed a human being." He told us he wanted to do the
play because it was critical of himself but we soon saw that he would
like the central character changed into a cantankerous young
curmudgeon, a sort of romantic theatrical "Grumpy," heart of gold in
the hard-boiled egg. It wouldn't be our play when he'd finished with it;
and Beatrice, from the first, loathed the prospect of working again with
Jed. We refused to revise.

By this time able, active men were selling apples in the street.
"Brother, Can You Spare a Dime?" was a popular song stenciled on
my memory. A once powerful and influential banking friend knocked

unexpectedly at our door one evening at twilight to ask for a loan of $300. We didn't have it. Landlords pressing for rent would be met by "I simply haven't the money and I can't get it."

Our able, prankish literary agent, Leland Hayward, by now head of American Play, helped keep us alive by encouraging us to concoct an absurd film plot. Quailing slightly when he heard it, he yet managed to fast-talk it to the movies for $1,000 which went for debts.

When our three-year lease on the Bleecker Street apartment ran out, with a year's rent, alas, still unpaid, we squeezed gratefully into the Hopewell farmhouse with Beatrice's parents. Our little nursemaid, Val, had already fled back to Ireland, where depressions are the common way of life.

The farm was a peaceful place to write. Sesaly loved the long walks, the quiet, ruminative cows, the restful country after noisy city streets.

But if we were to live in the country we would need a car, and rashly optimistic again because of the sale of two stories in rapid succession—and one by Beatrice, as well—we made a down payment on a delightful caramel-colored Nash convertible—very sporty —giving anyone the impression as we streaked across the horizon we were on top of the world. It nearly sank us.

My phenomenal run of beginner's luck with the *Post* suddenly failed. For one solid year I did not sell a single story.

Beatrice, too, stopped selling. For twelve months no check came in.

Mere memory of the snarling letters bill collectors can write still makes me cringe.

Our payments on the farm mortgage dwindled but the mortgage must not be foreclosed. Bit by bit we sold our Guaranty Trust stock, now down to $300 a share. Mrs. Blackmar's small income from her New York classes still held. She also did some writing for the Columbia Encyclopedia just being readied for production. The $35 a month from the farmer helped. So did my father-in-law's garden.

Neither Beatrice nor I had bought any new clothes since the 1929 crash. When her last evening dress was too shabby for her pride, she insisted on sending me out in dinner jacket to represent us, pick up news and gossip—keep us in circulation; fortunately men's clothes last a long time. Occasional parties our more solvent friends gave in

New York she evaded, murmuring of a cold or Sesaly's needing her. Since we had no telephone, not too many people bothered.

Eddie Blatt, after absorbing a great deal of one summer's time getting us to write a new second act he thought might attract an angel whose wings he was caressing, had disappeared into the anonymity of Hollywood. Hope of any immediate production of *The Terrible Turk* vanished with him. In spite of Nathan's generous pat on the back, no Broadway entrepreneur came forth. The Morningside Players, a Columbia University drama group, put on the play— bringing in no royalties but experience. An excellent amateur group in California, the Pasadena Playhouse, produced it on the same terms. After their opening, *Variety,* that hard-boiled bible of Broadway, gave *The Terrible Turk* a surprisingly good notice: "Here's rich fodder for Broadway where they know their theatre and some of its unique per- sonalities . . . play should have no trouble clicking . . . ought to be surefire for wise old Broadway," but, apparently, Broadway was too wise to touch it.

Mrs. Blackmar made Sesaly a charming green winter coat and hat for her first year in the Hopewell public school. The wool for it was our last still hopeful purchase at Wanamaker's. They liked to be paid reasonably soon for what they sold—and canceled our credit.

Even occasional trips to New York, staying with friends, had become too expensive. For Christmas that year we gave Sesaly some delightful lace-trimmed doll clothes made from bits and pieces, a hair clip, and some paper dolls from the ten-cent store. I bought Beatrice (and gaily wrapped for Sesaly's benefit) a slip, which Bibi had care- fully selected at the Grand Store in Trenton, costing ninety-eight cents. Her remaining old one had been mended too often. She gave me some homemade candy. My mother-in-law made me a bathrobe out of an old Navy blanket with gay plaid binding, and we managed a few cigars for Harry. It all looked very festive. The Christmas tree we cut from our woodlot. For it Sesaly strung popcorn and cran- berries and pasted loops of colored paper into gay chains.

Story after story I wrote was returned with flat rejections. What would we do when the last crumbs from the Guaranty Trust stock had vanished?

Fortunately Beatrice is a stout-hearted girl. She did not voice her fears. I think the thing that kept us going was confidence in our own adaptability. If worst came to worst—and it had just about arrived—we could turn to any needed work, and if we had to wash dishes, we'd wash them better than anyone else. So difficult were these times, during which I steadfastly wrote each day my usual stint of story, that when I later read in Samuel Butler's *The Way of All Flesh* about the lean period when his young hero nearly disintegrated for lack of funds, I could hardly endure the dismal passages where his spirit grinds to bitter dust. His feelings were too known.

I do remember, though, in this period, Beatrice's telling Sesaly half fancifully, half really (they both loved to walk), about the fun we could all have if we became hobos, walking along the highroad with our packs on our backs, seeing the world. We would sleep in barns, she explained, and work for our meals at anything people would give us to do.

"Daddy is a good woodchopper," she would explain. "He could always find some old people who couldn't chop their own wood, and do it for them."

She made it all sound like a gay adventure, and I think Sesaly felt a little cheated and let down that it didn't actually happen.

"I don't ever want Sesaly to be afraid of life," Beatrice told me. "There are always new chances, new things to do, if the old fail. I want to teach Sesaly the security of insecurity—the possbilities in not expecting anything, and starting from there."

In such a prolonged period of discouragement, when obligations without answers pile up, I suppose many men think of their life insurance. I never, even in the darkest night, actually looked up my $25,000 policy to see whether it was invalidated by suicide. Even the thought would have seemed to Beatrice like desertion.

In the early spring of 1933, with Depression fears still smothering us all, a letter arrived in the morning mail from *Cosmopolitan*. They wanted to buy "Women Have Loved Cads," which the *Post* had rejected. Moreover, they would pay me $1,200, topping the *Post*'s price, and would like to make a contract for half a dozen more stories at

$1,500. Beatrice cried when I showed her the letter—during this period, her only tears.

That afternoon I went out with my father-in-law to transplant some small trees along our driveway. I chose the finest, largest one we could possibly lug, heave, and lever into place and solemnly named it *Cosmopolitan.*

If *Cosmo* would buy my stories when the *Post* wouldn't, it deserved this sweaty tribute. Along our driveway, now paved, near the tennis court, Cosmo still stands, grown into a fine tree. He reminds us both of the changes and chances of life—the sudden joys as well as the dire disappointments Fate has in store. Sometimes I stand still at sunset and idiotically salute Cosmo.

Perhaps stimulated by *Cosmopolitan*'s interest, the *Post* persuaded me to stick with them. Again they began buying my stories, though Lorimer was too independent to meet *Cosmo*'s jump in price immediately. He had to be certain first I loved the *Post* for itself alone.

Lorimer had lost a dozen of his bright stars to *Cosmo,* which, when Ray Long edited it, enticed Irvin Cobb, Rupert Hughes, and others away with Hearst's inherited moneybags. Lorimer, bitter at the raiding since he had helped develop—as a good editor can—many of these writers, never took back an author who had strayed. My hard decision to play along probably recommended me to him as a loyal author with good sound sense.

Together Beatrice and I began some short stories about an engaging, unpredictable, fast-talking New York literary agent—the "Jimmie Faraday" series—at first against Lorimer's approval. He wanted nothing, he said, about literary agents, for whom, in the main, he had little respect and even occasional distrust. He'd had to deal with too many imperceptive ones, selling a writer's lifeblood as though it were pounds of cheese. Some, like Harold Ober, Carl Brandt, George Bye, he trusted. Moreover, Lorimer feared his readers were not interested in writers, whose intricate, whining, complicated, creative woes are hard for the average person to understand. But, for once, Lorimer was wrong. "Jimmie Faraday" proved strikingly popular. We wrote six or eight stories before we ran out of time.

Perhaps Lorimer wasn't really wrong. These were actually business tales—more about the selling of literary wares than about their creation. And the fabulous wheeling and dealing with the Hollywood-Broadway of Jimmie Faraday, based for the most part on Leland's charming antics, needed only slight dramatization to make good *Post* fiction.

Hayward brilliantly earned his Ten Per Cent (the title of the first story) by variety and ingenuity. He could peddle a manuscript, an actress, or even an idea; sometimes an idea would suddenly occur to his radar brain merely as he talked, and he would sell it over the telephone as if it were an uncut Kohinoor which he was foolish enough to give away for stage money when, by just polishing it himself, he could easily turn it into a fortune. Leland later became a successful producer (*Call Me Madam, The Sound of Music, Shot in the Dark*), proving innate polishing ability. Above all, he had taste. This alone set him apart in Hollywood and on Broadway from those with whom he customarily chaffered. His victims were always slightly bewildered, too, by his instinctive good manners. Good manners don't seem to come naturally to many of the most active denizens of the theatrical jungle, where a knife is something one uses on a friend rather than in eating peas, and a foe someone to be fawned upon.

Beatrice, too, on her own began to sell again. Several short-shorts went to *Collier's,* which clamored for more. A novelette was snapped up by *Cosmopolitan* with the editor flatteringly comparing Beatrice to Edith Wharton. A Christmas story sold to *Ladies' Home Journal.* Christmas was really Christmas that year, just as a Thanksgiving turkey lovingly roasted by Beatrice and her mother had nourished the spirit of Thanksgiving. For Christmas Beatrice received a much appreciated fur-lined coat. Sesaly got skates and real toys. I was given a new necktie and I needed it. Our car was really ours—the first thing we did was to pay all those menacing installments. I even, eventually, repaid to Liveright the advance ($750), received in 1929, on the novel, *Puritan,* I was never to write—the first time, Liveright said, an author had ever reimbursed the firm for work not delivered. As an editor I was later to find this reluctance of writers to pay for a dead horse quite universal; the excuses offered revealed brilliant creativeness and infinite individuality.

Row on, no matter what happens.
—RABELAIS

14 ❧

Missing a Train Starts a Long Journey

That agonizing year in which neither Beatrice nor I had sold a line and not a check had come in was over. The "Faraday" series was going well. Now I thought of an offbeat story. With a certain trepidation I took the train to Philadelphia to discuss my slightly exotic idea with Graeme Lorimer. "My" editor at the *Post,* he was assigned to a continuing relationship in developing my stories, and in warning me when I seemed about to run off the track.

This relation between writers and editors, many authors think, somewhat resembles that of a wary dog to a bad-tempered and uncertain master. The dog is never sure whether it's a kick or a bone he will receive when he faithfully drops a story at the master's boot. Refusal from an editor never seems just—simply capricious, bad-tempered and inexplicable. So, with a certain gelatinous assurance, I approached my editor's office. Would that day yield a kick or a bone?

The tale I hoped to write was admittedly a little odd for the *Post*—a Russian prima ballerina down on her luck. Ballet, then, was popular mainly with champagne-in-slipper-drinking grand dukes and a few home-grown aesthetes like me. The hairy-chested *Post,* many of whose heroes only shaved once a girl caught their eye, might consider a story about a prima ballerina as of dubious masculinity. (I could well remember my football-playing brother's contempt when he found me, a teen-age romantic out of funds, stealing a dangerous ride, blind baggage, from Grinnell, just to watch Pavlova's thistledown entrechats in our drafty Des Moines Coliseum.) There wouldn't be much use in trying to force such an effete story on the *Post* if Lorimer shared my brother's distaste, thought ballet too decadent for his he-man public.

With a show of confidence I outlined to Graeme the story. Leaning back comfortably in his heavily-cushioned swivel chair—which enabled an editor swiftly to turn his back or face you at will—Graeme listened gravely, twiddling the heavy black pencil with which editors beat a writer's prose into submission. The whole tale began to sound increasingly absurd as I sweated through my ridiculous plot. I never could, like some writers and story-creating producers like Walt Disney, speak a story. I have to write it. At the end, perhaps because he saw I was staking so much on its sale, Graeme excused himself to check with his father. He seemed in a hurry to get away, I thought. As if he couldn't face further hearing of my idea, he disappeared toward Lorimer's great corner office, where the Old Man sat thundering very little but "No!"

Left to mop my sweating palms with a service handkerchief from my hip pocket—a jaunty breast-pocket one camouflaging my doubts —I wondered why any man in his right mind took up the profession of writing when one might easily just read electric meters for a living.

In about ten anguishing minutes Graeme hurried back. "My father thinks it's a good bet." A little out of breath, he looked at me anxiously.

I stared at my wrist watch to avoid his gaze. The weakness of relief swept over me.

"I've missed the train back to Hopewell," I finally said, my head ducked down, as if still reading my watch. "You're stuck with me for another hour. Thank your father. I'll get right on that story." I still had to write it, but one need only take one hurdle at a time.

I could look at Graeme now, settled comfortably back in his chair, smiling. Himself a writer, he probably knew all too well the fog of misery blanketing the mind when creative efforts fail.

I relaxed. My spirits had soared with approval. We talked about the mechanics of writing—the methods each author uses to make easier his concentrated task.

Graeme, collaborator with his attractive wife, Sarah, on the amusing "Maudie" series then successfully running in *Ladies' Home Journal,* knew that every writer works differently. Some wrap up short stories at one sitting. Stimulating themselves with black coffee or enough cigarettes to stoke a funeral pyre, or bolstering themselves with liquor—one writer's formula was one bottle of Scotch, one night, one story—some authors can, in an intense burst of creativity, produce better stuff, and more stuff, than by steadily slogging every day as I had to do. Trollope, who wrote by his watch so many words in so many hours each morning before his full-time post office job, Arnold Bennett, a 1,400-word-a-day-man, Somerset Maugham slogged. O. Henry, always broke, presumably did not. Borrowing advances from one editor to pay back long-overdue advances from another, O. Henry could suddenly sit down and produce a kind of minor masterpiece. They aren't in today's fashion, when the depicting of a scene, or the evoking of a mood, if freshly and originally done, constitutes a story. The fashion will change—that is what makes it fashion. Maybe back to Maupassant and Kipling—who can read the future?

"I can only write from nine to one," I told Graeme. "That leaves me with time on my hands. A friend of mine suggested I start a book-publishing business with him. That would interest me."

"Have you ever," Graeme interrupted, "considered an editing job on a magazine? The *Post,* for instance. My father might take you on —we're short a man."

Short stories, he explained, could be written by energetic people like me on weekends. That is what he did, despite his manifold editorial chores, ably spotting and nursing along young talent.

"How about it, Bruce?"

Would a man already drunk like another drink? The answer was "Sure!" I didn't even stop to think what Beatrice would say.

"I'll speak to my father. See if he can see you now." Graeme disappeared again.

Although I had been writing for the *Post* more than two years, I didn't know much about the Curtis Publishing Company. Cyrus H. K. Curtis, the founder, had been dead a year. His son-in-law, Edward Bok, the famous editor of the *Journal*, had died several years earlier, after a thirty-year stint and writing a successful autobiography, *The Americanization of Edward Bok*—still read in schools as a kind of textbook on the opportunities of our democratic society. Lorimer, I knew, was now in absolute command. Last of the Curtis giants, he spoke, and everybody jumped. But he, too, was getting along.

Beatrice and I, as new writers, had been formally given lunch in the white-paneled eighth-floor dining room where so many really famous *Post* authors like Ring Lardner, Mary Roberts Rinehart, Booth Tarkington, Harry Leon Wilson, Joseph Hergesheimer, John Marquand had been honored. At these luncheons Lorimer, a charming, considerate host to whom women were instantly drawn, regaled us with stories about Arnold Bennett, Sinclair Lewis, Lady Astor, Calvin Coolidge, Al Smith, and other famous contemporaries, making us feel among the great.

It was obvious that Lorimer, in 1934, already despised That Man in the White House almost as much as he feared him. He had forgotten perhaps that, as a young editor, he had once published Frank Norris' radical novels exposing corruption, backed "Terrible Teddy" Roosevelt, supported reformer Wilson. He had even written an editorial he no longer remembered applauding the Russian Revolution as springing not from a palace clique but from a fedup people. But, growing older, growing richer, he had become as conservative as Herbert Hoover, both hoping to keep the world as they wished it to remain.

"Father can see you now," Graeme reported, interrupting my cogitations, and led me to the office big as a ballroom where Lorimer sat in lonely splendor. I began to wonder what it would be like to work for the most famous editor in America, who'd brought the *Post* in a dozen years from nothing to the best-known magazine in the world. Lorimer, I knew, was a dictator. Editors, I suppose, really have to be—anyway they are. I wished I were more naturally a courtier. I don't mind treating subordinates better than they deserve, my equals as equals, but I find it difficult to treat my superiors even with common decency.

Graeme introduced me hurriedly, "Father, you remember Bruce Gould." He, too, stood in awe of the Old Man, and quickly disappeared.

Lorimer, I noticed, wasn't actually as tall as he looked. His commanding presence fooled you into thinking he had great height. Sitting, he tucked one leg under his torso like a teenager, towering over his guest squashed down in a low leather chair facing the light.

I wasn't immediately bowled over by the salary offered me, $6,000 a year—after all I'd made more than that on newspapers before the Crash. However, it was certain money after years of uncertainty. Beatrice would, I suspected, appreciate knowing for a change where our grocery money was coming from. The black year was not forgotten by either of us.

"For once say nothing except absolutely necessary words," I told myself sternly. "Remember, $169.35 is at present your total wealth."

Besides the certain salary, since the *Post* staff was surprisingly small, perhaps the great man would not be too remote even from me on the foot of the ladder. I might learn a lot. Sometimes I thought I had a lot to learn.

The second in command, Tom Costain, had just left. Born a Canadian, he had incautiously admitted in public he could think of nothing happier than retiring to England in his old age. A shocked Lorimer immediately concluded a mind so warped could never be trusted to edit the strictly American *Post,* more tradition-bound than Thanksgiving turkey. Tom, told he'd never succeed to the throne, resigned. After a brief fling at Hollywood, where he speedily discovered it was hard to remain the gentleman he instinctively was, Tom demonstrated he could write as well as edit, in a series of successful historical novels. When he could afford to live in England like an old-fashioned lord, he did not.

I had still made no comment about the meager $6,000 offered me; perhaps Lorimer, acute as a woman weighing new neighbors, noticed.

"There'll be more money, if you're worth it," he remarked, apropos of nothing. He himself, I later learned, had started on the *Post* at $35 a week—so poor he'd picked up tobacco samples at corner cigar stores to keep his pipe supplied. He was now worth several millions. My beginning salary would have no bearing on my future; that would be what I made it, he indicated.

Looking into his lively, actinic-blue eyes, sizing up that countenance rugged as though carved out of everlasting hills by Gutzon Borglum, I believed him. A man who didn't yield easily, he looked as trustworthy as a pair of well-advertised President suspenders. What he said he meant—no more, perhaps, but definitely no less. In time I came to know him as a man of taste, of integrity, full of hearty humor and delicate perceptions, with enough weaknesses to make him human but none that threatened character—one of the men for whom I could have as complete respect as I had for my father.

I said I'd be glad to take the job, and thanked him for giving me the opportunity. Soon, I decided inwardly, he'd see I was worth more than $6,000, or I'd try my luck elsewhere. Meantime, I'd do my best for him, the *Post*—and myself.

Lorimer leaned back relaxed when I accepted his terms—agreeing I could live at Hopewell rather than make an expensive move to Philadelphia even though, commuting, I couldn't punch the time clock at nine and five with the rest of his clock-punching staff. So I blithely suggested I start work in three weeks, after Beatrice and I had slipped down to Florida for the short holiday we both needed.

He sat up erect as a cobra.

"I'd like you to start work next Monday. After you've been here a year, you'll have earned three weeks' vacation."

I perceived I'd better start at once.

I asked to whom I should report. "Well, I'm the boss," he said. "Report to me."

"Okay." I rose. "Monday. It'll be about 9:25. I like to walk from the station." His fist felt good as we shook hands and I left elatedly to tell Graeme, and report to Beatrice that we now had a weekly

As *Journal* war correspondent in 1945, Bruce meets
Chiang Kai-shek in Chungking. ALEXANDERSON (CNS)

Bruce, chatting with
General Eisenhower at
NATO's Paris headquarters
in 1951.

Madame Pandit and Nehru entertained Bruce and Beatrice
in the Prime Minister's New Delhi gardens in 1952.

paycheck for the first time since 1931, all because I'd missed a train.

I reported for duty, expectant, even awed. The *S.E.P.* had been preeminent in its field since my trudging brothers sold it for a nickel. I was exhilarated to find I would spend three weeks at a temporary desk in each associate's office, learning what that editor did. I wasn't going to join the staff and be forgotten. Only Wesley Stout, later briefly to succeed Lorimer, declined to have me. He was by nature convivial, an accomplished raconteur, quite the most amusing luncheon companion in our small group—but, in work, a loner. (Later, as editor, he often returned to the office evenings to type out his own letters.) I would wind up in Adelaide W. Neall's sanctum, next door to Mr. Lorimer, where she ruled, in effect, as managing editor.

There were unspoken questions around the office as to why an arrangement never before laid on for any new boy had been set up for me. I was as much in the dark as anyone. Sitting in on the main editorial conference once a week, asking questions at any time of anyone, I was privileged to poke my nose everywhere, with free access to all records, even Lorimer's. Since my training was journalistic and I am reasonably curious by nature, I did pry and poke—one reason perhaps Stout avoided my peering eye.

It was *Post* policy that every manuscript should be read by at least two, sometimes more, editors the day it came in. Stories and articles were distributed to associates by Miss Neall each morning, with rush jobs coming in occasionally by the midday mail. In late afternoon Lorimer glanced over staff comments—Yes, No, or Maybe, with brief amplifications if need be on the manuscript's manila envelope. Some he rejected out of hand—even though a few opinions might have been approving. Others he took home for reading and final decision though some selected might have been turned down by every associate. Next morning Lorimer brought in his manuscripts marked in great black pencil $\frac{OK}{GHL}$ or $\frac{NO}{GHL}$. When he spoke, contrary-minded editors never made an effort to change his decisions.

Post associates, I saw, sometimes discussed among themselves how He would likely react to an important manuscript, trying to line up their own opinions in advance; they feared they might think wrong.

"How," I asked Graeme, "can anyone expect to think like your father? How is it helping him always to agree, if it's not your real opinion you're giving?"

"You haven't yet crossed my father," Graeme reminded me.

Post submissions were read so promptly and often rejected so fast a legend grew among New York agents that manuscript bags were sidetracked at Trenton on the way to Philadelphia and rejected in bulk. Actually Lorimer, in his early days, had gained invaluable first-look at many desirable stories by promising immediate decision, a check to follow acceptance the next Wednesday. Established magazines, then, often paid only on publication, sometimes months later, sometimes never.

The last associate in whose office I spent three weeks was, of course, Miss Neall, a handsome spinsterish spinster with a humorous, sweet-natured look. She had been Lorimer's right-hand man ever since, an intelligent, alive girl, she had been graduated from Bryn Mawr. Starting as his secretary, for many years she had devoted all her waking hours, warm loyalty, and more than ordinary perception to seeing that what Lorimer wanted on the *Post* was done. It was a pleasure to watch them work together. His obvious respect for her judgment contrasted sharply with the little respect he seemed to have for most other opinions. She had no other interest than helping Lorimer edit the Post, though she could see through him as clearly as though they were man and wife.

"You were pounding the table so hard," she once said, "I could tell you weren't quite sure."

He laughed boisterously, caught out by someone before whom he needn't strut.

Miss Neall, a merry person with an incisive wit, perceived my genuine interest and sympathy. She gave me a very real close-up of the *Post* and of the man who dominated it.

Lorimer had built the *Post* solidly on the first law of life, self-preservation. Since most Americans preserved themselves by doing business, reading about business was, for Americans, reading about themselves in action. The more specific and realistic the details of how men made a profit, the better the stories. To show the way, he early wrote and serialized *Letters from a Self-made Merchant to His Son,* and *Old Gorgon Graham,* salty, shrewd reading. One could still make money today following their common sense.

Cyrus H. K. Curtis always said *Post* success could be explained in three words, "George Horace Lorimer." Just before Curtis died he had persuaded Lorimer to follow him as president. This task he loathed, I learned. It took time away from the sport and excitement of editing.

Lorimer knew one must have real intelligence to run a business, be extraordinarily intelligent to make it a roaring success. But editing requires different qualities and publishing houses are kept alive by editors—though good sense is crucial in the business office, too.

His voice had a special hard-timbered resonance. I have seen men lose control of their own voices when some difference occurred.

An inventor, I had heard, came in to thank Lorimer personally for an editorial praising his promising invention—turning cornhusks into newsprint. Fulsomely he assured the editor that once his product was in work, he intended to advertise extensively in the *Post.*

"I'm sorry you told me that," Lorimer stood up. "Now I can never mention your product again. Advertising must never influence *Post* opinions. Good day."

Led shaking from the presence, the awed inventor exclaimed: "What a man! What a man!!"

Post editors, I discovered, were choosing stories and articles for the *Journal,* as well as the *Post.* This struck me as strange. I thought each editor ran his own magazine.

"Why is that?" I asked Graeme, after a few days of puzzlement.

"The *Journal* isn't doing well, and my father doesn't trust Schuler's judgment," Graeme explained. Loring Schuler, since 1928 editor of the *Journal,* had before that been in charge of *The Country Gentleman,* a farm magazine so loved by Cyrus Curtis he spent a fortune futilely trying to make it successful.

"Why don't they get a new *Journal* editor?"

"You might ask Father."

"I'll wait a few days," I grinned. "But I also notice," I persisted, "the *Journal* gets only stories the *Post* doesn't really want. Except for the 'Maudies.' " Graeme grinned now. "Can that be helpful to the *Journal*—always getting second best?"

"You're learning fast," Graeme shrugged. "I'm not running Curtis."

"There is no doubt who's running Curtis," I agreed. "But isn't the poor old *Journal* being gypped? Getting only *Post* culls? Or can that be said aloud?"

Graeme raised his eyebrows.

Everyone walked in awe of the Great Man.. His iron hand was everywhere, in illustrations and the slightly old-fashioned writers he favored.

My apprenticeship over, I was assigned a small office next to Graeme's larger one, still without title, influence, or position. Brashly, Graeme and I tried to slip some of our young ideas into Lorimer's slightly formalized magazine; he growled at us to keep hands off when we attacked something too sacred, such as "Postscripts," a page of boisterous jokes selected to his own taste, scorned by sophisticates but much liked by readers.

One of our ambitious schemes was to rescue from the dustbin fiction he had rejected. He didn't believe in working with authors to revise unsatisfactory stories. To him an author's manuscript was either publishable or to be returned.

On this survival-of-the-fittest basis, Lorimer had built up a brilliant stable of authors. He watched our fussy efforts with skepticism, but not forbidding outright our half-charitable, half-selfish activities.

It is easier to show what is wrong with a story than to write a good story oneself. Objectivity often lets the editor clearly see the author's mistakes. Thus Graeme and I helped develop half-a-dozen limping young people into *Post* writers capable of standing on their own feet. Perhaps it's better not to list them. Many authors resent help so strongly they cannot benefit. They call it editorial interference. They speak of taboos, of writing to a formula. Certain authors accept rescue rather glumly, indicating they could have easily saved themselves. But some authors cooperated. We had the pleasure of securing an $\frac{\text{OK}}{\text{GHL}}$ on many stories which otherwise would have died stillborn.

Lorimer thought his sterner way best. Maybe it was. Essentially, a writer has to teach himself to write.

Calling me in one day, to tell me my salary was now raised to $8,000 (why not $10,000? I thought, but managed proper thanks) and my name was to go up on the masthead as an associate editor, he suggested I write some editorials. Of the two or three published in each issue, one was usually, and pretty obviously, his. My first editorial made him laugh heartily as he returned it.

"Sorry, Bruce. It's good. The point of view is perfectly permissible. But I've accepted a few honorary degrees myself. So I can't conscientiously condemn them as silly."

I went away kicking myself. Why hadn't I looked up Lorimer in *Who's Who,* where honorary degrees are always listed *in extenso?* Before I could write another, he asked my reaction one morning to a longish editorial of his own.

Scooter Rizzuto never had a hotter grounder to handle. The editorial was two editorials, not one. Right in the middle Lorimer had, strangely for him, wandered through a separate, scarcely related, theme.

Longing for dissimulation, I forced myself to his office; the distance from door to desk seemed a hundred yards. He listened without comment as I analyzed his faults in detail. He thanked me. Turning, I felt my back a dart board for his dagger eyes.

When advance copies came off the press, I immediately turned to his editorial. Had it been revised as I had suggested? It had. I could breathe. Later, from Miss Neall, I heard Lorimer had told her my views and grunted, "Gould isn't an associate editor—he's an *editor!*"

While he was on vacation I found myself recommending several manuscripts turned down by the rest of the staff. Miss Neall held them for the Boss's return. Several received his final $\frac{OK}{GHL}$, indicating he wasn't irritated by my temerity in holding out against the entire rest of the staff.

So it was within my first year at the *Post,* my salary again raised slightly, that Graeme one morning sounded me out about becoming managing editor of the *Journal,* with the tacit understanding I would succeed Schuler as soon as I proved ready.

My quick refusal was fortunately to Graeme rather than to the Old Man. I didn't wish to work under someone I was slated to supplant, I said. If he knew what was in the wind—and how could he not?—Schuler could easily reject any novel ideas. Since he would have final say I did not see how the *Journal* would be improved. Or, if Schuler didn't suspect I was to succeed him, he might turn down my suggestions simply because they didn't look good to him. I've always been better at deciding than at persuading. An editor must follow his own instinct, his own inner voice. If he begins taking opinions from others, opinions which don't agree with his own, he's a rudderless ship.

A little later the Old Man came up with a second suggestion—again through Graeme—that I take over directly from Schuler with Beatrice at my side and run the *Journal* as a man-and-wife team.

I learned later from Adelaide Neall and others that Lorimer had for some time thought seriously of putting me in sole charge of the *Journal.* The suggestion of adding Beatrice, too, was an afterthought, coming directly after an *S.E.P.* party at which Beatrice had not only looked very pretty in a wine velvet evening gown (copied by her mother from one worn by Lady Abdy in *Vogue*) but had also (deliberately) flattered the Old Man.

Beatrice is as honest as anyone I know—I'll amend that to more honest—constitutionally unable to utter a word of flattery unless it is deeply felt. But she is generous, too. When she admires she likes to express her admiration fully. Also, she had been sorry because the last time she had seen Mr. Lorimer she had argued with him, defending Walter Lippmann, whom the Old Man considered extremely far left. Since her liking for the Boss amounted as mine did almost to reverence she wished to express her admiration as warmly as she had expressed her disagreement.

While dancing with him she had said (she told me later that evening), "Mr. Lorimer, you have made a hero worshiper of my husband." From then on the conversation proceeded on understandably amiable lines. It was the following Monday that Mr. Lorimer proposed to Graeme that Beatrice join me in editing the *Ladies' Home Journal.*

Of course he knew her qualifications as writer and editor were sound. But I have always felt that the conversation that evening had persuaded him of her very womanly nature—valuable assistance in editing a woman's magazine.

When the offer was actually made, I couldn't forecast Beatrice's response. I said I'd like to stay home next day to discuss it with her —she never liked to decide anything important except in the morning when her mind worked most clearly.

Beatrice was not at all certain she wanted to take the job, flattering though it seemed to us both.

Her own writing was going rather more successfully than in the past. *Collier's* as well as the *Post* and *Cosmopolitan* were now buying her stories at increasingly better prices. She didn't care to be a big executive. She didn't fancy long commuting days away from home and child—our daughter was not quite eight. Beatrice's schedule was arranged so she could drive Sesaly to Miss Fine's school in Princeton, spend the morning writing in the university library, pick up Sesaly again and take her home for lunch. They were very companionable.

She could see, however, that I was more tempted by the joint proposal than by editing the *Journal* alone. I felt much more at home on the *Post.* George Meredith said: "I expect that Woman will be the last thing civilized by Man," by which he meant made over into smaller men, I suppose—what a loss to pleasure in difference! I didn't feel quite that strongly, but women were more of a mystery to me then than now. Even now, I'm not going to contend I thoroughly understand them—at least not while my wife is in the same room.

Beatrice finally said she would go along with Mr. Lorimer's idea provided she need appear at the office only three days a week—the rest of the time working at home as the first editor of the *Journal,* Louisa Knapp Curtis, had done before turning over the job to Bok.

Lorimer, surprisingly, said yes to her terms. He was, I believe, a little irritated that she did not accept his offer wholeheartedly. So he decreed Beatrice was to get $5,000 a year—I $20,000—that being his mistaken idea of our relative merits.

"It doesn't," he explained, "make any difference at what salary you start," thus making light of the modest sum offered. "If you're successful, you can write your own ticket."

Lorimer (starting in 1897 on the *Post* Curtis had bought for $1,000) had, when the *Post* suddenly became a success around 1912, written his own ticket. When Curtis suggested his editor buy some company stock, Lorimer somewhat hesitantly explained he hadn't any money. So Curtis loaned him, at no interest, $50,000— the principal to be repaid out of dividends on the rapidly rising stock.

"The next time," Lorimer told me, "I borrowed a million."

Lorimer, like Byron, thought the most beautiful words in the English language were "ready money," but could not foresee the Roosevelt era when mounting income taxes made it increasingly difficult to become rich. We didn't become millionaires. We did become unpoor.

In outlining his idea that our names were to top the masthead as equal editors, he said to me in a hasty but clear aside: "And, Bruce, don't forget—you're the Boss!"—thus indicating his unease and the company's at this unorthodox editing team.

Our editorship was to start July 1, 1935.

Lorimer was sparing of directions about how we should run the *Journal*. He did say: "Bruce, don't pay attention to anyone's opinions except your own. No magazine can stand the mistakes of more than one man."

He told me Curtis had once said to him: "George, my wife and daughter didn't like the last issue of the *Post* as well as usual."

"Mr. Curtis," replied Lorimer, "I'm not running the *Post* for your wife and daughter," and added to me, "He never said a word to me again about how to run the *Post*.

"As a matter of fact," he explained, "my resignation was always on the table."

I asked him how much Curtis, himself, had had to do with the success of the *Post*.

"He was a good businessman," Lorimer replied. "When you've said that, you've said it all."

The Curtis Publishing Company had staunchly weathered the 1929 Depression. Hard times were still with the *Journal,* however, and were to remain until World War II began. But Beatrice and I, in middle 1935, thought strictly in terms of sunrises not sunsets, and it was with lifted hearts, but with some trepidation on her part, that we looked forward to our challenging new job.

Honest labour bears a lovely face.
　　　　　　　—Thomas Dekker

15

The First Days

When I had telephoned my mother that I was taking over at the *Journal* all she said was, "Isn't Curtis lucky!" Laughing still, I can't deny my ego admired her percipience as we traveled down together that sultry July morning—our first as coeditors. (We disliked this term, and dropped it, even before we heard the crack traveling around Madison Avenue—"What the *Old Ladies' Journal* needs is less co-editing and more cohabiting.")

Possibly because of my mother's rather exaggerated pride in me, I have never lacked self-confidence, especially when I had little reason for it. Later, one realizes more and more that one knows less and less.

Beatrice has not the same full confidence, but she has a quality as important—courage. She will try her best to accomplish something even against a fifty-fifty chance she may not succeed. So, while she perhaps was not as assured as I that morning, she looked gay, demurely dressed as an editor should be in a navy-and-white silk dress, a white hat, and a red rose from Hopewell, for bravado.

We did not realize, right then, all the obstacles ahead—with our own staff, with our own company, with the outside world, especially Madison Avenue, which held the ace of advertising up its sleeve to play for us or against us.

We were aware, Beatrice, perhaps, with more apprehension than I, that a magazine is nothing but sheets of blank paper, until those pages are filled by means of ideas. The ideas you originate, the stories you buy, even the associates you choose, give those blank pages a personality vivid and real.

We hoped we had one clear asset. We felt a kinship with our readers. Beatrice was remembering her own dishwashing, bread-baking, poetry-loving mother. I recalled my family, straitened in money matters, never in intellectual aspiration or clear-cut moral attitude. Thousands of homes all over the country were like ours we knew in our blood and bones. We could never subscribe to that cliché of the moment—the idea of uniform "little people."

I had the rueful thought that liking our audience might be a handi-cap. At least, Bok, who brought the *Journal* of his day to world-wide fame, had written in his curious third-person autobiography: "Bok's intimate attitude towards women, was that of avoidance. He did not dislike women, but it could not be said that he liked them. Nor had he the slightest desire, even as an editor, to know them better, or to seek to understand them."

Soon after brilliant, arrogant Bok's death his widow briskly cut her hair, discarded the high net collar he had required her to wear even with evening dress at the opera, and shortly married Efrem Zimbalist, the violinist.

Bok, after his triumphant reign, had bequeathed his successors a magnificent office, large as a squash court. Beatrice's, next door, was suitably smaller, and I could even punch a bell to summon her —but, having tried it once, I found she didn't think that funny.

Bok, regarding his privileges highly, had installed the only wood-burning fireplace in Curtis' block-sized, classically-columned edifice facing Independence Square. Through the ceiling-high windows I could look far down to the Delaware River, sparkling half a mile away and curving off toward the sea in what seemed almost a world view. For years Bok had ruled here as the top magazine editor of America.

Since Bok's time, *Journal* editors had been less notable. One, installing an inviolate "thinking room" next to his office, had lasted twelve months. Barton Currie, after seven futile years, had retired with dwindling prestige and a million dollars, selling his Curtis stock at its 1928 peak. Because he had bought the second story Beatrice wrote, she retained an understandable affection for his memory. Schuler, whom we were succeeding, had lost his job with a big new house and a big new swimming pool to support while the Depression still lasted.

"Let's," I had said to Beatrice, "never build a swimming pool. Let's be able to walk away from the job, heads high, any time we don't like the setup."

"Fortunately, I don't like swimming pools," Beatrice rejoined.

An attractive young woman awaited me, introduced herself as my secretary, and explained a few needful things—who wanted to see me first, and who, perhaps, should be seen first. Then she lingered politely. I nodded.

"I should like," she said briskly, "to resign as soon as convenient."

She looked very determined.

"Are you getting married?" I asked, for I knew from *Post* days the absurd company rule that all secretaries and female clerks who married must quit their jobs immediately.

"No," she said, coloring slightly, "I'm not."

This was strictly true, though untrue in fact. She was already married, I later learned. Like many girls forced to act as though living in sin during the frightening Depression, she had, in self-defense, not told her former boss of her clandestine wedding. Later, we persuaded the board to change this rule, ridiculous anyway now, considering that a man and wife had just been made joint editors of the *Journal*. The company speedily discovered many of their supposedly single girls had become matrons overnight, another example of a prohibition against human nature blithely ignored.

I regarded my secretary, wondering if she had disliked me on sight —was this an omen?

"Very well," I finally said, "you can resign as soon as I find a girl as pretty as you to take your place."

She looked a little startled, but since my wife could be heard bustling about in the next room the situation must have seemed safe.

There was method in my madness.

The *Journal* had fallen on such evil days it was known, not only on Madison Avenue but even among its own personnel, as the *Old Ladies' Journal*. This odious nomenclature, bad for our public image and bad for magazine morale, must be changed; nothing is quicker than death from a snicker.

As receptionists, both in Philadelphia and in New York, we immediately hired the most charming young women we could find, paying them a little bonus for their pulchritude. In those Depression days beautiful girls were in ample supply. Since, with the naked eye, I can spot a pretty girl at a hundred yards, I selected the receptionists myself. Being attractive, Beatrice isn't jealous of my native skill, probably taking my interest in lovely girls as an involved compliment of sorts. The secretary I soon chose for myself was prettiest of all. (Beauty and intelligence are not mutually exclusive though some female office managers seem to think so. In fact, I have come to believe, if a girl isn't fairly good-looking nowadays, with all the beauty aids available, she can't be very bright—or else is angry at the world and wishes to avenge herself by looking dowdy.)

It amused us to see how our comely innovation affected visitors, roused the staidest officials in the company. Advertising and circulation men visited my office, I sometimes felt, just to see my pantherous young secretary glide about. Elderly executives, mysteriously stirred by our graceful personnel, found it impossible to think of the *Journal* as anything but provocative, young, and new, not to say nubile. *Old Ladies* sank without a trace.

But, on that first day, we soon found that lack of confidence was not confined to my secretary. Our Curtis advertising manager, head of the striving salesmen who must keep our magazine plump and profitable by persuading national advertisers to use its pages, came in to welcome us. His veneer of heartiness failed to disguise weights and measures in his eyes.

"For God's sake, what can you do to help?" his manner seemed to say.

Beside Bok's slim, almost feminine desk stood a cavernous cane-and-walnut wastebasket into which many hopes had dropped. Would we, the perceptibly agitated advertising director might well have wondered, end up in that wastebasket like the *Journal* editors preceding us?

The head of the circulation department also was complimentary but watchful. He had seen *Journal* subscriptions drop during several bad years. Fewer old readers wanted to renew. Fewer new women could be induced to buy. Newsstand sales were sluggish, declining. Even cheerful little boys going from door to door selling subscriptions and individual copies of the *Journal* to earn money for bicycles, baseball mitts, and air rifles were finding doors shut in their appealing faces.

To these department heads, new editors were all important. If we produced a magazine women longed to read, money would jangle in the till from advertiser and subscriber. By the editors' success this tired advertising man, this troubled circulation chief might once more become brilliant in their fields and be rewarded accordingly. But if the editors failed—we'd all be dragged out of the arena by our tails.

The *Journal* picture was gloomy, we realized, or new editors wouldn't have been appointed. We hadn't been told that Young and Rubicam had just completed a study of readers' preferences among the six leading women's periodicals. By such measurement, Madison Avenue decided which magazines got the advertiser's life-sustaining dollar. The *Journal,* the poll indicated, was a sinking ship.

According to the survey, run by the to-become-famous-but-still-relatively-unknown Dr. Gallup, women's preferences stood in this order:

1. *Good Housekeeping*
2. *Woman's Home Companion*
3. *McCall's*
4. *Ladies' Home Journal*
5. *Pictorial Review*
6. *Delineator*

The last two, once famous monthlies, soon merged, then died. The *Journal,* a poor fourth as we took over, seemed plunging toward the same oblivion.

Dr. Gallup, being a friend, had not so much as hinted at this disturbing information, once our decision to take over the *Journal* was made. It was known, undoubtedly, to the astute Mr. Lorimer, likewise silent. Madison Avenue, aware of the depressing statistics, was saying that all women's magazines were finished. The "formula" was worn out.

So, as respects were politely paid to us by our advertising and circulation managers, there was not great assurance in their eyes nor much confidence in their jovial manner.

Among our editorial associates, too, doubt, almost hostility, fogged the air. The unsuccessful Mr. Schuler had been likable, easygoing, courteous, more popular than Lorimer, who, to some, seemed grim— the hatchet man lopping off incompetent heads. It was a shock to associate editors to see Schuler overnight displaced by two brash young strangers. Since I had been with the *Post* only a year and a half, and in a low echelon, many people around Curtis had never heard of me, much less of Beatrice.

Fear of petticoat government, the fact that we were two, appeared to increase the risks.

"What will we do when Mr. Gould tells us one thing, Mrs. Gould another?" was the question repeated by an amused, needling Graeme.

Some of these associates greeted us with visibly shaking hands. Since an editor cannot always explain his decisions, but must operate on instinct—"People will like this, people won't like this"—no one can tell till long after whether he's right. His judgments often seem capricious; undoubtedly some of them are. A new editor frequently brings in a whole new staff, people he can count on to try to carry out his ideas. An editor of food or fashion tends to follow a certain pattern because she believes in it. If she doesn't fit the new concept, the editor must replace either her ideas or her.

So the atmosphere was not exactly cheerful as I installed myself in my grandiose, Mussolini-scaled office, paneled in Circassian walnut, one end of the room framing a giant copy of Rembrandt's "The Syndics"—Bok had liked to associate himself with the great.

My first thought that hot morning was the still-in-work October issue now being put up in dummy form on the walls in the art department.

It was exactly like all the *Journals* we had been seeing for years. To make the magazine look new, we must alter the old-fashioned, repetitive illustrations.

"Have we time to remake these two engravings?" I asked the art editor, briskly.

"Barely time—but scrapping them would cost about $2,800," said art editor, Frank Eltonhead.

"Make them over. Cut this one down like this—" I outlined in red pencil a rectangle slashing the proof. "This is a beautiful woman's face—enlarge it—make it strong—I want it to come toward you like a movie close-up.

"On this picture cut out everything except those two figures facing each other. There's clash there. Accent it! Let's make the *Journal* dramatic." Like a pale imitation of G.H.L., I made these authoritative, expensive decisions as if certain I knew what I was doing.

"But—the artists," stammered Frank, an engaging man with excellent conservative taste, always considerate of associates.

"I know, Frank, I know, but we must have change in the first *Journal* we put out. Let's make it different right away."

A fresh, gay, inviting layout was important at once, especially for men along Madison Avenue who don't read the text. Our bigger job was content—to win our readers' trust and affection. That would take longer.

The second day we attacked problems in our attractive New York office called the *Journal* workshop on the top floor of the RKO building, Fiftieth and Sixth Avenue. Here, with changing views of ships on the Hudson, scarlet New Jersey sunsets, and the Christmas-tree lights of Broadway at dusk, fashions were viewed, apple pies baked and pictured, washing machines operated under the eyes of their appropriate associate editors. Here, yesterday's attitude of polite, show-me skepticism met us. Mr. Schuler had treated these editors as experts,

let them do as they pleased. Experts, I feel, are people who can do
well what has always been done. We wanted innovators. A natural
lack of enthusiasm for Schuler's prying successors, one of them an
interfering woman, was evidenced. Soon they thought they had reason.

In the homemaking department, we saw plans being drawn up for
an ideal, labor-saving kitchen. Small, efficient, antiseptic as a laboratory, every step from here to there had been proudly measured, as
we were proudly shown.

"Where can you sit down for a cup of coffee?" Beatrice asked.
"There ought to be a place for the children to make cookies, or to
crayon while Mama is working. Most people live in their kitchens.
Let's plan one big enough for the kids and a rocking chair."

Our rocking-chair kitchens eventually became famous. Millionaires,
sans servants, now build $100,000 houses with living kitchens—a
"family" room with charcoal grill for chef-hatted papa.

Drawings for "minimum" houses—suitable, we were told, for the
"average American income," then about $1,600 a year—were shown
us, each with two bedrooms. Our architectural editor, I recall, had
a waxed mustache. Mustaches are bad enough—I have one myself
—but waxed!

"These homes are fit only for the elderly or young marrieds," I
sweepingly declared, as the waxed tips rose in horror.

"Are our readers doomed never to have more than two children
of the same sex? And where is Grandma going to sleep when she
comes to visit? Let's get the best domestic architects, have them
design the best minimum-cost houses they can—with at *least* three
bedrooms. Some people have families!"

We had already agreed between ourselves that *Journal* fashions
were dowdy. From her mother Beatrice had inherited an eye for
elegance. And I knew the most attractively dressed women in New
York were Wall Street secretaries earning about $40 a week, and
mostly dressing on that—not as many were kept by money moguls
as *The American Weekly* would have had its readers believe. That
morning we saw average-priced average clothes, photographed on
average women, fitting them averagely well.

"These are the dresses our readers can afford and will like," our fashion editor responded, superiorly, to our protest. "They are suitable for the ordinary housewife."

"Let's have one beautiful spread of dream clothes in each issue," Beatrice suggested. "Then let's try to get as near the same effect as we can, with inexpensives."

In changing the magazine's appearance, we persuaded illustrators to concentrate on one figure or two, catching them at an intense moment. Most of our illustrators were men. They, especially the talented John La Gatta, loved to draw feminine bodies—clad in revealing, soft, styleless clothes.

"Women aren't interested in women's legs, bosoms, hips," my wife remarked. "They know they have them. But they love clothes. Let's get some fashion in our illustrations, not just females."

Some artists like Coby Whitmore and Jon Whitcomb had a natural sense of style. We asked others to pose their models in dresses loaned by Bergdorf, Bendel, and Hattie Carnegie.

On a fall fashion page one head stood out strongly, a vivid drawing of a woman's face under a striking red hat.

"That artist has real fashion," Beatrice said. "Let's get all he can do."

Thus Al Parker was launched as our favorite illustrator and most popular cover artist. And soon we replaced our market-minded fashion editor with elegant, Paris-wise, imaginative Wilhela Cushman, whose pages speedily proved immensely popular with our "average" women.

But it rapidly became apparent that people at Curtis expected us to change the *Journal*'s battered image, make the magazine loved by readers, approved by Madison Avenue—while altering practically nothing. Innovations were met with quiet resistance, sometimes open hostility. Doubting editors and surprised company officials seemed disturbed as we rapidly moved away from the old *Journal*. We didn't want to lose old *Journal* subscribers either—and tried not to jar them unduly, while we won new, young readers by a more contemporary approach.

Our predecessor, we felt, had envisioned his audience as statistics rather than persons—all alike, less intelligent than we with our Iowa youth among the un-average average believed. Moreover, I had the advantage, irritating often, of a woman's true point of view—a woman who dared talk back, who didn't think women were dolts, shrews, or angels sheltered from the facts of life. My wife is feminine, but remarkably stubborn in defending her femininity. Her presence, also, protected me from the natural desire of female editors to flatter the male boss by yessing him. (Later I discovered a way to detect outrageous flattery—I never discovered a way to not like it. When appreciation and compliments seem just about your due, that's flattery. If praise leaves you hungering for more, perhaps you're getting all you deserve.)

We both agreed that, as we took over, the *Journal* had three marked assets. One was Ann Batchelder, food editor, winning friends by her warm humor. "French pastry," she commented, "is a ruffle on the sleeve but a good baked potato is a two-pants suit." To make sure Annie's food was as good as her prose, each month we turned over her recipes to our Hopewell helper, attractive Eleanor Faherty, straight out of high school, and ate meal after meal strictly from *L.H.J.* until satisfied that our recipes were excellent and practical.

Splendid mouth-watering color pictures produced by supporting editor Alice Blinn illustrated Annie's delectable fare. Even skeptical Madison Avenue asked for a second helping.

A subdeb department, hugely popular with the teens, was edited by Elizabeth Woodward. And the gay "Maudie" stories, relished and quoted then, are still chuckled over by daughters today.

One of our more grueling early experiences was to visit throughout the country Curtis branch offices, staffed with men whose livelihood depended on selling pages in forthcoming issues to advertise soap, bath towels, and canned soup. We must persuade these yearning men that we were the longed-for magicians—a trick we had not yet demonstrated even to ourselves.

We were shepherded to key cities by an anxious advertising manager, ostensibly treating us with the fulsome honor due great editors, actually there to warn, rather than comfort—occasionally almost to command. Our youth, of course, was desirable—but might it not be rash? Honesty, surely, was in order—if not too outspoken. Originality was a good thing, perhaps, but it should never become daring. Like a raw orchestra under a worried conductor we were fortissimoed, pianissimoed, day after day beckoned in, waved off, or suddenly brought to a full stop by our harried guide. Beatrice's only comfort was a charming suit from Bergdorf made to order for the gantlet we had to run.

Advertising is full of shibboleths—and men in the profession often seemed the most timid in the world. At that time they feared nude art (even if great), babies' bottoms, the mention of snakes in a story lest pregnant women miscarry. Words like contraceptive, coitus, even childbirth, were unthinkable. They would have swooned away at the mention of venereal disease in print. The only four-letter word from which they didn't shy was *sell*.

I recall earnest men around a table, courteous, attentive, but unpersuaded. They seemed to be saying, as in the popular song Julie Andrews was one day to sing, "Don't tell me—Show me!—Show me!" How right they were! Who, for instance, could have predicted *My Fair Lady* until it was produced?

While early trying to prove to a doubting organization that we were directly in the Bok-Lorimer tradition—though still learning the rudiments—two enormous tasks faced us. One, the constant day-by-day challenge of finding, or creating, first-class, fresh material. The other, to read everything on the copy list. Called the inventory, this collection of serials, stories, and articles is the pantry shelf from which supplies are taken down for the next issue. Already bought and paid for, it included a few gems and all the previous editor's expensive mistakes. Through the long humid weeks of that summer we read, on trains, at desks, till midnight in our beds. So absorbed were we eating *Journal* food, eyeing *Journal* fashion, rejecting or accepting submitted ideas and inventing a few ourselves, we scarcely spoke or thought of anything else. One day, after the hot ride home, we were enjoying a slow, pre-dinner swim, side by side in the cool, deep water of the vine-clad Hopewell quarry. Suddenly we realized we were pacing our strokes by discussing earnestly as we swam the new Faith Baldwin serial. We burst into laughter and that night we had champagne for dinner and spoke of other things.

Some $380,000 worth of manuscript had to be scrapped; and their now useless illustrations added some $170,000 more. For young people who had never thought of bigger money than $10,000, this was a drastic decision, and the business office must have thought so, too. In deference to Curtis tradition they accepted the editor's ukase without an audible "Ouch!" But we felt sure that Mr. Lorimer was in the background, lending support.

It was magnanimous of him. Our belief that the *Post* could not choose fiction for the *Journal* was strengthened by reading the copy list. Many second-best stories by established *Post* authors were included in the slash.

"Women don't care about stories of the rugged Northwest, with pictures of unshaven men in plaid mackinaws" was Beatrice's firm dismissal of some.

A struggle was forming, one which we would not enjoy.

As a few months passed, we were heartened that the first cover we chose ourselves, our first shorter, livelier cover lines, won favorable comment, even within the company. Food we enjoyed our readers seemed to like. Parker's red hat was widely admired. Newsstand sales showed the nubbin of a rise.

Our readers were surprised when we ran Van Gogh's "Sunflowers" as a *Journal* cover. Soon a superb collection of French Impressionists from the National Gallery was reproduced, with short interpretative essays by that excellent critic John Walker, who writes so clearly where many write so opaquely. We continued to print good pictures as long as we were editors (even, in 1956, from Leningrad's previously inaccessible Hermitage Museum). Art museums everywhere were happy to work with us because of the excellence of Curtis' color reproduction.

We printed more poems and better, frowning somewhat on those that dotingly counted Baby's fingers and toes, beloved by male editors as sure-fire female fare.

From the first, Beatrice and I agreed without words that the *Journal* should express our sense of the heaped-up riches, the enormous excitement provided by sheer presence on the human scene. We didn't plan this as a formula. We didn't think of it as the popular thing to do. We did it because we couldn't help it. We were born that way. Enthusiasm and enjoyment are often contagious. Our readers seemed to share ours.

Areas of feeling, of interest, which link all mankind are wider than many acknowledge. Most of us admire courage, humor which punctures pretense; we struggle for excellence, in gardening, in a job, in artistry, in conquest of self. We experience love, man-woman, of family, of friends and clan; we know temptation, lust, jealousy, and envy; we struggle for existence, for food, for money, for prestige; we try to understand our society, the foibles and strengths of human character; we attempt to probe riddles of existence—why am I here? what is the purpose?—answers sought in religion, in philosophy, in cracker-barrel discussion.

These vast shared areas of feeling and thought—acres of diamonds to an editor—can widen horizons, inform as well as entertain millions of readers.

We knew early that we didn't want our magazine to be that deadening thing, a catalogue for advertisers. Ham recipes published opposite a page advertising ham arouse some skepticism. Uncritical puffs for dishwashers without realistic discussion of their home performance may please manufacturers, but owners of failing appliances may begin to feel, "You can't believe what you read in the papers." This philosophy had the advertising director's verbal support, too. But most salesmen like to get the business. Hard decisions are left to the editor. Our advertising chief had said to me fairly early, "This job will take the guts of a bear."

Problems of maintaining independence of the advertiser were more difficult on a woman's magazine than on the *Post,* which did not have pages of beauty aids or show pictures of ideal laundries (with trademarked automatic dryers), did not use recipes (cake mixes, canned soups, coffee are advertisers). Personable advertising salesmen wheedle and flatter women editors—"Use more tea. Lipton's is planning a big campaign," "Don't find flaws in washing machines—they're our life blood."

We criticized one associate—who had come to the *Journal* from a department store—as being geared more to "merchandising" than to the reader's needs. This editor promptly formed a cabal, trying to line up other staff members against us. She complained: "These people are against the advertiser. Advertising pays our salaries."

Our career might well have ended before it had fairly begun. But Mr. Lorimer, to whom the perturbed advertising director traveled with the editor's rebellious wail, gave the intriguer not even a right to resign.

"Fire her at once!" he suggested to me.

His moral support in those dangerous days sustained us, though one could understand the erring department editor's bewilderment. Under the sheltering shade of the advertiser's friendly branches, she couldn't see the forest of readers we were really out to please. Mr. Lorimer had no doubts. Advertisers, he believed, as did Bok and Curtis before him, profit most from a magazine enthusiastically loved and trusted by its readership. No "commercials" should be slyly slipped in to weaken the readers' faith. The associate editors who remained with us on this basis began to feel like a team.

The Old Man stood by us once again. Brisk housecleaning of inventory trash had left us desperately needing a serial. I begged the *Post,* through Graeme (his father was in Europe), for the gift of a lively mystery novel by Mignon Eberhart—one which had her usual shivering heroine delectably reduced to jelly by a juicy murder at the end of each installment.

Graeme refused. He took high ground.

Mignon, he said, had aspired to the *Post* for years, finally made it. She would feel "humiliated" at having this serial transferred to the second-rate *Journal.*

If he'd cast aspersion on the ancestry of my favorite aunt, I couldn't have jumped him harder.

"Never," I roared in the voice reserved exclusively for office roaring, "never do I want to hear such nonsense! Authors are delighted to appear in *Journal* pages! I'm sure she'd rather be in the *Journal* than the *Post!*"

If I said it often enough, and worked hard enough to make it come true, maybe I could someday make people believe it, I thought, laughing inside. Graeme looked at my stern visage as if I were out of my mind. Such blasphemy!

"Cable your father!" I roared again.

Back came Lorimer's cable.

"Give Gould what he wants."

Those first weeks were fun, though harrowing. There was some compensation. We were so busy we had to give up playing bridge.

Beatrice and I are not exactly crusaders; but we do believe the world can be made a better place in certain areas, gradually, if one persists. At least you can work hard to keep it from getting worse. When I think my wife is getting too serious, I have been known to refer to my slightly flippant self as the "run in Beatrice's blue stocking." But to both of us our audience of millions was a public trust. Grateful for an opportunity to crystallize the *Journal's* potential in a worthwhile cause, we began "Why Should Mothers Die?"

At that time the maternal death rate in the United States was six per thousand live births, higher than in most civilized countries. These needless deaths were due mainly to medical and hospital neglect, in the opinion of Dr. Joseph B. De Lee, who had written an influential book on obstetrics. Paul de Kruif, the crusading author we'd inherited from Schuler, wrote three outspoken articles on this subject—suggesting that each hospital set up a board of inquiry to review every case of maternal or infant death, probing facts, judging whether that life might have been saved. Both the doctor's and the hospital's efficiency would be put under impartial scrutiny.

An organized protest from physicians exploded in our faces. We were accused of frightening pregnant women into losing their babies, charged with undermining faith in the doctor. Our own family physician, a close friend, was reproachful, "Women must believe in their doctors," he said. "Doctors can't help them otherwise." Wives of physicians protested vehemently. Some friends refused to speak to us at all. We printed indignant doctors' letters, to which our answer was:

"The United States ought to have as low a maternal death rate as England or Sweden has. Even at some cost we must have it."

The series, we said, would continue. We even made a prediction:

"Five years from now—in 1941—fewer mothers will die in the United States giving birth to their babies than died in 1936."

Beatrice flew to London to see why East End Maternity Hospital, built of three converted tenements, with few modern facilities, staffed by nurse-midwives rather than doctors, had a lower maternal mortality than many good, modern American hospitals. The supervising sister, explaining to Beatrice how meticulously her nurses were trained, said:

"The important thing is to teach our girls to care—enough."

Her visit strengthened us to continue our campaign "Why Should Mothers Die?" Doctors in America must care—enough.

By 1941, the maternal death rate had dropped in the United States so precipitately it more than justified our campaign. The *Journal* was proving it had useful power.

Discussions of pregnancy and childbirth Mr. Lorimer found distasteful. "Ladies" of the *Journal* should avoid such subjects. He might very well give us more difficulty than anyone else at Curtis, both because he had absolute power and because what we were doing with the *Journal* seemed continuously upsetting.

A test occasion soon arose. Brilliant, acidulous Alice Roosevelt Longworth had been hired to castigate That Man in the White House monthly in the *Journal* while Lorimer belabored him weekly in the *Post*.

"The number of 'get-well-quick' policies tried out and then soft-pedaled because of their undeniable failure is distressing," she was writing.

Not wanting to publish a partisan magazine intemperate in statement and myopic in view we journeyed to Washington. Received royally, regaled wittily with palace anecdotes and dry comments about cliff dwellers—Alice Longworth was more amusing in the drawing room than in print—we gained her agreement to broaden the column. But if she continued to please Mr. Lorimer, she may have felt, she needn't worry too much whether she totally pleased these newcomers; in any case her next page on Cousin Eleanor read:

"Though people have a tremendous interest in the family side of their Presidents, I don't think they care to see that side too much out asking for votes for Father."

Dropping Princess Alice quietly as a handkerchief, we heard a total but ominous silence.

Lorimer, our staunchest supporter, still wanted a finger in the *Journal* pie. He had told me a magazine could not be run by committee. Nevertheless, he had been running the *Journal* by committee. Once a week, in his office, it advised what we should do next. *Post* associates went on buying *Journal* fiction; I had not been empowered to deal directly with literary agents for stories and serials.

Lorimer had said, "Bruce, you're the Boss!" He really meant it, but he couldn't quite let go.

Our next committee meeting seemed the time for a declaration of independence. We must free ourselves; no magazine could succeed under two generations, under two such differing points of view.

My first brush with Lorimer was mild enough, though I noticed Miss Neall looked up quickly when I suggested opening the book ("the opening" is where main editorial material begins) later than page 5. The *Post* had opened editorially on page 5 since time out of mind, and, because it did, all Curtis magazines did.

"I want," I explained, in answer to Lorimer's look, "to use short editorial pieces there, too small for the main section—and also have room for some full-page ads. Some advertisers seem to think front-of-the-book positions are better than back-page ones."

Lorimer growled his dissent. The advertising director, I noticed, was silent; if he'd agreed with Lorimer, he'd have quickly added his "Yes."

"If anyone wants to advertise in the *Journal,* we don't want to throw up any roadblocks," I suggested.

It made a kind of sense.

· "All right, Bruce," Lorimer nodded. "We won't change the *Post,* however."

"Another important thing—I'd like to use more full-color pages in the *Journal,*" I went on. "We need four-color for decoration, certainly for fashion, more for food. All fiction illustrations should be in color."

"Can we afford it?" Lorimer interjected. "The *Journal*'s losing money—"

"We can't *not* afford it! That's the trend."

"*Post* two-color pages look pretty good," countered Lorimer warmly.

My mission wasn't to update the *Post*—that was his. *Post* two-color looked weak and artificial, I thought.

"You know what's best for the *Post*," I cajoled. "The *Journal*'s different. Women want color." I could see Miss Neall nodding to that. "They want to see their lipstick red—their rare roast beef, too. Dresses and rooms without color tell them nothing."

Lorimer turned to the advertising director.

"Can you get the ads to foot the bill, Fred?"

"With circulation and editorial leadership, we'll get the ads." Stoutly Fred Healy passed the buck to the editor.

I exuded confidence, more than I felt. "If we want to turn the *Journal* around, make it a success, we have no choice."

"Well," said Lorimer, evenly, still in command, "see that it pays."

"Thank you."

"Anything else?" For one day at least, his grim tone suggested, he'd had enough.

"Yes, there is," I took the high dive. "These two stories—"

In the manila envelopes I held up were two stories by favorite *Post* authors. Lorimer had commented in bold, black pencil that the pair, not quite up to *Post* standards, might do nicely for the *Journal*.

"Beatrice and I have read these two stories carefully." I hoped my voice was unshaken. "For the *Journal* they're not right. You may decide you want them for the *Post*. We can't use them."

I slid them with attempted casualness to where he sat at the head of the table. No one, except Mr. Lorimer, was looking at me—all eyes were on him. This might be war.

The glance from Lorimer's piercing eye was a hurled lance, like that of Alexander irritated by his friend Cassander, an angry glance so vividly remembered that when, later, unexpectedly, turning a corner in Adelphi, Cassander faced a mere statue of Alexander, "he was smitten suddenly with a shuddering from which he could scarcely recover."

Lorimer ruled his little world as Alexander had his great one, both conquering absolutely at about thirty. Like Cassander, I have never forgotten Lorimer's extraordinary eyes. I, too, may have shuddered.

Mr. Lorimer rose, gathered his papers together, including the two rejected short stories, and indicated that the meeting had come to an end.

"Mr. Gould," he said, "you're the boss. I'm sure we can use these two good stories in the *Post*. You may buy *Journal* fiction for yourself in the future." I saw Graeme eye me quickly. "The *Post* will keep hands off."

That was the last committee meeting ever called. We were on our own.

I went directly to Beatrice's office.

"How did it go?" she asked.

"Great!" I said. "Great! We're free!"

Suddenly, the crisis over, I felt shaky as a motorist who has narrowly avoided collision on a rise.

"To have to fight a great guy like that! After he's made us!"

"He understands."

"Sure—and so do I."

By March of the next year we hoped the tide was beginning to turn. But, if so, we were alone, apparently, in sensing it. Madison Avenue certainly hadn't noticed. On the train for a brief needed winter holiday in Mexico City, which, now in charge, I could allow us, I slept for thirty-six hours.

As we sat waiting for the first bull to trot into the sunlit Mexican arena, Beatrice asked me if I hadn't been frightened by the enormity of the challenge confronting us.

I wasn't quite sure whether I had or not.

"Why should I have been?" I finally countered, playing the Superman bit. "If we fail, Curtis stands to lose millions. Publishing companies on the skids can lose money faster than the Mint can print it.

But it isn't our money in jeopardy. What can we lose but our jobs?"

Into the shimmering sandlot trotted the afternoon's first bull—it was the first such spectacle we had seen. Tossing his horns, the magnificent bull pawed defiance at the high, encircling crowd. Back they glared with death in their eyes.

To the bull the threatening crowd must have looked remarkably like the subscribers of a magazine as seen by a new editor of a failing publication.

Man is the only animal that blushes. Or needs to.
　　　　　　　　　　　　　　—MARK TWAIN

16

The Journal Gets Airborne

When Beatrice and I returned from our Mexican holiday, we realized we had hardly begun our task—and there was need to hurry. Editors, like prime ministers, last only as long as the public vote of confidence holds. Macy's window is the inside of a black velvet bag compared to the spotlight under which a new editor works.

Mr. Lorimer planned to retire January 1, 1937, but in spring, 1936, he hadn't found his ideal successor. He wanted someone fiercely determined to save America from That Man in the White House. Had a young man very like the radical Lorimer of 1897 come along just then, old Lorimer might well have thought that promising youth too leftish for his beloved magazine. By default, oldish Wesley Stout was finally nominated. Stout indicated he would try to think like Lorimer. Adelaide Neall obligingly stayed on to help Stout think right. Her idol, G.H.L., would never have imitated anyone.

What was happening to the *Post* directly concerned Beatrice and me. A strong company is needed to resist unsuitable pressures.

We did not realize fully the dangers ahead. Editorially-oriented

178

publishers like Luce, Cowles, the Wallaces, the Ochs-Sulzbergers
have been the great successes of our day, as were Curtis and Lorimer
before them. Their eye was always on the excellence of the product
itself, the publication. Business, advertising, and circulation people
often feel that this devotion to the readers' interest can be trimmed
down here and there. Readers are smarter than such people think.

Within a few months of Lorimer's departure an ingenious advertising campaign threatened our subscribers. Its attempt was to frighten
women into using a daily douche with a strong disinfectant. The idea
was somewhat akin to the "Halitosis" campaign which made Listerine
famous. This proposed advertising was not only distasteful; its advice,
a daily douche, with a liquid whose smell is too familiar in hospital cor-
ridors, was against sound medical practice, we believed. The series
was conceived and energetically backed by the pharmaceutical firm's
advertising agency. Millions of bottles of this popular disinfectant
were sold for household use; the company wanted more business.
Strictly as a selling idea, it would be successful. Profits should run to
millions.

The *Journal* was told that all competing women's publications
would accept the campaign if prestigious Curtis would. Along Madison Avenue the word then was "If Curtis will take it, everyone will."
Strong pressure to accept a year's campaign was brought to bear
on us by our own advertising department and other hungry magazines.

It was pointed out to us how welcome twelve full-color pages would
be, an extra quarter-million dollars' revenue at this thin time. More
could be expected if the campaign succeeded. Supported by all the
magazines women relied on, the scheme could hardly fail. It depended
on us, the editors.

Neither of us was an expert in the field of feminine hygiene. Our
immediate reaction, however, was negative. Not only did a daily
douche seem unnecessary, quite possibly inadvisable, but the antiseptic was harsh, potentially dangerous. The use of fear compulsion,
the comparison with "cave women" in the copy was repugnant. There
was a faint hint, also, that the douche promised birth control as a
side effect—a suggestion discreetly within the law, as then interpreted.

Thinking this might persuade her, our advertising director suggested Beatrice confer with the medical expert of another woman's magazine, one ready to accept the campaign.

I was in Chicago when Beatrice, escorted by two top *Journal* salesmen, visited this doctor. He showed her a letter from a gynecologist asserting that the proposed douche was "not harmful" and assured her his magazine, for which he wrote a medical column, was prepared to publish the series.

"Have you queried any other gynecologists?" Beatrice asked. "It's an important decision to make on the basis of one opinion."

"No," the doctor-columnist replied. "We did not feel it necessary to go further."

After leaving, Beatrice and the two anxious Curtis men walked three blocks without speaking, she told me later. Finally she broke the chilling silence: "I don't see how we can take this advertising unless we get a representative cross-section of leading gynecologists to say that such a douche is not only not harmful but *actually useful.*"

"We will have to take this to the president," coldly replied one of the men. It was a declaration of war. At Curtis, the editor's opinion was supposed to be final on what advertising was acceptable.

"Certainly," said Beatrice.

This was one of the times she was glad we had no swimming pool—we could risk all and walk away if necessary.

That evening, a little tremulous, Beatrice telephoned me in Chicago to relate the events of the day. She felt, she said, like the Dutch boy with his finger in the dike. Her proposal seemed to me eminently fair. It assured full medical protection for our readers and gave us sound reason to accept or reject the advertising. I told her to stick to her guns.

Walter Fuller, president after Lorimer's retirement, backed us. He had been brought up in the company tradition that the editor must rule his own publication; and, a fair and honest man, he did not wish to lower Curtis' reputation by accepting dubious advertising.

We queried fifty gynecologists from the best medical listing. A few said that, if used exactly as specified, the practice might not do actual harm. Others felt even a daily water douche was inadvisable. Some

The Hopewell farmhouse was a refuge from the world's clamor.

In the Bahamas, Hope Town, too, offered beauty and relaxation.

Both born on May 19, eighty years apart; Beatrice's mother with her great-grandson Dean.   JOE DI PIETRO

suggested involuntary sterility might result from careless measurement of such a harsh preparation. None felt the suggested douche should be recommended.

We refused the proffered advertising. Other women's magazines hastily backed away, blaming us. The million-dollar campaign was dropped—manufacturer and advertising agency furious.

Not only had we lost the quarter-of-a-million dollars; the firm abruptly canceled all legitimate advertising it had been running in the *Journal*—and *Post* as well. Thus Curtis magazines, our pained advertising director pointed out, lost nearly half a million dollars that year—the pharmaceutical company's quick reprisal. Other women's magazines were not similarly disciplined for following our negative decision. *Journal* and *Post* bore the full burden of the drug company's wrath.

Being young, and eager—some might say a little quixotic—we had, during this episode, made the mistake of trying to win another successful editor to our idea: that all women's magazine editors standing together should refuse any advertising not in the public interest. After sharing with us a pleasant and seemingly harmonious lunch, this editor briskly confided to the publication's advertising head—who spread the word rapidly on Madison Avenue—that the new editors of *Ladies' Home Journal* "would not support their advertisers." Gloomy salesmen brought back the report.

The world of advertising has been intimately bound up with the world of publishing since the advent of mass magazines, radio, and TV. A hard, competitive world, advertising, except in the hands of its best practitioners, gives little consideration to matters not directly connected with profit. Being forced to spend weeks and months devising vivid, new ways of saying that Ne Plus Ultra soap is gentler, purer, whiter, softer, more regardful of woman's innate femininity while his wife steadfastly prefers Everywoman's soap tends to turn the best ad man into a cynic. More than half-a-dozen great men have come up through this difficult school maintaining high standards as they did so, among them Raymond Rubicam, William Benton, David Ogilvy. But it is a grinding labor, its results measured in dollars and cents, with fewer accompanying satisfactions than most other good work brings—the profession I would least like to see a son or grandson of mine enter. Men at the top can profess noble sentiments, while in their own agencies men in the middle may be squeezed into less than honest claims by the unending requirement to sell. Pressure on editorial text of all publications is constant—to tout uncritically motorcars, synthetic fabrics, new foods, kitchen appliances. Some of these products are genuine news. Many enter a gray area—freckle creams which scarcely remove freckles, reducing machines which do not reduce. Decision as to which "plugs" are valid, which claims are false, even dangerous, lies with the editor and is never questioned under a strong editor. With weaker publications, financial retaliation is an unspoken threat.

"Advertising is a tool. It has no more morality than a hammer. Its purpose is to sell goods, maintain business prosperity," Thurman Arnold, one of President Roosevelt's early braintrusters, once said to Beatrice. Many advertising men defend this thesis. Indeed, it does seem a superficially rational point of view. It fills me with deep social misgivings. If advertising is a tool to sell goods and has no more ethics than a hammer—if a vital economy and a high standard of living are aims unaffected by moral considerations—then man is purely an economic animal, and a full plate before a TV set fulfills his highest needs.

Our editorial conscience was clear; our advertising pockets empty. We felt that Curtis, Bok, and Lorimer would have cheered. By early insistence on high standards in advertising that doughty trio of editorial pioneers had time and again risked their own money. We had risked only our jobs.

Beatrice had, to her sorrow, become a chain smoker during our tense, nerve-racking play-rehearsal days in New York. She hated this slavery. Suddenly throwing her cigarette into the fireplace in 1930 she said, "I will not smoke a cigarette for a year." She didn't—indeed, never smoked again.

After release from this two-pack-a-day habit, Beatrice slept better, felt better, all her senses more alive. An early study by Dr. Raymond Pearl, of Johns Hopkins, published in the late twenties, supported her belief that cigarettes are bad for you. Moderate smoking tended to undermine health even more than moderate drinking, he had shown. At this time, the question of our accepting cigarette advertising in the *Journal* arose. To find out whether medical opinion agreed with Dr. Pearl, a cross-section of doctors was asked if they considered cigarettes harmful.

We were too early. Practically none saw harm in smoking. Many said, "It's good—a release from the tensions of modern life." We decided we could not presume to know more than the medical profession and accepted the few cigarette advertisements offered the *Journal*—not many, since then women did not smoke and drink like men without fear of social censure.

Later when study after study revealed the link between excessive smoking and lung cancer, we were to see again the dangerous power of advertising. The regrettable connection between excessive smoking and painful death was denied by cigarette companies, who spend millions advertising their product. All media were slow to publish adverse reports. Free discussion was blanketed for some time. When the case against cigarettes became unmistakably demonstrated, a few strong editors led the way. Others, safe in the multitude, followed. The press record was finally creditable, though slow in the making, and too often qualified by printing "the other side"—claims, that is, by manufacturers, that the cigarette-lung-cancer connection was not fully proven, that more research was needed before conclusions could be final.

During this period, a group of young trainees at Curtis were heard in the elevator deploring an article in our *Journal* on how to stop smoking. "There goes the *Post*'s cigarette advertising," they lamented. Youthful, they were acquiring the attitude held by many in their profession that truth, even involving the public good, had better not be spoken if it might interefere with business.

Having with our stand against the douche cost the company so much money, having frightened some of our advertising salesmen into fiscal fidgets, we tried harder than ever to win our readers— and through them solid financial success.

As we sought new and exciting features, we read and edited every line of copy ourselves.

"Everything can be made better," Beatrice sometimes sighed after a hard day.

We tried not to let our food and fashion editors speak as worldly women talking from a New York skyscraper to those little people way below. "Their interests are the same as yours," we would urge. (Later, when our editors were sent to "How America Lives" homes all over the country, they found again the truth that Judy O'Grady and Westport's lady *are* sisters under the skin.)

My wife would not read competing magazines.

"I want to think of our readers as I know them in Iowa, Hopewell, Princeton, New York," she said. "I don't want to be confused by other editors' attitudes toward women, especially when those editors always keep one eye on Madison Avenue."

Beatrice's philosophy was to present the best we could find in clothes and decoration, then let our readers imitate as they wished according to tastes and finances.

Fashion—about which Beatrice herself had been slightly mad on Main Street, Ottumwa, Iowa—meant, she felt, two things to women. Glamour—something to dream about—and the nice little $29.95 which would go a fair way to realize the dream. Under Wilhela (pronounced Willa) Cushman's talented editing, the *Journal* showed women exciting and beautiful pages of clothes from Hattie Carnegie, Balenciaga, Dior, Chanel, Mainbocher, and followed them up— thanks to Wilhela's discerning eye, her perfectionism, and her prestige on Seventh Avenue—with the best of ready-to-wear. The secretary and the young married with taste could look almost as well dressed as the Duchess of Windsor, she demonstrated—and frequently prettier.

Richard Pratt's marvelous color pictures of distinguished Early American houses became in book form later a true treasury, a service to the scholar, a decorator's delight, a rich chapter in the history of American colonial days.

Leading domestic architects were persuaded, too, by Pratt to try every new method to create the most house for the money. Perhaps we foresaw the population explosion, in our insistence on three, even four, bedrooms, and a kitchen roomy enough for coffee and a chat. We even favored the dining room. "Family meals and conversation are part of children's education," Beatrice maintained. "How can people talk in a civilized fashion if they sit in a straight line at a counter and speak out of the sides of their mouths?"

We designed beautiful rooms as well as some simple attractive ones to be achieved with paint, ingenuity, and a modest expenditure. Sometimes we were in conflict with our advertising men; they spoke of our do-it-yourself rooms as using "orange-crate" furniture, complaining when we did not show the glossier Grand Rapids types.

Feeling better acquainted with our readers, we decided to introduce ourselves and our views to them in 1936. That credo, to our surprise, we still believe in today.

Here are some excerpts:

> Political and racial intolerance begin in the home and can be nipped in the home.
>
> We believe in marriage—that it's an art and an adventure.
>
> We like walking better than horseback riding, tennis better than golf, swimming better than badminton. We like games and having fun and people who like those things.
>
> We adore personal conversation—an honest curiosity about human beings.
>
> We think some of the things in life to get genuinely excited about are:
>
> Improving public health.
>
> Throwing every resource of health open to children, whether they can pay for it or not.
>
> Stamping out preventable diseases like childbed fever, tuberculosis, syphilis.
>
> We believe in faith: in religious faith, faith in our fellow men.
>
> We think war is the most menacing, senseless factor in our civilization; but we don't believe it can be done away with by hissing munition manufacturers, or by urging young men simultaneously to lay down their arms. It must be prevented earlier than that—in its first seeds of prejudice, race hatred, intolerance.

We had our mistakes, one near disaster. An article on Edward VIII's Coronation was scheduled to appear in early December, 1936, with a glamorous picture of the king in full regal uniform. Just as we closed our forms, with a hazardous eight-week interval before newsstand release, the story of Wally Simpson broke. The fact that she was Edward's great friend had long been known, but few had believed she was ambitious, also, for a throne. We held our breaths and waited as the time span narrowed. Would Edward abdicate or renounce his love? Would our issue look ridiculous? Finally, by a magnificent effort, our circulation department brought the magazine to the newsstands ten days ahead of its scheduled date, while Edward still delayed decision. With Wally's story on everyone's tongue, coronation or abdication the question, our issue with Edward resplendent in royal robes sold out just before he actually abdicated. Luck, that time, was with us. (We were children of luck, then and often.)

Dorothy Thompson suddenly flared across the sky. She became, in the field of politics and public affairs, women's international spokesman. Beatrice said to me, "We must have Dorothy for the *Journal*."

So busy she could hardly give presidents, dictators, or even her problem-beset husband, Sinclair Lewis, much of her time, Dorothy ignored my importuning letters. Urgent telegrams were not answered. Persuasive personal messages received no response until, one day, I did manage to catch her attention with an agonized telephone cry: "Dorothy, I'm having trouble with my wife!"

Her always womanly interest was engaged. "Come and tell me about it."

My trouble with Beatrice, I told her, was solely that Bibi would give me no peace unless I could hire Dorothy to write a monthly piece for the *Journal*.

Amused, Dorothy agreed. We set a mutually satisfactory price for her column, thus starting, May, 1937, a lifelong association.

Eleanor Roosevelt's autobiography, *This Is My Story,* beginning in April, 1937, attracted to our magazine approving attention of columnists and critics from the powerful New York journalistic world. Mostly liberals, they admired this intrepid woman, subject of so much controversy in early New Deal days, jested at for her moral earnestness. Now that she is a world-wide symbol of forbearance and brotherly love, it is hard to recall the derision then frequently poured on her head. Since her husband was an enemy to entrenched Republicans and conservative Democrats, and she was his eyes and ears, his reporter, his agent, she was disliked, if possible, more then he. Cartoons proliferated. These were the days when two coal miners deep in their shaft were pictured exclaiming: "My God, here comes Eleanor Roosevelt!"

Had the *Post* not been so anti-Roosevelt, the *Journal* would probably never have had first look at Mrs. R.'s memoirs. Her agent, George Bye, usually fed his best stuff direct to the *Post*. The amiable George, a good friend, knowing we were now buying independently, offered the series first to us, rather than risk from Stout a certain turndown. The story was excellent. It was by the wife of the President. We bought it promptly for $75,000.

The Curtis building was shaken. Considered red radicals by some, traitors to the sound business principles of the company by others, wretched opportunists at best, we rode out the storm. One incensed board member thought our political affiliations should be investigated —we were perhaps "Communist!," that last desperate epithet to hurl at someone who disagrees with you and may be winning the argument. Miss Neall felt we were betraying all that G.H.L.—that grand old man and our benefactor—had fought for. She was too staunchly my friend to complain to me directly.

Eleanor Roosevelt's book in its early portions is moving and veracious. With startling honesty and courage she set down full details of a painful childhood—an alcoholic father, her conviction she was an ugly duckling, crippling shyness, the domination of a mother-in-law who planned her house for her, interfered in the upbringing of her children. After her husband's illness and entrance into politics, the narrative became understandably more superficial and hurried. Like most great stories, hers was a tale of courage, of obstacles overcome, of gradual growth to triumphant days as America's revered First Lady.

On the day before *This Is My Story* hit the newsstands, we gave a promotion party in our Manhattan workshop for New York's feature writers, columnists, book reviewers—those garrulous public figures whose talking makes something "talked about"—inviting them all in to meet Eleanor Roosevelt. Acceptances were immediate. A number asked if they could bring their wives, as well.

Mrs. Roosevelt arrived early, beautifully dressed as always (this day wearing a handsome black suit with white satin blouse and wide black hat). Tall, overcoming awkwardness by magnificent poise and genuine, warm interest, she stood in line shaking hands and chatting with everyone—her face smiling, flushed with pleasure. In deference to her known dislike of alcohol, we served only the mildest of wine punches, an unusual procedure at a New York publishing party. Even so, everyone stayed a long time, as did she.

After the last lingering guest had departed—each carrying under his arm an advance copy of the *Journal,* with its dramatic first install-ment—Mrs. Roosevelt, still radiant, thanked us glowingly.

"I can't tell you what it means to me," she said, with touching sincerity, "to have this wonderful recognition for something I have done myself"—and her voice rising in its characteristic high crescendo —"not on account of Franklin's position."

Even the great are human.

This Is My Story was a smash success. Copies vanished from the newsstands like whisky at an Irish wake. People talked who had never talked about a woman's magazine before. Soon, other features made the talk even louder.

To the anger of many physicians, we had continued our articles demanding that childbirth be made safer, both for mother and infant. Some younger men in the profession, however, and thoughtful oldsters, shared our conviction that too many mothers still died in childbirth.

Hospitals began to follow procedures laid down by Dr. Herman Bundesen, who had joined our staff as baby expert. Health com-missioner of Chicago, he had instituted a formal, full-dress inquiry into the "why" of every maternal death and every baby death in his city's hospitals. This practice, which we publicized in the *Journal,* had so changed the picture in Chicago that by 1936 it had the lowest infant mortality of any large city in the country, whereas in 1922 when he became commissioner it had had the highest.

The lowest maternal death rate in the United States was found in a clinic in Chicago's slums where babies were often delivered on newspapers on kitchen tables. Its rate was second only to the London East End hospital Beatrice had visited. My wife, never one to let an important *Journal* story go by without her firsthand acquaintance, visited the Chicago Maternity Center Clinic started by famed Dr. De Lee, carried on by able Dr. Beatrice Tucker. She became friends with both and learned all she could about why mothers and infants unnecessarily die. From them she heard much about combating syphilis in the unborn. Realizing its importance to mothers and babies, we decided to tackle the subject of venereal disease.

Straight sex, leg art, fashion shown in its striptease aspects, how the bad girls titillate in foreign movies—these have always seemed to editors of men's magazines legitimate circulation-pulling gimmicks. I used to say to Beatrice it is only on a woman's magazine that an editor can't stand on women's legs—successful stilts for many masculine publications.

Thirty years ago, "nice" men tried to protect women from realistic facts about sex in a manner many women found charming but slightly absurd. While sex may seem to many men an end in itself, as well as to some a form of mystical unity with a loved being, to a woman it is more than unity, it is a link in the remarkable chain of creation, life renewing life, earth's promise of immortality, her final fulfillment. As Henry Adams has said, "Woman is tied to the life cycle." So, to a woman, knowledge and understanding of sex are important in her role as wife and mother, and in the education of her children. She tends to approach the subject far more realistically than squeamish men, whose timidity becomes almost comic at times.

Since venereal disease causes so much suffering, Beatrice sensibly felt that women would welcome honest discussion of ways to lessen this threat to family life. So, when the surgeon-general of the United States, Thomas Parran, revealed to us his lifelong ambition to eliminate syphilis and gonorrhea, and asked our help, we decided to back him up.

Some of our editors questioned our exposing women to the grim actuality Dr. Parran knew. What was there to gain? Nice women, women who read the *Journal,* didn't have venereal diseases.

Beatrice scoffed at such an attitude. Women wanted to end *endable* evils, she felt. This evil—even if not immediately endable—could be lessened by the light of knowledge played on its dark distress.

"Don't let's rail at things we can't help—like wild youth," she would say. "But let's inform, where information may lead to action."

We began in August, 1937, by reprinting Nancy Hale's "Blue-Muslin Sepulchre," a short story of syphilis in a well-bred family with marriageable daughters, unable even to acknowledge its dread existence in their home. In the same issue we published a piece by the surgeon-general, "We Can End This Sorrow," and an editorial, "Shall We Keep Silent?"

In the eight-week interval between going to press and actual publication date, our tremulous advertising men had time for nightmares, hoping as usual for an extraordinary magazine with nothing extraordinary in it. Even we began to wonder if this frank discussion in a staid woman's magazine would bring a deluge of protest.

On the first morning after publication we opened our mail with curiosity, if not trepidation. There was just one letter on the subject —from an indignant male.

He wrote that we were clearly against the working man. Our article had implied that venereal disease was more common among the poor. Surely that could not be true. The rich had more money to spend, hence more opportunity for illicit sexual adventure than the poor, he contended. Obviously we were prejudiced—fascists to the core.

Outcries of shock and horror failed to materialize. *Journal* readers simply had too much realism to question our effort to illuminate this murky subject.

Soon the surgeon-general again appealed to us for aid. Although it had not yet been discovered that penicillin would make syphilis and gonorrhea more easily curable, and the administration would not back an all-out public health campaign against venereal disease, Dr. Parran believed that with an appropriation of only a few million dollars a year syphilis could be made as rare in the United States as smallpox. Men in government backed away from the subject, unwilling to ask Congress for the money—Parran had to go it alone.

The surgeon-general's plan called for widespread education and asked that syphilis and gonorrhea be made reportable diseases. When a case was reported, public-health workers in every state would then try to discover and cure all possible contacts. Dr. Parran expected to be opposed by apathy of the public, by women's reticence, and by the strait-laced, who considered social diseases suitable punishment for sexual sin. Most prostitutes and promiscuous teen-agers, resenting their own infection, might resist his program. He told of a young girl in a small Vermont town who, informed she had syphilis, vengefully deferred treatment until she had infected each of the thirteen men from whom she might have caught the disease.

But the most surprising resistance came from the President of the United States, Dr. Parran's long-time friend, Franklin Delano Roosevelt. Because of well-bred masculine conservatism or fear of public opinion, Roosevelt declined to put the program in the budget. Only if Congress forced the President's hand could Dr. Parran get the money he needed. Dr. Parran wanted us to enlist the public, make its voice activate Congress. He thought the *Journal* with its readership of millions could persuade the President that the plan should at least be tried.

We agreed that if Dr. Parran would assure us a bill would be introduced in Congress, timed with our publication date, we would help him to the utmost of the *Journal*'s power. But he must give us his solemn word nothing, not even Presidential disapproval, would cause him to back away once our presses were started. For we must print our article eight weeks ahead, mentioning the bill as though it were actually being presented then to Congress. In that interval Dr. Parran might be urged to abandon his program for fear of scandalizing the electorate. We must count on his promise to protect our timing. Dr. Parran gave us his word.

Senator La Follette and Representative Bulwinkle introduced Dr.

Parran's bill, with requests for money to implement it, in each chamber. The bill's presentation was timed exactly to the newsstand appearance of the April, 1938, *Journal*. That issue carried a double-page editorial titled "By Reading This You Might Save Your Child's Life."

Around the border of this editorial appeal were printed names and addresses of every Senator and every Representative in the country. Each reader was asked to write a personal letter to her Congressmen explaining why she felt Dr. Parran's bill should be passed, the money appropriated, and a program set in motion to eliminate syphilis and gonorrhea.

At Dr. Parran's request, Beatrice, her courage bolstered by a new violet hat from John & Fred, appeared before a Senate Appropriations Committee—somewhat reluctantly—she doesn't like cameras or having her picture taken. It was a very becoming hat; but the obdurate income-tax people wouldn't let her deduct its excessive cost as the legitimate business expense it was. Her photograph widely reproduced wasn't too bad, and the sight of such an obviously womanly woman, representing as she did millions of other "average" womanly women, speaking out publicly against v.d., probably influenced Congress.

Senators and Representatives were deluged with mail. Not floods of uniform postcards, nor letters, mimeographed, all alike, and all sent out by a hard-hitting lobby group, such as Congressmen were conditioned to ignore. Not at all. More than 300,000 individual persons back home wrote their thoughts, posted their letters, and requested action. The snowflakes fluttered down on Washington in such swirls that Congress had to take notice of the blizzard.

Suddenly everyone seemed to be against syphilis. The President relaxed his opposition. The spotlight was on the hapless victim of all social diseases, the innocent child.

Dr. Parran got a $6,200,000 appropriation, sufficient to finance the job, as if from the start everyone had been on his side. Social diseases dropped encouragingly in a matter of months.

Recently there has been an upsurge of syphilis and gonorrhea, partly because, since cure, with antibiotics, is now possible by prompt medication, these diseases are no longer as frightening as they once were; partly because much in today's printed and spoken word seems to encourage promiscuity among teenagers; partly because birth-control methods are supposed to be more infallible than they actually are; but mainly because, as victory seemed near, funds were withdrawn from the Public Health Service. To continue the battle another crusading magazine must take its turn, insist that money be appropriated and the fight renewed. Now, at least, syphilis and gonorrhea are mild words in our outspoken age.

The *Journal* received general acclaim; a few, of course, charged us with sensation seeking. As part of his program, Dr. Parran wanted Wassermann tests more generally taken—at that time many people, especially women, had never had one. We supported his idea editorially, and worked for an appealing advertisement to call attention to his campaign and our endorsement of it.

Our agency was conventional and pussyfooting, as men often are and advertising men especially, in suggesting ads for this editorial promotion. Fearful that "taste" might be violated, they let their squeamishness show, and the results were tasteless indeed. In a long coffee-drinking evening session at the office, Beatrice and I wrote a promotion ad showing a straightforward, pleasing young girl saying, "Yes, I'll take a Wassermann test." We even selected the model— a wholesome, any-man's-sister type, more straightforward than sexy. The ad, running in the *Times* and *Herald Tribune* and other big city newspapers, not unnaturally attracted considerable attention. It also won a prize for the agency handling *Journal* promotion as one of the year's best.

While many of our articles were serious, lively short pieces lightened each issue. We recalled Havelock Ellis' "Dancing is the loftiest, the most moving, the most beautiful of the arts, because it is no mere translation or abstraction from life; it is life itself . . ." and we compared the dance to modern marriage: "Two moving in harmony, the man leading, but so imperceptibly that the impulse seems to come almost equally from both."

Modern paintings selected from the San Francisco Fair exhibition gave us a pleasurable excursion to that engaging town—unquenchable memories of the fair's exotic island, a shimmering jeweled fantasy in the night of the Golden Gate; memories, too, of Elsa Maxwell's gay parties; of a lunchtime discussion with handsome Douglas Fairbanks, weighing French tolerance of infidelity versus the American choice, divorce rather than a liaison; of thrice-married Fairbanks saying, "Don't you think ours is the cleaner way?"—a question, certainly, which it would take the wisest and bravest of marriage counselors to answer definitively.

As the Twig Is Bent by Johns Hopkins psychiatrist Dr. Leslie Hohman, ever studying and learning from children, presented such wise views on their upbringing that we ran his book complete in short chapters over a two-year period. "Many parents, consciously or unconsciously, reward children for unsatisfactory behavior. Not unnaturally, this behavior becomes fixed," was the gist of his warning.

Munro Leaf's "Watchbird" cartoons delighted parents and spoofed even hard-headed children into mending their barbaric ways.

"Your Chance of Making a Success of Marriage," based on a wide study by two well-known psychologists, informed readers that men who cry at movies are good husband material. Scientists, too, are good bets; traveling salesmen the poorest marriage risks, which is why there are all those traveling-salesmen jokes. Sooner or later science usually verifies what earliest man knew instinctively.

André Maurois wrote of "The Art of Love," and Lilly Daché offered paper patterns of her celebrated $50 hats for just three cents. while Joseph Alsop and Robert Kintner recorded the Nazis' appalling drive through Poland—preparing readers' minds for war.

In March, 1941, we began breaking up pages of solid type with short quotations. Through the years we gave our readers, in small takes, La Rochefoucauld, Montaigne, even Abe Burrows.

Aphorisms, being short expressions of long experience, are memorable, wise, often amusing. Since many editors delight in the cynical, disillusioned remark as testimony to their own sophistication, I, being naturally believing, chose these quotes myself. I didn't want them to poke fun at women, easy target for hack humorists. Some we use in this book over chapter headings.

Here are other samples:

I have always noticed that deeply and truly religious persons are fond of a joke, and I am suspicious of those who aren't.—ALFRED NORTH WHITEHEAD

In the game of tennis both persons use the same ball but one of the players is better than the other.—PASCAL

Let me have my own way exactly in everything, and a sunnier or pleasanter creature does not exist.—CARLYLE

To understand your parents you must have children yourself.—CHINESE PROVERB

An enemy can partly ruin a man, but it takes a good-natured, injudicious friend to complete the thing and make it perfect.—MARK TWAIN

Whoever loves is in no condition old.—EMERSON

Show me a family of readers, and I will show you the people who move the world.—NAPOLEON

With the decline of the religious life, neuroses grow more frequent. —JUNG

Atlas had a great reputation but I'd like to have seen him carry a mattress upstairs.—KIN HUBBARD

The quotes served a practical purpose too. About 60 percent of our women leafed entirely through the magazine first just to look at the quotes; hence ads, to the delight of our advertising department, were better read.

In February, 1938, Mary Carson Cookman, recently added to our staff, suggested "What Do the Women of America Think?," based on Dr. Gallup's polls. With beauty and a feminine frou-frou masking her clear head and respect for hard work, with sympathy, charm, and a flashing intuition from which sprang her many editorial ideas and real promotional flair, she went on to become our executive editor.

Women's thoughts about marriage and divorce were explored in the series, and we soon tackled the hushed-up subject of birth control, expressing in print for the first time that a majority of American women definitely approved family planning. Catholics favored "birth control"—the method not indicated— by 51 percent.

Our New York advertising agency, certain our figures could not be true, pleaded with us not to print the article. We risked being caught in egregious error, they said, and we risked offending the Church.

Advance proofs of editorial matter were always sent, before publication, to circulation and advertising men to keep them abreast, and to the New York agency that handled our editorial promotion. These men, it sometimes seemed, thought of themselves as Watchbirds watching us. Our birth-control article was considered by many both shocking and inaccurate. Polls are never accurate when they run counter to one's beliefs.

Direct observation is an excellent quality in an editor. Knowing other women's opinions on birth control, a woman editor applies her immediate observation to a larger scene. People are not as different as many people think. Thus the results of the poll came as no surprise to us.

But, in view of the opposition, we decided to recheck. Some birth-control clinics had inquired into their clients' religious affiliations. Their percentages of Catholic women tallied almost exactly with the Gallup poll. So, over protests, we printed the article. Our women readers did not protest. Not unnaturally, they were interested.

We experienced, then, for the first time, the occasional attempt of the Catholic Church to influence publishing it does not approve. From churchmen we had many critical and disapproving letters. Some advised parishioners to cancel subscriptions.

Most organized groups, sooner or later, try to control the press by threats of boycott or withdrawal of advertising. Labor, Catholics, Jews stand out among the most vigorous protesters. The NAACP has now joined these groups. Few of them hesitate to try to suppress comment they dislike, even while sometimes admitting the comment may be true.

Within our first three years on the *Journal* we had discussed two unmentionable topics, birth control and syphilis. Not only had we offended the Catholic Church and some leading advertisers—and lost the company considerable money—we had also shocked executives in our own company. A comment reached us from the *Post* floor, using our experience in the theatre against us: "They're not

editors—they're showmen!" Only in staid Curtis could such a hor-
rendous accusation be considered damning to a publicist.

From time to time we returned, in the *Journal,* to the subject of
syphilis. Many battles will have to be fought before this particular
war is won. Besides the satisfaction we had in helping a good cause,
we reaffirmed, for ourselves, the power of the *Journal,* but even more
the power of women, average women, when properly addressed. To
speak to such an audience, we felt, was a privilege we must constantly study to deserve.

17

Winning Readers

An editor knows instantly when his magazine is doing better. The circulation manager stops complaining about how bad the magazine is in his monthly report to the board; he begins, instead, to point out how good a circulation manager he is. By early 1937, we were feeling the first change of tide. Subscriptions were easier to sell. Before long, the circulation department began to record a profit on *Journal* subscriptions. Some newsstands sold out.

Readers' letters expressed warmth: "When my husband came home last night and found me lying on the sofa, the breakfast dishes still piled in the sink, he asked at once, 'Did the *Journal* come today?' "

Gradually our total circulation passed that of *McCall's* and, finally, of *Woman's Home Companion;* newsstand sales began overtaking *McCall's* single-copy lead.

Even more pleasing than this liking expressed in numbers was the exciting discovery that Eleanor Roosevelt's autobiography was read, in effect, by everyone—in government, parlors, and slums. There must be more material of this sort: valid enough to interest the sophisticated, human enough to appeal to all. It was our job to find it.

We urged our editors not to use foreign phrases, exclusionary allusions. We tried to persuade contributors against the We-and-They theory—the assumption that because We are more widely read, more knowledgeable about art, music, classics, finance, the stars, more accustomed to a sophisticated society, or graduates of a better college, We are basically different from Them. Subjects of wide concern, if clearly written about, could interest the Emmetsburg housewife, the file clerk with four years of high school, and the Ph.D. at Smith.

We quoted George Orwell's comment about "the emotional overlap" between intellectual and average. "The intellectual," he says, "is different from the ordinary man, but only in certain sections of his personality, and even then not all the time."

When we had become editors, a friend had said to Beatrice: "Do make the *Journal* better."

"In what way?"

"Oh, more intelligent—more like *The New Yorker.*"

"Well, we'd hate to shrink its circulation down from 2,500,000 to 250,000," replied my wife.

Even then, we valued our enormous audience and hoped to enlarge it. The great challenge, the constant, absorbing excitement of our job was to try to find the highest common denominator of interest which would link, in enthusiasm and respect, these diverse millions.

David Lilienthal once criticized us for seeking a way to make an article on atomic energy "popular."

But to print a worthy piece on economics, foreign affairs, nuclear fission which will be read by only 2 percent of one's potential audience is poor editing, wasteful of a precious opportunity. To find a way to make the subject of atomic energy fascinating, lucid, and comprehensible—in short, interesting—can be itself interesting, though difficult. Publishing of this sort has the joys of any imaginative project. I shall always remember the glow of amused pleasure on Walter Lippmann's face as he worked with us on an experimental effort to translate the basic ideas in his *U.S. Foreign Policy: The Shield of the Republic* into so-called comic-strip cartoons by able

Joel King for our August, 1943, issue. "It almost makes my ideas clearer to me" was his half-serious comment as he viewed the finished drawings, seen and understood by millions instead of thousands.

Our readers began to welcome the *Journal* like the visit of a trusted friend: they felt we liked and respected them, that we were "on their side." An editor feels this—in letters, in the glow on a woman's face as she speaks of "her" magazine—has it verified in a rising newsstand sale.

We had now passed all the competing women's magazines. Month by month, we were gradually overtaking the *Post,* still leader of all.

Newly confident *Journal* advertising salesmen began to speak of our successful campaigns against maternal mortality, venereal disease, even, where it might not be untactful, of Mrs. Roosevelt's story, to hard-headed Madison Avenue, listening in spite of our intractable editorial attitude. Advertising men respect the successful magazine which does not cater to them, while still pushing weaker ones to become advertising catalogues if they can.

Throughout these pages it will have been apparent that the editor regards the advertiser with what might be called a guarded friendliness. It is proper that this should be so. An editor must never be so affected by gratitude that he forgets his advertising ally is only a junior partner in the enterprise of a free press. When that junior is more, he begins to call the tune.

Partners though these two be, their aims are substantially if not totally different. The editor's purpose is to inform as well as to entertain; the advertiser's purpose is to sell. If the advertiser is to accomplish his intention, it sometimes seems to him desirable not to inform. He may want to withhold essential facts, as in the case of cigarette smoking and lung cancer. He may want to misinform. Surely, at all times, he wishes to avoid the scrutinizing criticism for advertising itself accorded most institutions, criticism without which politics, business, and the arts tend to become unhealthy. The editor who yields, distorting his responsibility for truth as he can discover it, is perhaps more at fault than the advertiser, whose function is a different one.

Such a conflict of aims keeps an editor on his guard. No medium, newspaper, magazine, TV, or radio, should ever be so dependent, financially, on selling goods that the free discussion of any subject whatever is inhibited by commercial considerations—whether that subject is washing machines, cancer, the position of the Jew in America, or the questionable power of advertising itself.

In spite of, or maybe because of, our firm attitude, Madison Avenue was beginning to support the *Journal*. An amusing campaign —cartoons by Lionni published in *The New Yorker*—gave sparkle to our burgeoning image.

"Never Underestimate the Power of a Woman," devised by N. W. Ayer, was designed to persuade Madison Avenue that advertisements of cake mix, household appliances, Beauty Rest mattresses would be more effective in a woman's magazine than in general weeklies claiming a "dual audience." It pointed up, with humor, the *Journal's* slogan, "Men and Women Are Different."

Each ad illustrated a difference in taste between men and women, the conflict ending amusingly in the woman's favor. But women are the favorite target of male wit. It soon became apparent that the agency's wit must be watched. A latent masculine hostility kept trying to find expression. Women were envisaged as powerful Katinkas— making men see Clark Gable movies they hated, forcing hot rodders to settle for a practical Volkswagen.

Never having been subject to domineering women, I have always believed with Havelock Ellis that woman's charm is her greatest strength, as man's strength is his greatest charm. Persuasion, the quiet, amused revealing of another point of view, perhaps preferable, was woman's power. Absolute equality was our view—with the male slightly more equal than the female, but both equally enjoying the unequal arrangement. We never let the hulking, overbearing, Amazon type get by.

"Never Underestimate the Power of a Woman" became one of the top ten promotion slogans of our times. Our lively subscription and newsstand sale made it more and more apparent we would soon pass the *Post*. While Mr. Lorimer remained at the helm, it would have saddened us to leave behind his great magazine, long basic in Curtis' financial structure. If the *Journal,* for women only, and a monthly, passed the *Post* in circulation, the famous old weekly's preeminence would be gone. Madison Avenue would begin to say, "What's wrong with the *Post?*" perhaps even before it added, "What's right with the *Journal?*"

But we did not think the solution for Curtis was to maintain two weak magazines. The *Journal* should not be held back to make the *Post* look better.

Some company officials seemed to feel it somehow disloyal to push the preeminent weekly aside. Still, month after month the *Journal* rolled on.

Tacit help from the company's circulation head we could count on. Pointing out how well he was doing with the *Journal* might save his neck. The better the *Journal* sold the easier it was to explain that the *Post's* sluggish sales were not the fault of his department, responsible for both.

Finally, in March, 1940, with pride even if with some regret, we printed on our cover:

THE JOURNAL NOW HAS THE LARGEST PAID
CIRCULATION OF ANY MAGAZINE IN THE WORLD

With good fiction and lively articles the *Post* could appeal both to women and men. We were limited to women readers. The *Journal* would have been quite happy to be tops among our direct competition, and, in proper feminine fashion, tag along after big brother. But the *Post* needed fresh, original, vigorous editing and Wesley Stout was paralyzed by a tradition.

People, even the most intelligent, have always been curious about people—often learning more through other humans' experiences than from books. The endless variety of real life relates directly to us all. Marvels of love, joy in birth, suffering in loss, triumph and bitter defeat are felt by the average person on that ordinary street. "Nothing worth having or caring about in this world," Walter Scott pointed out, "is uncommon." Money, sex, adjustments to marriage and children, daily toil, are of uncommon interest to us all because they are common to us all. No two readers meet their problems in the same way, and individual response provides infinite plot and subplot. With these beliefs we started "How America Lives" in early 1940.

We were returning from beaching, surfboard riding, and attempting to hula in Hawaii when we thought out this series, original, but based on the ordinary. I had always been an addict of vacations, feeling that life should be one continuous vacation with little short, sharp intervals of necessary work. From that Hawaiian holiday on we could justify vacations. They clear the mind, set it free, rested, for original thought. Magazine editing, like many occupations, is always in need of original thought.

Working together in a comfortable compartment on a transcontinental train, our peaceful seclusion walled in by the wheels' click-clack, we conducted our own "brainstorm" for two. Our brainstorms tended to be argumentative. Crossly we probed each other's minds, tentatively suggested, scornfully rejected, went to sleep, tried again, until the pattern for our new project came clear.

Each month we would tell about an actual family, their necessities and struggles: four people to be fed well on $10 a week, life-insurance payments to be increased from a budget already strained, an ill-adjusted teenager, a harried housewife snatching a few precious hours for reading or community work, the drama of daily living set out on the stage of our pages. In a year's time we could by carefully choosing our families reveal a tapestry of American life—small town, city, farm; poor-to-rich; California-to-Maine-to-Alabama. Our editors, faced with problems straight out of life, would keep homemaking, food, and fashion material close to the realities of ordinary existence.

"We're all trying to learn how to live," said Beatrice. "But every problem jumps out at us before we're quite ready. Adolescence— the boy next door. Marriage, for better or for worse—little, demanding, children—swiftly they, too, are rebellious teenagers. Soon worrisome elderly relatives. This is why women talk to their neighbors. We all need to learn. Men in their working day discuss details of their professions. Women, in a sense, all have the same profession. They learn constantly from others."

Mary Bass, when we explained our idea, saw at once the potentials of "How America Lives." Mary was asked to find the first characters in our play. We wanted a family in America's population center, Cedar Rapids, Iowa; of middle years (late thirties) and middle income (then around $1,900 a year); a middle-sized family (two or three children). Thus we would at once dramatize the representativeness of the series. Keeping closely in touch with us by telephone, Mary combed Cedar Rapids for just the right family and came up with six, any one of which would have been good. We chose the Aulden Griffins, who effectively demonstrated how unaverage the American average could be. Mrs. Griffin, president of the woman's club, did her own washing, made her children's clothes, and fed her family good solid meals on $7 a week. She soon became the talk of America, her food budget discussed at dinner tables, skeptically or believingly, according to geography and the speaker's own talents.

Our first story came out February, 1940. At the beginning of the war democracies were spoken of as muddling, soft, decadent, especially by those who admired the "efficiency" of dictatorships. There was value in showing how our people, sprawled across a vast continent, actually lived. Madison Avenue soon recognized the vigor of the fresh idea, which was popular with readers right from the start.

We intended the series to run for a year—then added a second and a third. Ever renewing itself, ever dramatic, it ran for twenty-one years and has since been revived by the present editors. During our time the *Journal* told the stories of more than 250 families, whose cash income ranged from a quarter of a million dollars (Chicago packing tycoon) to $26 a year (colored tenant farmer with seventeen children in Mississippi).

We told of an alcoholic trying to reform, a widow bringing up children by taking in washing, even the despairing cry of one reader, "I'm a Punk Housewife!" A majority of our families lived within their incomes—most families more or less do.

In the first year we included the family of a Negro doctor in Philadelphia, whose wife we referred to as "Mrs." This natural courtesy resulted in thousands of denunciatory letters and thousands of canceled subscriptions from the South, even torn-up copies of the article in the mail. Because we had called a Negro woman "Mrs.," not just Sadie or Jennie, as was the custom, our circulation for that issue fell off 200,000 in the South. But the drop was only temporary.

Laws of libel kept us from telling of many women whose husbands flatly refused to give them enough money to run a house, although we could hint at not too flagrant cases. Nor did we try to portray a *ménage à trois*. Nor a Mafia family, nor even a husband in prison. All are part of the "How America Lives" picture, of course. But our spectrum was broad enough. We checked inconsistencies with banks, employers, ministers. Even so we were twice grossly deceived by families who turned out to be crooks, and once or twice charged with inaccuracy. Families were not permitted to read stories until they were out on the newsstands, lest they try to delete warts, cosmeticize freckles, modify facts to upgrade their community position. Usually before there were hurt feelings at the unretouched photographs, neighbors' congratulations and sudden fame poulticed any wounds.

After December, 1941, we adapted the series to war problems— the lonely wife, the parted sweethearts, the disabled veteran.

Diplomats, sociologists, students visiting America for the first time were advised by many to read the series as background in understanding our country.

"H.A.L." educated our editors, too. Visiting ordinary homes in Ashland, Ohio, or Cody, Wyoming, our food editor picked up some excellent recipes and learned what people actually ate. Our decorating editor realized how often women did over a room with paint and slipcovers for $219.23 rather than spending $1,000 at the nearest department store. And Wilhela Cushman, elegant, metropolitan, schooled in fashion at *Harper's Bazaar,* Hattie Carnegie, and Paris, delightedly discovered how an average woman could have grace and style of her own. Her perceptive cry after helping select a $200 wardrobe for the wife of an auto worker in Detroit was "But, Mrs. Gould—she's a lady! She could go anywhere. She could be an ambassador's wife!"

In America a lot of workingmen's wives have been, often with remarkable distinction.

There were gains we didn't foresee. Madison Avenue, perennially unsatisfied, hopefully scans the skies for something to give its products a better break, sometimes even going to the length of writing better ads. The picture magazine format was then in fashion. Since in "How America Lives" pictures and text ran through the back of the book we too benefited from the favored format of the moment.

Some other magazines tried to copy "H.A.L." but, geared to glamour, the sensational, they did not see the story quality in daily living, humdrum to them.

Our gratitude goes to Mary Bass for imaginative coordinating and editing of "H.A.L." She never got tired of people, was sensitive to their aspirations, amused by their inconsistencies, and sympathetic with their problems. The drama in ordinary human existence continued to fascinate her, us, and our readers.

Russia, later, would not let our *Journal* in—doubtless because "H.A.L." gave a picture of democracy so different from what Stalin (to say nothing of Hitler and Mussolini) portrayed. But in the USIS libraries elsewhere copies were thumbed till frayed and fragmented—and from strange spots in Africa, Ceylon, South America we had gratifying letters from women thanking us for introducing them to the human side of America.

Later, we did stories abroad. In India, after the war, when Beatrice was supervising a story, our staff was nearly stoned as they searched mud villages for an appealing girl of the Untouchable caste; our proposal to photograph her for an unknown magazine in far-off America apparently seemed to illiterate villagers to mask the most sinister design. We had to start afresh, more tactfully, in a distant village. Our resulting articles contrasting the life of a college-educated girl and an outcaste extended understanding of India's needs and problems to a large audience.

But all this was to come later. Soon after the *Journal* had passed it in circulation in 1940, the *Post* faced even more complicated problems—how to handle the Hitler-Mussolini drive to dominate Europe, Hitler's flagrant anti-Semitism. Stout threw the *Post* editorially on the side of those perhaps patriotic but, to us, mistaken America Firsters who thought the United States could and should keep out of Europe's war. Like too many others he seemed to believe Germany was certain to win. America should keep out of the whole European tragedy, the *Post* insisted. Its editors seemed to miss the moral implications in Hitler's ruthless thrust for power—his genocidal mania. The *Post* was simply backing the wrong horse. Life was backing the right one—and riding hard.

In these troubled months, Dorothy Thompson, brilliantly against Hitler, through her newspaper columns something of an international oracle, explained in the *Journal* the basics of the oncoming conflict: "The greatest living master of the propaganda of the lie is Adolf Hitler. . . . The doctrine that the end justifies the means and that a lie can serve useful social purpose is primarily what has brought the world into chaos and, at last, War. . . ."

Foreign correspondent George Seldes, writing about Mussolini, and his wife, quoted Mussolini's father as having warned Donna Rachele in 1907: "Do not let yourself think of that man. It would be better to throw yourself under a train."

Of the first fortnight of the war Rebecca West wrote for us: "When this War has proved how stupid and beastly humanity is, let us remember that a part of it was loving and kindly," telling how people were suddenly helping their neighbors.

We had already published Stephen Vincent Benét's scathing anti-Nazi story, "Into Egypt," a parable on Hitler and the Jews. We began printing Dorothy Black's inimitable letters about England under siege, beginning October, 1940, with:

> The French have laid down their arms. It is not a surprise to us.
> So now what? So now we are in it alone, and the lion is picking the moths out of his coat. Out comes the blunderbuss, the assagai has been taken from the wall, and those whose ancestors left them a cannonball over from The Battle of Waterloo are even looking thoughtfully at that.
> One feels the sympathy of most of America is towards us.

Edward Mead Earle, distinguished historian, wrote for us "Hitler and Our Future," warned, "We, too, may have to choose guns instead of butter."

After the disastrous spring of 1940, a note in "Journal About Town" said that Iver and Lucille Drummond, eight and six, were expected by the Goulds in a convoy from beleaguered England. My mother disapproved of our taking the evacuees—"Children should stay with their mother," she said. Many psychiatrists, after the war, agreed with her when they studied the frequently damaging effects of family separation. We, however, were grateful for the presence of two lively, attractive children for nearly four years, offering Sesaly some of the give-and-take of the brother and sister she had not had.

Feeling a deep distress about the *Post*'s editorial position on the war, I attempted through Miss Neall, with some diffidence, to dissuade Stout from his fatal course.

I was warned "to shinny on my own side."

Unexpectedly, in 1942, I had to make a difficult choice. Curtis suddenly (suddenly to the directors at least, though outsiders had predicted it for some time) needed a new editor for the *Post*. Stout's replacement was precipitated by an ill-timed controversial article by Milton Mayer—although his damaging mistake about World War II had let *Life* get halfway around the first turn in war coverage before the *Post* could spring from the starting gate.

The immediate cause of Stout's resignation seems, in retrospect, just a case of bad nerves among advertisers and jitters among Curtis directors. The article, about fundamental Jewish beliefs and ideals, was published to help combat Hitler's destructive anti-Semitic propaganda. Stout, not himself anti-Semitic, welcomed the article, but, perhaps in order to attract attention, ill-advisedly retitled it "What's Wrong with the Jews?". There was very little wrong, Mayer said, except that many Jews in a predominantly Christian society did not value highly enough their own great religious tradition.

I remember our friend Dr. Hohman, arriving to spend the night with us at Hopewell, reported that half New York was seething about the *Post*'s "What's Wrong with the Jews?" This seeming anti-Semitism at such a critical time was unbearable. A brilliant psychiatrist, Leslie Hohman wore his Jewish heritage with charm as befitted the intelligent man he was. Nevertheless, he was angry at the *Post*, long a favorite magazine—if only for its bad timing.

"Have you read the article?" I asked, when I could get in a word.

Leslie said he had not, but didn't need to, as he had "heard all about it." "I'll put it in your room tonight. Right now I can see you need a drink."

Next morning Leslie agreed the article was far more laudatory than critical. Stout had been guilty of a grave mistake in changing to a foolishly provocative title.

Incensed Jews, however, weren't as rational as our old friend or perhaps had read only the title. After Hitler, they were not in a forgiving mood. Headed by Albert Lasker, of Lord and Thomas advertising fame, some militants threatened that not another line of advertising would be placed in the *Post* if Stout remained. Newsstand dealers in New York hid that issue under their counters, refusing to sell it. There was talk of boycotting the *Post* forever.

The Curtis board decided to let Stout go. It was the right decision but, I felt, made for the wrong reason.

I was asked if I would become editor of *S.E.P.*

Stout's mistaken attitude toward World War II—though hastily revised after the Japs bombed Pearl Harbor—had put the *Post,* for the first time, really out of step. Heroic editing might get it back in the parade, but no one could tell if it would ever again lead the procession.

The *Journal,* on the other hand, was at last being accepted by Madison Avenue as having truly staged a comeback—a rare thing in either magazine or newspaper history. That was why, of course, Mr. Fuller was suggesting I now take over the *Post.*

But what would happen if we left the *Journal,* just beginning to feel the thrill of life? Since an editor's personality becomes the magazine, changing editors is always a chancy business. We were devoted to "our" magazine. We had put so much into it our pride was now involved in seeing the *Journal* fully successful and recognized. We couldn't just put it into unknown hands—and no successor had been thought of.

Beatrice was adamant on one point. She would not, she said, edit the *Journal* alone. With our daughter still young, she did not wish to accept such a full-time, compelling responsibility. She didn't want to be coeditor of the *Post* either, she told me. It wasn't her cup of tea.

If I wanted to take her on just as a *Post* associate editor, she would do what she could to help me in that capacity. But she would be perfectly willing to retire, go back to writing, and have more time with Sesaly. She urged me neither one way nor the other, having stated her position. I could decide for us both.

What I finally decided probably struck everyone as quixotic—more sentimental than sensible. I would, I said, edit both magazines, but I simply couldn't desert the barely revived *Journal*. If I could get the *Post* off and running—and I felt fairly sure I could—then, perhaps, we might turn one magazine over to a successor, someone who had shown initiative and drive, who was rooted in American traditions, who had faith in and respect for middle-class America.

Mr. Fuller was a bit taken aback by my decision, thinking probably I would leap at the chance to edit the *Post*. He would discuss my proposal with the board, with whom I wasn't sitting because I was involved.

Next day Mr. Fuller said the board wished me only to take on the *Post*. Beatrice could edit the *Journal* if she wished. If not, the board would find someone else for the *Journal*.

After a night's consideration and a morning's discussion with Beatrice, I turned down the *Post* editorship. I did it in writing, for the record—my record at least—explaining to Mr. Fuller I was tempted by the challenge but couldn't desert the *Journal* so abruptly. I was perfectly content to stay at the *Journal* with Beatrice.

I had gained a secret satisfaction demonstrating—not at all to my surprise—that a mere woman's magazine could be an intelligent magazine, could win the respect not only of its readers and advertisers but of sound journalists and eminent educators, even though directed to what many men continue to consider the second sex. Editing the *Post* successfully, I thought, wouldn't be half so difficult as editing the *Journal*.

Rejecting the *Post,* I felt a sense of relief. I'd simply have been working harder with two magazines to carry; once more trying to build up another magazine from scratch. I certainly didn't want to abandon a task I'd learned to love. Moreover, Curtis at that time was opposed to stock options, and income taxes were so high I wouldn't earn any more. I had a normal appreciation of money but it has never been a determining factor in decisions about work I wished to do.

"We're working hard enough as it is," I said to Beatrice. "Who knows, maybe the double task would have made us old before our time."

"Yes, let's have fun while we go along," said Beatrice, always a child of pleasure.

"Of course, editing the *Journal* hasn't the kudos editing the *Post* would have," I warned.

"Well—?" Beatrice replied.

The next day Mr. Fuller asked me what I thought of several other possibilities for *Post* editor, among them Ben Hibbs, then editor of *Country Gentleman,* and Bob Fuoss, the *Gentleman*'s alert promotion man. All of Mr. Fuller's suggestions for an *S.E.P.* editor came from within Curtis.

"Walter," I asked, "have you considered going outside the company? There are some good men in New York. Some new blood, a fresh viewpoint, might be valuable for Curtis."

Mr. Fuller did not seem impressed. Yet I knew the *Post*'s position was precarious.

"Walter," I said finally, having decided in those moments of silent cogitation to express what I really thought, however awkward it might sound, "whoever you choose must be someone who can put the *Post* back in first position. I cannot conceive of being satisfied with anything less. There is no substitute for being first, Walter. Madison Avenue only pays off on the winner."

Mr. Fuller had a compulsive way of anxiously tapping his teeth with two fingers of one hand when he was concentrating. Those fingers now played a light tattoo on his dentals.

"Walter, I know there's a tradition of coming up from the ranks at Curtis. You did. Most of the officers did. But there's nothing sacred about it. Lorimer was an outsider. So was Bok. For the matter of that, so were Beatrice and I. The man you now choose for editor of the *Post* will make or break it. It may make or break Curtis. You can't afford to be wrong. The world is wider than Curtis, wider than Philadelphia, Walter. Look around for someone who will be satisfied with nothing less than putting the *Post* back on top."

Fuller sat in silence for quite a spell, except for a little more tooth-tapping. . . . "Well, thank you, Bruce. I'll see, thank you."

I'm sure he felt my sympathy. Whether he quite realized that on his decision that day might rest the whole future of Curtis, I'm not sure. In all his dealings he tried to do his best.

The next day, unannounced, Cary Bok walked into my office. Cary, son of the famous editor, grandson of Cyrus Curtis, representing his family's controlling block of stock, was looked upon throughout the company as owner. Somewhat hesitantly, he explained his thinking: "The *Post* doesn't have to be in first place to get along, Bruce. *Collier's* has been second to the *Post* for years. It is doing all right."

As complacent as if he'd just enunciated Newton's law, he awaited my agreement. I regarded him with astonishment. How could the son of Bok and the grandson of Curtis hold such an attitude? Where was his pride? To look forward to such retreat without distaste seemed unbelievable. At last I replied:

"There is no substitute for first, Cary. None. Your father knew that. Lorimer knew that. So did your grandfather. One reason they all got to first place. It's the only place to be. There's no future in being second."

"Well," he insisted, "we'll see."

"I'm afraid we shall," I agreed.

When he'd gone I gazed through the great windowed expanse of my office and apostrophized Beatrice: "Well, Bibi, we'll make the *Journal* a magazine women can be proud to read. Through the *Journal,* we'll get done some things that need doing. And we'll have fun."

Cary, I suppose, didn't want editors to have too much power. He had resented Lorimer—as he had resented his own father. Good editors are autocrats. They seem overbearing and arrogant to those whose minds are not in tune. Cary respected business minds. He became treasurer for a while. He told me, later, he didn't think editors should be officers—businessmen should run Curtis' affairs. Probably

The ducks had a better than even chance to escape,
but Bruce enjoyed shooting at them.

Bruce and Beatrice ready for a country ramble.

Visiting the Korean warfront, Bruce and Beatrice rejoiced to learn how quickly helicopters flew wounded back to medical care.

Beatrice's continuing interest, like Lady Astor's, was the welfare of women and children—in the next block or far-off Africa.

he considered my suggestion to run two magazines only as another instance of editor's arrogance—perhaps a sheer bid for power.

Ben Hibbs, in the event, did a better job than I had predicted or foreseen. Never receiving the solid promotional support his steady editorial job merited, he built up the *Post* to where its newsstand exceeded the combined newsstand for *Life* and *Look* (after the war's unique bulge in favor of picture magazines subsided). Only the *Journal's* and *Reader's Digest's* newsstand exceeded the *Post's* from then on.

But the brilliant onslaughts of *Time-Life*—to say nothing of *Look,* as Fleur Cowles joined her undeniable flair to Mike Cowles' business and publishing acumen—made the *Post* seem stodgier than it actually was. The *Post's* promotion men, defeatist at heart, never initiating, always defensive, seemed futile by comparison with *Time-Life's* men and *Look's* to say nothing of *Reader's Digest's* imaginative promotion. Ben's magazine, solid, well-liked, consistently maintained a good circulation. It stopped just short of being tops. But only after Ben retired did the *Post's* really bad days begin.

All good ideas have already been thought;
the point is to try to think them again.
　　　　　　　　　　　　—GOETHE

18

Women in the World

We had continued a friendly and admiring relationship with Mrs. Roosevelt and printed several articles by her after the success of *My Story*. One day George Bye suggested that Mrs. Roosevelt write a monthly page for us.

Mrs. Roosevelt was not a good writer—a fact she cheerfully admitted in print. Her autobiography had succeeded because she told an honest, moving story. But, as wife of the President, little she had to say was entirely without interest, though some of her newspaper columns, full of inconsequentialities, approached inanity. The question-and-answer technique, we decided, would require her to speak to the point about significant subjects. We asked for the right to select questions she should answer from among our readers' mail, and stipulated that all selected questions must be answered.

At this time there were more than the usual rumors, innuendoes and backstairs gossip about the inhabitants of the White House. Mrs. Roosevelt could answer in her *Journal* page such queries, about which the public, rightly or wrongly, thinks it has a right to know.

"What people say behind your back," as Ed Howe put it, "is your standing in the community."

Mrs. Roosevelt must have been brought up on "Speak the truth and shame the Devil." She accepted the plan with alacrity. Our terms were $2,500 a page, twelve times a year, to be terminated by either party, at will; the contract was never other than a verbal one. (Incidentally, much of the money Mrs. Roosevelt earned through her writings went to various charities and philanthropic institutions.) Her *Journal* column began June, 1941, and was an instantaneous hit. With eight or ten questions in each issue, her answers had to be succinct.

Here are some samples:

Do you mean by "racial equality" intermarrying of the races?

Not of necessity. Marriage is an individual thing and each person must decide for himself. Equality of the races, however, can be established whether individuals decide to marry or not. There must be equality before the law, equality of education, equal opportunity to obtain a job according to one's ability and training, and equality in participation in self-government.

Do you believe in a fourth presidential term?

No, I do not believe in any presidential term. It is an office which carries so many burdens that, as far as I am concerned, no one human being should ever be willing to undertake it.

What do you think of the increasing tendency of novelists to use so many "four-letter words" not spoken in polite soceity?

I did not know there were any words left that were not spoken in polite society.

At various times I have heard that you and Mr. Roosevelt are separated, but that you live together to keep down scandal in the United States. I do not believe this at all true. Will you please answer this so I may read it in black and white?

You are young, I imagine, and therefore your question is neither impertinent nor malicious. It is the kind of question, however, which, when I was young, we were taught belonged to the realm of things about which one might speculate, but never talk. Gossip of the kind which you have heard is whispered about almost all people in public life, and no one should notice it.

Mrs. Roosevelt's answers were shrewd, well thought out, and an indication of a magnanimous character. Often they cleared the air of noxious gossip. Here, as in other activities, she became an invaluable political asset to her husband.

Her page was not only widely read but made "newsbreaks" in the press. The *Journal* became almost required reading for liberal columnists, and even won a grudging admiration from some brash young critics of the press, who often prefer contempt to praise and are especially supercilious when women's affairs are concerned. (I shudder as I remember my own critical youth, when to be superior, in print, seemed more delightful than bags of gold pieces.)

With a warmly interested Mrs. Roosevelt we discussed many future ideas, a school-lunch program for our many depression-hungry children—nationally organized rather than relying on sporadic volunteer effort—improved health conditions and better educational facilities in impoverished areas. Several times she would ask us to discuss these ideas with "Franklin." Beatrice remembers, almost with anguish, being seated next to Franklin, beside his deaf ear, at a large round-table luncheon, when she was supposed to help sell him on the merits of feeding hungry children at school, while a most vivacious, energetic lady on his other side claimed all his attention she could get and Beatrice, never an aggressive saleswoman, found herself striving to talk, quite literally, into a deaf ear. The fact that the school-lunch program, which we had urged so strongly in the *Journal,* developed as a program to use agricultural surpluses instead of being shaped, primarily, for the pitifully undernourished of our country, distressed us. "Children don't vote, farmers do," we were told, unofficially.

As our circulation grew, our ideas became more cosmic. We tended, perhaps too largely, to refer to our audience simply as "The Women of America." It is true the *Journal* had an enormously wide and enthusiastic readership, cutting across all classes in all sections of the country. Our concern for maternal and infant health, for hot school lunches expanded naturally into a concern for children everywhere.

After the war started, people suddenly began thinking globally— even our former yard boy, never before twenty miles from Hopewell, was now an aviation mechanic somewhere in India. With Mrs. Roosevelt we talked of the possibility of uniting leading women of the democracies into a committee or group (perhaps I was daydreaming again); each would tell of the interest of women in her own country for the well-being of women, children, and homes throughout the world. While men were divided politically, economically, territorially, women shared a wide common denominator of interest. In a war-ravaged world, with the masculine, aggressive principle dominant, such an expression of human regard for others, concern for the undernourished, the neglected, the suffering, especially the young, might help link women everywhere in a bond of sympathy.

Nowadays, after the successful Marshall Plan, the Peace Corps' widespread aid to distant peoples, our Great Society speaking of an obligation to keep Southeast Asia free, India from starving, and South America developing and literate, our puny, wartime "talk" project may not seem so ambitious as it did then. Then it seemed almost as revolutionary as Henry Wallace's pint-of-milk-a-day for all children.

Talk of itself may accomplish nothing, but it has always preceded action. To many statesmen our womanly project must have appeared, like other of Mrs. Roosevelt's efforts, an undue intrusion into masculine affairs. In those dark war days, when the light at the end of the tunnel appeared at times hardly more than a glimmer, our vision doubtless seemed a marsh-fire glow. But the concept that the United States could not exist "an isle of plenty in a sea of misery" should be widely expressed, we believed, before it could emerge as the shape of things to come.

The almost unprecedented contribution of women in Europe to the war effort (less marked, as less needed, in the U.S.) had given women a new sense of importance. Perhaps they began to think that maybe, after the war, the world might conceivably do with a little help from the distaff side. Women, with their instinct to cherish, not to destroy; to love, not to hate; to nurture, not to oppose, might legitimately ask for a part in ordering this new, loving world.

Teilhard de Chardin says:

Love alone is capable of uniting living beings in such a way as to complete and fulfill them, for it alone takes them and joins them by what is deepest in themselves. This is a fact of daily experience. At what moment do lovers come into the most complete possession of themselves if not when they say they are lost in each other? In truth, does not love every instant achieve all around us, in the couple or the team, the magic feat, the feat reputed to be contradictory, of "personalizing" by totalizing? And if that is what it can achieve daily on a small scale, why should it not repeat this one day on world wide dimensions?

Mankind, the spirit of the earth, the syntheses of individuals and peoples, the paradoxical conciliation of the element with the whole, and of unity with multitude—all these are called Utopian and yet they are biologically necessary. And for them to be incarnated in the world all we may well need is to imagine our power of loving developing until it embraces the total of men and of the earth.

Mrs. Roosevelt, not uncosmic in her own thinking, and, like Beatrice, a do-gooder to her toes, approved our Women in the World idea highly. She would write for America, and try to enlist Queen Elizabeth and Queen Wilhelmina to do articles for their countries. Mme. Chiang, then at the height of adulation, could speak for China, and Eve Curie, we thought, might be a representative of the Free French. Mme. Pandit could represent India. Each would do an article about the bonds of sympathy which unite women everywhere, their concern for the nourishment, health, and education of children in their own lands and in every nation. They would suggest a universal spiritual Esperanto—philosophical, nonpolitical, but promising sympathy and, if possible, aid in the postwar years.

Mrs. Roosevelt planned to go to England in the fall of 1942, partly as a warm symbol of United States support to that hard-pressed land, partly to do several articles for the *Journal* on the devoted war work of women in Great Britain. She won her husband's approval of our tentative plan, and suggested we accompany her, to help develop her own articles and be ready to carry our project further, if possible.

[Beatrice writes:

In the summer of 1942 Mrs. Roosevelt had already
arranged for us to meet Queen Wilhelmina, who, with
her minister of foreign affairs, Eelco van Kleffens, was
then in the United States. Close to the throne one learns
a careful tongue. Van Kleffens, like many skilled diplomats, was handsome, elegant, utterly courteous and as
cool as a polished piece of marble. One could almost
hear words clink against his smooth, impervious surface. Queen Wilhelmina was even more difficult. I talked
to her for a few minutes at the White House before
a luncheon given in her honor. Plain, dowdy, yet majestic, she had a terrifying presence—that guarded air,
almost suspicious, which easy politicians learn to cover
with smiles and humor, but which the shy never manage
to conceal. If Mrs. Roosevelt had not been there to help
me stumble through the audience, words would literally
have failed me, I fear.

Later, across an enormous round luncheon table in
the state dining room I watched handsome, relentlessly
affable Wendell Willkie in easy conversation with Her
Majesty. Suddenly the Queen broke into warm laughter.
Later, I wondered to Mr. Willkie how he had managed
to thaw this difficult lady—then living in England. "I
asked her," Mr. Willkie said, "if she had explored the
English character enough to get a joke. Then I just
told her the simplest possible joke: It seems there were
two Scotchmen—"

Later, when we published Grace Tully's *My Boss,
F.D.R.* I was delighted to learn that even President
Roosevelt regarded the Queen with cautious respect.
"I'm scared to death of the old girl," he said to Miss
Tully.

Under Secretary of State Sumner Welles, already

slightly hostile to Mrs. Roosevelt's pervasive influence on her husband's business, apparently thought well-meaning but ignorant women should not intrude into matters of state. We had been warned of his cool attitude. Once when we waited in the White House to see Mrs. Roosevelt, his tall, spare, elegant figure emerged from the President's office, and with a bare greeting he remarked, "This is impossible! Impossible!" almost with clenched teeth, as he hastily passed by.

However, Mrs. Roosevelt, though her husband sometimes slighted her in personal matters, maintained great suasion in political affairs. With the strength of the meek—or the power of the person who believes doing good is possible—she prevailed over Secretary Welles' objections. We were granted White House visas, 1A, for England, and transport on a somewhat ancient flying boat, looked at a bit askance by Bruce, experienced in aviation.

There is always, I suppose, some tension about a first flight over the Atlantic, and especially in the uncertain secrecy of a wartime journey. No one would know how or when we were going. Only a few hours' notice would be given us.

Embarking in gray pre-dawn in the huge flying boat, in the dark, too, as to our next landing, we alighted in frigid northeast Canada. There we laid over two days— held up by uncertain weather above the ocean. The previous flying boat, sister to ours, had crashed on its watery takeoff, unofficial word got about, drowning all hands as it dived to the bottom of the bay. Instead of being daunted by this information, my husband seemed to perk up. "You very seldom," he told me, "get two bad crashes in a row. I don't know why this is—but there's always an interval. We're playing in luck." Our flight to me was eerie adventure, rushing headlong through darkness toward the dawn. Portholes were densely curtained, though there was no way of hiding from an air raider the blue-green glare from belching exhausts against the black. The men sat up reading, playing cards, many doing a little quiet, intensive drinking. Mrs. Robert Bingham, widow of our former ambassador, and I, the only women, were given berths. I slept fairly soundly above a poker game. But one almost shed tears of relief to see emerald Ireland below us on a sunny October morning, and the hearty breakfast of bacon, two eggs, toast, and plentiful butter was almost like a reprieve—the last such ample meal we were to see for weeks.

In London the once-luxurious Ritz was cold and dingy, with patched bedspreads, darned sheets. The late-afternoon blackout, exact, painstaking, of two heavy curtains allowing no chink of light, held ominous suggestions. Drab, sparse meals were served by the halt, infirm, or alcoholic. All who were fit had more arduous service. Butter on one's plate was a circle thin as a worn penny. Bread and potatoes abundant, a small ragged piece of meat soon told us what our fare would be, as did next morning's powdered eggs, scrambled for breakfast.

Mrs. Roosevelt had arrived a day or two before us, staying at our embassy with brooding, enigmatic Ambassador Winant. In that curiously close society of official England, where everything and everybody is known, and everything heard about almost before it happens, our arrival was expected. The Minister of Information, Brendan Bracken—looking as if he'd snatched Harpo Marx's orange wig and clapped it on his own head, where it had taken root—called to ask how he could be of help. All doors were open to us. Mrs. Roosevelt, of course, was involved in many official occasions with the Lord Mayor of London, with their Majesties at Windsor Castle, but she also visited factories and studied the war effort of women with us. Just as to America Churchill was a symbol of courage and strength far above human stature, so President Roosevelt seemed to the English, in their desperate need, a human expression, without flaw, of the strength and rescuing support of the great American nation. Mrs. Roosevelt bore this banner well. Veneration met her everywhere she went, stately and tall, attentive and sympathetic. I remember, after she had passed, a small, worn woman in a Spitfire factory touching my arm, whispering reverently, "She has such a beautiful face."

We visited these weary women in their homes, neat working-class houses in a brick row, a skimpy bomb shelter in the back yard, tidy front parlor, kettle on the hob, rudimentary kitchen with one tap for cold water, two bedrooms above. Doing ten hours a day, six days a week in a factory, they would tell, without self-pity, how they managed their housework, washing and cleaning on one day off. To one whose husband was a paratrooper we spoke with sympathy of his courage. "Well, we've got to get it over, haven't we?" she answered sturdily.

We knew that Mrs. Roosevelt had discussed our project with Ambassador Winant and found him sympathetic, and would speak about it, at the first favorable moment, to the Queen. But even Mrs. Roosevelt could not hurry the formal procedures of royalty.

So we waited, observing wartime work on the farm, in day nurseries, in the services. The shock of the first few days was to realize how little people complained. An amazing number had been bombed out, sometimes twice, even three times. Almost every family had lost a home or a near relative—a husband or a son. How proud they were if they had a boy in the RAF—that heroic, lonely few, who hurled themselves night and day against the German bombers. London's scars showed on every street, whole blocks of houses gone, a crazy exposed staircase ascending nowhere, the skeleton of a church, gaunt against a moonlit sky.

We visited Plymouth, which had been disastrously bombed. Lord and Lady Astor (she was Plymouth's M.P.) had instituted, to lift spirits, evening singing, music, and dancing on the Hoe esplanade. One old man there said—by this time American bombers were over Europe—"Well, they plastered us. Now they're getting it themselves, poor devils."

Surprisingly, bombing had grown almost casual to many. An attractive young secretary, helping Bruce, told us how she had managed to buy a charming yellow coat with sparse clothing coupons. Wearing it to work she heard an alert. "Fall flat on my face, as we were supposed to do—and ruin my new coat? Never!—I huddled in a doorway till it was over."

Later, I watched women volunteers after a buzz bombing. Sometimes going without sleep from one job to another, these quiet uniformed women set up posts, served hot coffee or soup to survivors, found temporary shelter, helped rejoin scattered families. I remember a little boy near the rubble of his East End home coming hesitantly to a motherly woman: "Did anyone—anyone, happen to see a canary in a cage?"

Since buses were crowded, taxis almost unheard of, one walked everywhere, in 1942's autumn's early dark, with hooded flashlight, through blackened, muffled streets, grateful, if fog was absent, for the pinpricks of stars, welcoming the moon's return with the awe our forefathers must have felt, when it was their only night light. Even the shadowy, skirted figures waiting in Piccadilly doorways for the lonely soldier had been sifted out by age or vigor from those who might perform a more useful war service. A cruel incident told me by a friend scars my memory. Coming up a subway stairs, he saw a soldier, accosted, strike a match and light the near features—apparently revolting. He shrank back and away, walked hastily off down the street.

Though cold was so pervasive that even in the Ritz men sat about evenings in their overcoats, and women snuggled in bits of fur, with blankets over their knees, it was rarely spoken of—just as little was said about hard darkish bread, omnipresent potatoes, unidentified bits of fish. But if someone had a chicken, brought by friends from the country, it made a party, parceled out among many. Bruce remembers Lord Harcourt in the Ritz eating his unappetizing fare while cheerfully reading a French cookbook, in memory of better times.

Learning of our presence early through the grapevine which surrounded E.R., Lady Astor telephoned to invite us to Cliveden for a weekend. Having never met Lady Astor, we expressed a hesitation to accept, to Mrs. Bingham, staying, too, at the Ritz, and an old friend of the Astors. Next day Mrs. Bingham reported that Lady Astor had said, "Tell Mrs. Gould I'm sure I've met her on a yacht someplace." So palpable a fabrication, our introduction to Nancy Astor's breezy and outrageous humor, left us nothing to do but laugh and accept.

At that time, the so-called "Cliveden set" was in disrepute in America, as "appeasers." Neville Chamberlain had been a friend, and criticism clouded those who had supported his policies. We were not sure we wanted to go to Cliveden. However, talking to English friends, we realized again that the Atlantic had exaggerated an attitude. The "Cliveden set" was an easy journalistic label, linking individuals who, as Christians, as civilized people, feared and hated war, possibly not fully reckoning the consequences of continually yielding to force—together with politicians who, knowing England's unpreparedness, sought time to arm. No more pro-Nazi

than many America Firsters, this group included Lord
Halifax among others, lacking foresight perhaps but
motivated by what they considered their country's best
interest.

Lady Astor, we found, was admired by many for
sponsoring in the House of Commons measures benefit-
ing the welfare of women and children—though she was
loathed by some men for the sharpness of her tongue.

Cliveden's splendid house of tawny stone, high on
its terrace, with formal gardens now orderly with rows
of winter cabbages, was calculated to make us shy as
college freshmen. The stately, high-ceilinged hall was
sparsely warmed by logs big as trees roaring in the huge
fireplace around which all had gathered. Nancy Astor
greeted us with her captivating blend of warmth,
spirited, mischievous humor, her interested, curious,
but friendly blue gaze. With that direct, clear look, her
teasing smile, she set up no barriers between yourself
and her. Her friendships were spontaneous, her antip-
athies strong, and frequently expressed in lacerating
words. Her tongue was quick, audacious, and unruly,
and unfortunately those she loved sometimes felt its
rough side, as well as those she disliked. With a dashing
air at sixty, she still had the bone beauty of the famous
Gibson Girls for whom her older sister, Mrs. Charles
Dana Gibson, was model. Waldorf Astor, gentle, with a
frail, sensitive face, was a quietly considerate host. Their
oldest son, Bill, rather plump, with prominent brown
eyes, little resembled either parent. Lady Astor's out-
going humor melted away strangeness and Bruce, rarely
inhibited, was as given to the unexpected, often startling,
remark as she. They set each other off like a pair of pin-
wheels as we consumed a hearty tea (breads and
starches were plentiful), our large oval table set close as
possible to the fire. Lord Astor himself showed us to our
two adjoining bedrooms, large and frigid.

"What is that little stream down there?" asked my unwary husband, looking across gardens sloping toward Windsor, and not yet geographically oriented.

"That," replied Waldorf Astor with unwavering courtesy, "is the Thames."

My huge bathroom was heated, I had been told. A tepid towel rack served as radiator and I ventured a quick, tepid bath, then down to dinner with a low-necked sweater under my dress, wool underwear as complete as outer garments allowed, flesh-colored wool stockings under my nylons, and a shawl. The dining room had no heat at all. One could have hung a leg of lamb there and kept it fresh all winter.

That evening we were taken to a staff dance at the Canadian hospital on Cliveden grounds, its steam heat full on. A kindly nurse took me wadded and dripping to her bedroom, where I stripped off layers of wool to enjoy the party. Next morning with Lady Astor we visited the war wounded. Her kindly teasing, her outrageous jokes could spark into laughter a whole ward of bedridden men.

Cliveden was a welcoming house then, and always during Nancy Astor's residence a haven for visiting Americans—students, ambassadors, journalists, Rhodes scholars, even Senators.

When Nancy told us of her old Negro nurse from Virginia come to visit her crying, "Lawsa, Miss Nancy, you shuh married outside yuhsef," two Middle Westerners could appreciate Mammy's wonder.

Warmly hospitable as she was, Lady Astor set up a tollhouse by her gate (not unlike the octagonal stone ones guarding old roads in Scotland), exacting a modest fee from guests. "Isn't this good ham?" she would say, over her thin wartime slice. "Friends from Virginia brought it. And we couldn't possibly have this dessert if my last visitors had not sent me that wonderful sweet chocolate. Americans are so generous." The moral was plain. One never appeared at Cliveden's friendly door without luxurious sweets and goodies; hams and tinned tongue were welcome Atlantic freight.

She was a bit of a brigand, too, in matters of feminine attire. Beginning gradually, she borrowed, to be copied by her own milliner, a John-Fred dark brown jersey turban brightened by topaz pins. But on our way to an evening party at the American embassy she said, "What is that enchanting thing on your head? I must have it. You can get another when you go home." The tribute was paid, but alas the mold was broken. The little whiff of black lace from Carnegie was never duplicated. Small sacrifice to a woman who gave us so much shrewd advice in our work, and such warm and always amusing friendship.

At Cliveden our hostess walked with us, always running up the steep flight of stone steps at the last terrace —"Just to be sure I still can"; gave us cozy cups of tea in her own sitting room, elegant, with pale walls, pale chintz; asked about our families; told about hers—Bill, in Parliament, Jakey recently surviving a commando dash on Dieppe. In the midst of her English life, active in the House, she kept great warmth for her American family, her Virginia home. After this visit, the first of many at Cliveden, she never forgot the name or whereabouts of our daughter, followed her career, school, college, marriage, children, with remembering interest and once, telephoning me on an unexpected arrival, asked, "How are your grandchildren?"—briefest pause —"You don't need to answer, I can just see that silly grin on your face."

With or without her varied store of false faces, kept in a handy cupboard, she was an amusing mimic as well as anecdotist. Her impeccable butler remained impeccable on entering the drawing room to find her transmuted into blackface or a ringleted Southern belle. Her cousin Joyce Grenfell, who later gained fame for her impersonations, was considered in the family their least talented member, Nancy told us.

Wherever Nancy went she must be star of the show. Years later, at lunch with her and Lester Pearson in the UN dining room with wide river view, Nancy entertained, joking, then mimicking, charmingly but just conspicuously enough so that soon, at neighboring tables, people inevitably looked, stared, nudged, "Why, that must be Nancy Astor!"

Many Englishmen were not amused by Nancy Astor's sharp tongue as Churchill, notably, made clear:

"If I were your wife I'd put poison in your tea."

"If I were your husband, I'd take it."

As we waited for word about our project, Nancy proposed taking us to call on George Bernard Shaw, her great friend and Bruce's idol since youth. Driving through London's streets, Nancy and I could not resist waving at newly arrived American boys in uniform, begging to stop the car and speak to them. Bruce, correct with strangers, refused, unmoved by our plea that we wanted our soldiers to feel welcomed and appreciated. "Why are men so stuffy?" I wailed to Nancy. "They are, aren't they?" she replied. "I suppose it's because of their collars."

On that chilly autumn day, we drove to Ayot-St.-Lawrence to be served tea around a lively fire in a pleasant suburban house. Mrs. Shaw presided, short, plump, strongly individual, with aware, perceptive eyes, not at all a subordinated shadow. Shaw, overbearing in print, must have been milder in the home. Already fatally ill, she seemed as merry as he. G.B.S., eighty-six, sat lean and upright as an exclamation point, his form fitted to his exclamatory mind. His prankish boy's vitality suited his knee-length knickers. Mrs. Shaw, unruffled, poured tea, as he and Nancy exchanged outrageous badinage, Shaw's electric eyes darting everywhere to see what mischief he could stir up.

He reiterated his insistence that Stalin was the greatest man in the world. Bruce said he didn't like dictators. Shaw said he didn't mind them if they moved people in the right direction. There seemed to be more than a hint that the world might have been in less sad state if Shaw had been a dictator himself.

Since he was a man of paradoxes, it didn't seem to strange that immediately afterward the great Socialist mourned that the wartime government, allocating labor, only allowed him two servants in spite of the millions he had brought England in taxes, when he really needed three.

Blanche Patch, Shaw's long-time secretary, urged old friend Nancy to go upstairs before our departure: "It's cold. You've miles to go. And with this heavy traffic and rolls of barbed wire people can't slip into the woods the way they used to."

In the bedroom she confided: "The articles he's writing now are so far left even the Communist papers won't accept them."

Dorothy Thompson told us later she had once confessed to Rebecca West, "I can't see why brilliant G.B.S. and a flighty woman like Nancy Astor should have so much in common."

"Don't you see," replied Rebecca, "they're both old Southern beauties!"

The friendship lasted. Nancy comforted Shaw in his loneliness after the death of Charlotte, and was with him at his own deathbed. I suppose he loved her for the goodness under her too tart tongue. She, witty herself, revered him as the wittiest, most original mind of our time.

We often visited Nancy later at Sandwich, Kent, and

and at her town house in Hill Street. After our first
meeting, she and Bruce kept up a spirited correspondence (Nancy claiming that after my death he would be
her next husband). Her letters started bravely with four
or five typewritten lines, then trailed off into a two-page
postscript in her appalling, hentrack handwriting which
might have been Sanskrit and required several secretaries to decipher.

In these tense weeks in England during the late
autumn of 1942 we awaited some word from the palace
—and word from the palace is always slow. Mrs. Roosevelt, faithful to her articles, also kept faith in our project,
about women in the free world, as did Ambassador
Winant. In the meantime English doors swung wide, so
English coldness we did not experience.

This was no credit to us. The Roosevelts were rever-
enced. And America had come to Britain's aid at her
desperate hour. In hotel lobbies, in trains, even on the
street, strangers came up recognizing us as Americans
(we knew not how), insisted on talking, offering us
hospitality if we were going their way.

We met many women doing valuable war work. Lady
Reading, head of thousands in the inspiring and efficient
Women's Voluntary Services, herself compassionate,
ruled and directed her helpers with an iron hand to insist that compassion was always given compassionately.
Mrs. Walter Elliot was a member of the committee
advising Ernst Bevin on the wartime employment of
women, similar to but more influential because England's needs were greater than my corresponding committee in Washington (mine chaired by Margaret
Hickey, later one of our editors).

In these cold, dark days, finding cheerful courage
everywhere, we formed not only lasting friendships but
an admiration for the British people, staunch under
stress, an admiration so great that we knew, when we re-

turned home, we must express it temperately, not as glowingly as we felt, lest cynics or American Firsters dismiss our praise as if we had been "sucked in" by British propaganda.

It was a pleasure, too, to Bruce to renew his friendship with Daisy and find her safe after fleeing the Nazi occupation of France. She was at the Dorchester in an apartment made cozy by rare needlepoint rugs, her own pictures, and again a lustrous mink throw.

We had time to meet publishers, editors, and writers all eager to know America's "point of view." We renewed acquaintances with contributors and friends, among them Dorothy Black, who brought us occasional fresh eggs from the country and always brought laughter wherever she went. She lost a son in the war and had two daughters in the services, but her letters in the *Journal,* describing with humor hardships of wartime life, revealed the sturdy determination of her countrymen. While Churchill stirred the English to their highest effort, Dorothy Black, almost as famous among American women, pictured their effort in human terms to every hamlet in America.

Mrs. Roosevelt told us she had found the Queen charming but noncommittal, saying she must consult her advisers about our proposal. We, in the meantime, talked about it to Brendan Bracken, Lady Reading, Lady Astor, whoever might have the palace ear.

In this November of '42 the African invasion took place. For days there was a sense of stir and bustle in the air, but guarded, muffled, as the lighted interiors were by thick curtains of the blackout. Then correspondents, friends simply disappeared. On the morning of November 8 joy swept London with news of the successful landings. Everyone spoke to everyone on the street in their elation. In the "Strangers Gallery" of the House of Lords, where Commons was sitting (its own house had been bombed out), we heard Churchill tell the first good news he had been able to bring in a long while.

He slipped in an aside: "Hitler says we are military idiots and," he paused to make certain he had every ear, "drunkards."

The House caught its breath—Churchill's fondness for Scotch-and-soda was well known. A slight smile played about the antic Prime Minister's mouth. He leaned forward confidingly: "You know, that man can be very impertinent at times."

The House roared—the gaiety of the man again lifted all hearts.

Word on our project was indefinite, though Ambassador Winant seemed to feel that attitudes were "not unfavorable." Bruce, discussing the matter with Home Secretary Herbert Morrison, found that Labour stalwart wary lest women be given too much "say." They had had so much recognition for their war work, often holding positions of unusual influence. Didn't Bruce think that after the war women might become "a little hoity-toity"? American women were, perhaps, already "hoity-toity." It was obvious he couldn't bear to think of the good English housewife taking on such an alarming character. About this time even conservative Churchill, in a speech outlining what victory might mean, conceded that most, not just some, children were entitled to a daily mug of milk along with the prospect of getting a bit more education as well. Many favored an all-out expression among democracies indicating concern for the well-being of peoples everywhere. From the first, Nancy Astor, always sensitive to the welfare of women and children, approved our plan. She could not resist having a finger in the pie. Now she proposed that we meet the Queen and her daughter Elizabeth at Cliveden for luncheon. We, in person, could explain our proposal to Her Majesty as no intermediary could do.

Even for Cliveden this was a great day. Nancy Astor, that skilled and accustomed hostess, seemed to be up and about earlier than most mornings, fussing more than usual with servants, arrangements, flowers. We were all given our instructions: "You be in this room by 12:30." "Must I curtsy? I can't." "Ignorant Americans can get by with a bob."

About a dozen of us were assembled in Lady Astor's sitting room, filled with fresh flowers touched by a pale sun—the Astor daughter, Phyllis, Countess of Ancaster; Bill, M.P.; the other son, Jakey, in uniform, home for a day on leave; the head of the hospital on Cliveden grounds. I think all of us felt some awe as the Queen— she and her husband carried a weight of wartime sorrow—entered, with her special gift of unstudied poise combined with warm friendliness. Her simple gray-blue suit and hat intensified dark-blue black-lashed eyes. As she circled the room greeting us in order, she turned on each a deeply personal glance of such interest it seemed for a moment that she saw only you and would remember you always.

Bruce told me later he had observed her consideration while we were all being introduced. Standing beside him was the Canadian doctor, a handsome, middle-aged colonel who, as he was presented to Her Majesty, could not speak, was struck entirely dumb. He trembled.

Probably Queen Elizabeth had seen this happen before—an adult, presented to royalty, suddenly mute as an embarrassed child. Without seeming to notice, she turned back with a courteous word to include Bruce in the threesome until the colonel, at last recovered, found his tongue and hesitantly joined in the conversation. Whereupon, she bathed them both in the warmth of her remarkable eyes, and, with the dignity and ease of a large swan, floated on.

Sixteen-year-old Princess Elizabeth, slim in a sky-blue wool suit and matching beret, seemed almost rigid with shyness. Resembling her father, her flowerlike pink-and-white skin and azure eyes gave her a beauty her photographs did not show.

At a long, handsomely set table, in the noble, chilly dining room, with an excellent wine but that sparsity of food and service England's most luxurious homes offered in those austere months, the Queen had been placed at Lord Astor's right, with Bruce on her other side. This most popular of royal figures (in a family given to constraint) proved an easy conversationalist. Bruce was relieved to find they speedily got on the subject of differences between English and Americans. He sought to illustrate some divergences with a famous story about Lincoln. During our Civil War, an English major, bringing a diplomatic message, had found our great President in a dusty army camp, foot up on tent peg, polishing his boots.

"Mr. President," cried the astonished major, "do you shine your own shoes?"

From his great height Lincoln looked down contemplatively at the incredulous major.

"Whose shoes," he responded benignly, "would I be shining?"

A little startled, Queen Elizabeth (she is a Scot) laughed after a bit politely, checked herself, laughed again, but then mused sadly: "It is hard, isn't it, to get one's shoes shined in wartime?"

Bruce agreed it was, a little startled himself. The old saying is that you must tell a joke three times to a Scotsman. He tried less American ones next time, and was rewarded by spontaneous gurgles.

After lunch, while the young people went for a

walk, and Bruce was shooed away with Waldorf—
"This is woman's business," Nancy declared—I had my
opportunity to outline our project to Her Majesty. The
Queen listened with warm concentration, but with noncommittal ease, explaining again that she would need
to consult her advisers.

Just recently, twenty years later, we sat directly facing
the royal family at morning service in the little church
near Balmoral—the young Queen in a severe beret, the
expansive Queen Mother in a flower toque, Princess
Anne all in pink, and Prince Philip masculinely impos-
ing. My grandson, only twelve but already susceptible
to feminine charm, after studying them closely, whispered to me, "I like the Queen Mum best." The charming young Queen, born to the purple, has not yet
attained the womanly radiance so spontaneously ema-
nating from her lovely mother, born a commoner. Our
little granddaughter said, with some disappointment, "I
thought the Queen would be wearing her crown."

I suppose one thinks of a queen as always in a sense
wearing a crown. Certainly I was amused that day at
Cliveden by a very feminine colloquy just before good-
byes. Nancy Astor said, "You know I've known this
girl ever since she and my daughter were in dancing
class together." Queen Elizabeth, regarding herself
closely in her compact mirror as she powdered her nose,
replied, "Sadly changed since those days, I fear." "Not
at all, you are lovelier than ever," her hostess asserted
stoutly. Even Queens, apparently, like reassurance. And
it was true then and still is, that a magic charm does
radiate from those amazing eyes.

As the pair were about to climb into their shining
Rolls, to be motored in state back to nearby Windsor
Castle, Nancy, never in awe on any occasion, presented
them each with a brace of lollipops we had brought
from America. The Queen beamed her thanks. "We'll

suck them all the way home." Inside the Rolls, they proceeded to do so.

Mrs. Roosevelt had already gone home and Bruce soon followed—flying south to Lisbon, to Africa, to South America in a roundabout circuit to escape unwelcome attention from German fighter planes. I stayed on. If the Queen of England would sponsor one article on the world women wanted after the war, we would have, we felt, no trouble in persuading Queen Wilhelmina, Mme. Chiang, and others to speak also.

I think our plan was seriously considered because of Mrs. Roosevelt's influence. The "no" was long in coming. But with Mrs. Roosevelt, to whom so much was owed, well out of the way, I was finally called upon at the Ritz by Viscount Lascelles, the Queen's private secretary, with the courteously told decision that the Queen, being above and beyond politics, could not speak on this matter to other nations.

Our project had failed and I sailed for home. Our battered, war-weary *Queen* slunk furtively through fog and rain across the North Atlantic, carrying men invalided home, men on leave, ferry pilots returning to ferry planes again across the ocean—a ship so crowded that meals were served in continuous shifts; in the lounge evenings, one half had to stand. There I learned a skillful soldier's game of gin rummy. Our darkened, secret voyage on an evasive route reached New York one day too late for Christmas.

But, though our main project had failed, the germ of another idea had formed in our minds after that luncheon at Cliveden. How does one bring up a young, shy girl to become Her Majesty; how does one educate a princess to be a queen?]

Kings are . . . made by universal hallucination.
—GEORGE BERNARD SHAW

19 🐾

The Little Princesses

Following our wartime meeting with royalty at Lady Astor's, I had
said to Beatrice:

"Young Elizabeth is about the same age as Sesaly. They're both
trying to learn to be first-class women. But Elizabeth has to grow up
to be a queen, too. Why wouldn't it be fascinating to tell the story of
how a young girl is educated for a royal role?"

"It would," agreed Beatrice, "but could we get it?"

"There must be ways," I said, not then quite realizing how rigorously majesty tries to preserve its luster, discouraging all publicity save
that which emanates officially from the palace.

We discussed the idea first with Ambassador Winant in London,
and then, at his suggestion, with Brendan Bracken. We pointed out
how much, in the depth of the war, England needed America's understanding and good will. A story of this young girl in an endearingly
affectionate and high-principled family being taught her duties as a
queen—such a sympathetic story reaching millions in our magazine—
would help Americans understand the English, and even their mon-

archy, which often seems to our countrymen a meaningless, almost absurd institution.

As that average American, I think monarchy somewhat obsolete in our modern day. Beatrice believes royalty gives the English a symbol of their unity as a nation, a symbol not tarnished by political and partisan differences. She also thinks royalty, revered, can set standards for good behavior. Jacqueline Kennedy, young, attractive, intelligent, once suggested such standards in the White House. In any event, the English on the whole seem better mannered than we. Even when they're deliberately bad-mannered they are bad-mannered with punctilio.

During the war, most officials were too occupied to give attention to our precedent-shaking proposal. But we kept on talking to any who might be influential—Lady Reading, familiar with American attitudes; Lady Astor, whose children had grown up with the King and Queen. We dropped several words to Mrs. Roosevelt. The fact that our own First Lady, exalted abroad, was published by us gave prestige to our magazine in English eyes.

All this time the suggestion, I suppose, was being discussed quietly behind the scenes—by all those officials who really make palace decisions—but any matter involving royalty moves slowly as a TV replay. Finally, we were told that the royal family had agreed to break precedent. They would allow us to gather material for our story, *The Education of a Princess.*

Permission was hedged with limitations. We were to accept an author chosen by the palace—Dermot Morrah. An editorial writer for the *Times* of London, also official ghost writer of King George's speeches, he was known to "help" other members of the royal family draft their radio talks. (He has recently written the "official" biography of Prince Charles.) The palace, it was stipulated, must see and approve the final manuscript. Knowing that an official biographer would tend to be more awestruck than human, but hoping to persuade him to put in as much veracious detail as possible, we agreed. We invited Dermot Morrah to fly to Hopewell for a weekend conference.

A handsome man, rather formal, erudite—a fellow of All Souls—

he possessed a delightful sense of humor. He deeply respected the monarchy, the Roman Catholic Church, and good wine, though not necessarily in that order. In hours of delightful, increasingly friendly talk, mellowed by some fairly good wine, we filled him to the brim, we hoped, with suggestions on how to give a human portrayal without constant genuflection. But weeks went by and Dermot did not seem to be making progress. Several times he wrote that everyone he approached—the Queen, Grandmother Queen Mary, teachers and aides—all said, "But you must see Crawfie. She is the one who has lived with these little girls, who brought them up. She will know all that."

Crawfie was Marion Crawford, long-time governess to the little princesses. She had come to them at the request of their mother, then Duchess of York, while Elizabeth and Margaret were small. When their father became King, she shared their adjustment in moving to the palace. After teaching them for over a dozen years, she seemed to know almost more about them than the Queen herself. Certainly she had more time to give to the telling. But Crawfie was proving strangely elusive. She was hard to see. She wouldn't make appointments. She couldn't be pinned down.

The situation had reached an impasse when we received, at Hopewell, a long-distance call from England. Our friend Dorothy Black spoke: "Bruce, is this a private wire? Can anyone overhear us? I have just got on to something interesting."

Through a source "close to palace circles," Dorothy had learned that Crawfie was extremely vexed. Recently retired, (her fledglings having outgrown her care), she had been given a modest "Grace and Favor" cottage on the grounds of Kensington Palace, and a pension even more modest. Now she did not see why she should give her story away to someone else, who would be paid handsomely for writing it, when it was *her* story.

"Dorothy," I said, "do you think she would do it herself?"

"I think she might," replied Dorothy.

"We will fly right over."

Crawfie had married in middle years, after retirement. Her husband, Major George Buthlay, a minor executive in a large bank, did not feel that Crawfie, considering her service in forming England's future Queen, had been generously treated financially. His resentment fostered hers.

When we met Crawfie in the low-ceilinged sitting room of her small, charming, shabby, eighteenth-century cottage within earshot of Wren's historic Kensington Palace, we found her a rather pretty Scotswoman in her early forties. She was willing to tell her story and she would tell it with love and with loyalty to the royal family. But, living barely above penury, she did not see why she should not profit by it, if the story was to be told at all. Persuaded by her husband, she hoped to sell it for a good, round sum. Not only had her salary and pension been small, but—and this had hurt her—her wedding presents had seemed inadequate rather than generous. A few plates and platters, a picture, nothing rich and rare. She adored her two charges. Now that the girls were grown, after years of devoted companionship, she felt pushed aside, forgotten. However, her awe of the royal family almost paralyzed her. Even in her own sanctuary, close as it was to Kensington Palace, she would hardly speak these words above a whisper.

It soon became apparent that Crawfie had no skill with the pen. Writing, she became formal, stilted, sparse, with the inadequate grammar of one who could firmly correct "Between you and me" to read "Between you and I." But she could talk. Reminiscence and anecdote in rich detail gushed from her lips.

It was agreed that Crawfie would tell her story to a stenotypist, with Dorothy Black in the room asking questions, drawing her out. "Tell about your first meeting. What did she wear? What did she say?" Then Dorothy would shape the material, putting it in time sequence, deleting repetitions and irrelevancies, keeping Crawfie's own words—except ungrammatical ones—probing memory for forgotten bits.

Crawfie feared to work with an English typist—terrified lest rumors would fly, her secret would leak, and the palace would pounce. Hurrying home, we engaged an American stenotypist recommended for discretion in recording wartime secret conferences. A day later she flew to England. Dorothy Black set her up in a quiet Hyde Park hotel. Sometimes there, sometimes even in Crawfie's "Grace and

Favor" cottage—but rarely lest palace neighbors should notice unusual activity—Crawfie told all her story. The stenotypist took it down
verbatim. Dorothy, an experienced writer, nightly shaped it up. After
a few weeks, when the work was well under way, Beatrice and I flew
again to London, settled in at the Dorchester, right around the corner
from Dorothy's club, read the story up to date and from then on suggested and revised till it was finished.

As we approved it, bit by bit, we airmailed it home. Influenced by
Crawfie's fears, we weren't sure but that the royal family might stop
the story once and for all by intimidating Crawfie, or, exercising some
royal prerogative we knew not of, have the secret manuscript seized
and banned. At last the story was done. We felt sure it was good.
Airmailing the final chapter, we ordered up a bottle of champagne for
the four of us—maybe it was two bottles.

We felt certain the royal family would frown on Crawfie's domestic
tale of life in the palace. They had only agreed to a much less informal piece.

It was all innocent enough, from our point of view. Even the King's
enjoyment of dancing with youngish Crawfie, the fact that the servants
in the royal household were expected to fatten on prestige rather
than high wages, the excitement of the underprivileged little princesses
at their first ride in the Underground, the King's reaction to his brother
David's abdication for Wallis Simpson, seemed well within the bounds,
we felt. Actually, so great was her awe and so loyal her nature,
Crawfie told nothing disparaging except things which had been
printed in the papers—that servants had struck for higher wages, that
their rooms in the palace basement were little over five feet high, that
a rat catcher made regular rounds, since mice were rampant. Only
one passage, we were told later, left hurt feelings. Queen Mary felt
the girls' mother, Queen Elizabeth, was not sufficiently attentive to
their education, and occasionally that formidable old lady interfered
behind the scenes to ensure a higher intellectual content in their teaching.

But such a story had never before been written from inside the
palace! Crawfie would probably be ostracized, we realized, banned
from the royal presence. She would certainly lose her "Grace and

Favor" cottage and possibly her all-important pension, around £300 a year.

Wanting to protect Crawfie from any dire consequences of her rebellion, at least financially, we investigated English income-tax laws, and found that if we bought only the customary North American first serial rights to Crawfie's manuscript she would have to pay nineteen shillings income tax out of each twenty-shilling pound. But if the *Journal* bought the story outright, an unusual procedure, she wouldn't have to pay a shilling. No tax at all. Not even a halfpenny. Because it was her life story—a capital asset—it would be considered capital gains, on which the English levied no tax, so the tax lawyers (with the charming English names of Vertue and Churcher) advised us. We proposed to Crawfie that the *Journal* buy world rights, paying $80,000. If she'd sold just the American rights to the story for $1,600,000 on a straight royalty basis (an unlikely offer in those days), she would have cleared approximately $80,000 after taxes. Crawfie was delighted with such a fortune. In her modest thinking, it made her independent for life. Even her banker husband, George, was satisfied. She soon bought a house of her own, well distant from the palace, in Scotland, where money goes far.

With the manuscript safely bought, and printing started, we had a difficult task. We must let the royal family know what we had been doing. Lady Astor was given the unwelcome task of acting as our emissary. At her Kent summer house by the sea we lunched on a hot August day, gave her a copy of Crawfie's story. Someone must tell the royal family. Would it be she? She turned almost white, was, surprisingly for her, speechless for a moment, but rallied.

"I'll give it to David Bowes-Lyon, the Queen's brother, and let him tell her." And after she had read the manuscript—"It's a charmin' story—but they'll never forgive Crawfie—never!"

We told Lady Astor that after the royal family had read the manuscript, we would, of course, correct any errors of fact. We wanted the story to be accurate.

Royalty are as curious as anyone else. There was no delay in the reading. Within a few days, thirteen minor changes were suggested by the Queen. We altered mistakes such as the name of a long-past

French teacher, but did not delete, as was requested, passages about the servants' strike, since this was a matter of record.

Because Dermot Morrah had been so generous in recognizing that Crawfie could tell a realer story than he, so amiable in not insisting on his "rights" in the matter, we asked him to do a supplementary piece on the history and significance of the monarchy. He became a valued contributor and a warm friend.

Some of our editors at home had thought *Journal* readers too democratic to be interested in little princesses, and were not sanguine about the story's reception on the newsstands. But we felt that a fairy-tale quality still surrounded young royalty, especially delightful little girls like these, sensibly brought up with gaiety and love.

And, when we published the first installment in January, 1950, newsstands sold out to the last copy. Learning that princesses had a playhouse, loved their Corgis, quarreled, resisted lessons, romped with their parents—were, in fact, like little girls everywhere—seemed to be peeping into an unknown, magic world. Thousands of women subscribed to the magazine to make certain they wouldn't miss the next chapter. Vandals, who couldn't get a *Journal* any other way, razorbladed *Little Princesses* sections out of reserved drugstore copies to the great indignation of the ultimate purchasers. Interest never let up through all eight installments. We held the increased circulation after the series ended; our new readers had found other things in the magazine they liked.

The fact that we had purchased Crawfie's manuscript outright benefited the *Journal,* too. For when I finally let an English editor read the story one evening in our New York apartment, just before our publication, he tried to keep his expression impassive, but the light in his eye flashed "Buy!" He could buy, we said, English rights for $90,000. He accepted instantly—and wisely—for when it was published in England, his magazine's circulation soared 500,000. Thus the *Journal* got the story almost free—we had to pay taxes, of course, on our sales. A question was raised in Commons about why an American magazine could get a story an English magazine couldn't—but we weren't called on to give the answer.

During serialization of *The Little Princesses,* we received news—

from friends in England who were "close to the palace" or knew others who were—of the royal family's reaction. Shocked and angered at first by Crawfie's rebellion, they began to realize, from personal friends, from information officials, and from emissaries of many kinds, how favorable a climate of opinion the story was creating. Throughout the simple narrative shone qualities of family love, of devotion to duty, and high standards of conduct which no fulsome, official, awestruck account could have conveyed. By revealing the wrinkles as well as the glossy surfaces, the informality as well as the tiaras, the story gained a sense of truth, and inevitably created admiration not only for the King and Queen, but also for England and its customs. The result was a friendlier understanding in America of modern England's constitutional monarchy. Millions, having known her as a little girl, already had a sympathetic attitude toward England's present Queen when she ascended the throne.

The royal family did not forgive Crawfie but they forgave us. To show that they were not angry, but were actually appreciative of what the story had accomplished, we were invited to tea at St. James's Palace on our next trip to London. It was there we met Peter Townsend, the King's equerry. For almost an hour I found myself in absorbed conversation with this dark, slender, sensitive flyer, for whose Battle of Britain heroism I had immeasurable admiration. Beatrice, as we departed, echoed my thought, "What a charming person!" Princess Margaret fell in love with him, as Desdemona with Othello, "for the dangers" he had passed. Often "this only is the witchcraft" necessary.

A few years later, at a big gala in one of the handsome state rooms in London's Lancaster House, the royal party entered. On such occasions certain persons well-known to royalty are spotted at conspicuous places so the eminent personages can easily stop and warmly greet old acquaintances. Our friend K. Elliot, soon to be Baroness Elliot of Harwood, was asked to stand at the right of the wide entrance door in the second drawing room. "Come on! come on!" she said with her sense of an occasion, of life as a spectacle. "Stand here with me and you'll talk to them all."

With Mrs. Blackmar and golden retriever Yankee, the Goulds enjoyed their Martha's Vineyard terrace view: no works of man, only trees, rocks, sea and sky.

While Bruce solemnly promised Beatrice their first child would be a redhead, he hadn't guaranteed redheaded grandchildren—five of them.

Collaboration was not a marble cake, Bruce and Beatrice felt,
each person's part sharply traced. To each other they rarely
credited whom with what. So when they quarreled it was invariably
over something trivial—ending in a laugh.   JOHN ENGSTEAD

Each in the royal party halted and chatted. Beatrice made her American bob to the young Queen, entering almost shyly, slightly tense, her tiaraed head a little bent. The Queen Mother, magnificently poised, all in white, with her radiant, sharing smile, swept up like a galleon in full sail.

Princess Margaret seemed a distrait satellite of the royal entourage. Two days before she had broken finally with Townsend. Her dark eyes burned with that "Saxon sadness" which made the young Prince of Wales so appealing until, in later years, he began to look like an aged John D. Rockefeller. Margaret's gaze swam stonily over that glittering assemblage as if she were searching only for that special one of those matchless few to whom England owed so much.

During many visits, our love for England grew as we renewed old friendships and formed new ones. Even though we were working hard, reading manuscripts, seeing writers and agents, we gained by being apart from two busy offices, with leisure to talk, to go to theatres, to weekend. Somehow, the English pace seemed rewardingly unhurried. And learning a different society well gives perspective to views of one's own country.

After the war, a friend took us to meet Attlee at 10 Downing Street, the eighteenth-century house from which England once ruled the world, slightly shaky from wartime bombing in those still stringent years. As we climbed the narrow old stairs, Attlee, diffident, friendly, showed us the framed photographs of his predecessors, lined in order up the stair wall. Only Churchill was out of his own time sequence. His portrait, on the landing, commanded attention each step up from the hall below. Modest Attlee was paying his silent tribute to a political opponent whose crack that Attlee "has a lot to be modest about" disturbed Attlee, apparently, not at all.

In Scotland we visited the Elliots, who had become warm friends there and here, where K spent several sessions in the UN, representing her country. Walter, former Cabinet member, M.P., was famous as a wit and according to Nancy Astor and Rebecca West was the best conversationalist in England.

Harold Nicolson in his amusing diaries disparages American talk: "They are so slow in conversation it's like being held up by a horse dray in a taxi."

Americans, he says, are so concerned with offering fresh tea, fresh hospitality they never listen to what one says. The English do, and reply in a flash. Good talk in leisure seems more appreciated there than in our brisk society. Harold Macmillan had some particularly memorable dining-out stories.

The Labour Party, he said, always wanted to claim the best of everything—or, as he called it, have it both ways. In a radio campaign speech he had wished to say, he claimed, but had been sternly dissuaded: "The Labour party says the atom bomb will render your husbands impotent and your children imbecile. That is just another example of the Labour party wanting to have it both ways!"

Another story concerned the brother, a prominent clubman, of Sir Stafford Cripps, whose daughter was marrying an African. After the wedding, the brother hurried back to his club, appropriately called White's, mopped his brow and ordered a stiff drink. A sympathetic friend remarked: "Rather an ordeal, eh?" Cripps' brother: "Well I *was* a little unprepared when they asked me at the door, 'Which side of the church? Bride or groom?' "

K Elliot, elevated to the peerage after Walter's death, was one of the first four women, Lady Reading another, to go into the House of Lords, melting, we were told, by her friendly common sense some of the peers' tradition-bound resistance to this female invasion. Beatrice asked her, early, how it went.

"I feel," she replied, "like a very new girl at a rather elderly boarding school."

Daisy, living in a handsome Gothic country house, elaborately Gothic in furnishing, once owned by Beau Nash, entertained us with her always rather unexpected, naughty wit.

Faithful to marriage in her fashion as to those few lasting friends she had chosen, Daisy was quietly loyal to her dashing Reggie, now fatally ill. Though their intimacies had long been separate, Daisy gave up travel, most parties, played endless games of chess, read beside his wheelchair, during those final months he bore with unassailable good manners, never paining others with his pain.

After his death, Daisy made her last home in the Faubourg St. Germain of her ancestors, redoing a distinguished French town house, but filling it for piquancy with fine old English furniture. Enormously rich, she resumed her role as *femme fatale,* surrounded by an adulatory circle, a few celebrities like Duff and Diana Cooper, Beaverbrook, Maugham, fashion editors, and many of those whom *Vogue* calls "the beautiful people."

But, for the most part, Daisy had lost faith in happiness derived from deep personal relationships. Still sighing that she had never known "true love," she had sought for her daughters marriages arranged as hers had been "within their class," without those "generous feelings" which, as Balzac says, "are so fruitful."

She died in 1963 after a few years of bad times. I read again a letter she had written me from London in the dangerous days of 1940:

You are a wonderful friend, and all you are doing for me and mine show me that our affection for each other has always been a real and deep-rooted thing; living on, quite steadily, regardless of events, distances and the usual *contracts.* . . .

Thanks to you I carry a little gold bag of sugar with me when I go out— and this I use parsimoniously in my coffee. Merci, Dear Bruce. I think of you daily and happily, (and it's a great help.)

Give my love to your dear ones. . . .

Your
D.

She was sending me a copy of her will, just in case. Happily, no bomb struck.

Our friend Nancy's later years, too, were saddened by Waldorf's insistence that she give up her seat in the House of Commons she loved, never admitting that her tongue, always a rebel, had grown more untrammeled with the years—and that injudicious tirades on such matters as temperance, the Catholic Church, or any but her own Christian Science one, aroused much hostility. Some occasionally laid her open to response in kind. Nancy sorrowed over Waldorf's death, even more since it necessitated giving up beloved Cliveden, where she had shone so brilliantly. It is now a National Trust—a few rooms reserved for future Lord Astors. Nancy Astor will be remembered by those who loved her for her humor, her verve, and her generous friendship—even, by the unregenerate, for that too tart, amusing tongue.

On these many visits to England, finding stories like Margery Sharp's *Cluny Brown,* Mary Stewart's *Nine Coaches Waiting,* visiting Enid Bagnold at Rottingdean, arranging for Lord Halifax's gentlemanly memoirs and futilely trying to get Nancy Astor to write hers, sipping wine with Dermot Morrah as we angled for Dowager Queen Elizabeth's reminiscences—on these visits we gained an ever greater admiration for the staunch standards, the "good behaviour" in Nicolson's phrase with which most of these overseas friends accepted so uncomplainingly a stringent economy, a lessened British glory.

Those who write obscurely have great luck; they will have commentators.
The others will have only readers, and this, it seems, is worthy of scorn.
—FROM THE NOTEBOOK OF ALBERT CAMUS

20

Why Editing Is Fun

No editor has ever found a secret way to create writers any more than baseball managers can make a whole baseball team hit like Mickey Mantle and field like Willie Mays. Some book editors, notably Maxwell Perkins, and Harold Ross among magazine wizards, possessed a personal magic inspiring writers to do their best.

Perkins spoon-fed Hemingway, Fitzgerald, and Thomas Wolfe. Ross chose good writers and rode herd. Lorimer belabored George Randolph Chester of *Get-Rich-Quick Wallingford* fame, refusing an advance to finance a trip abroad, suggesting alternatively that Chester lock himself in a hotel room, write a story a day until just time to catch the steamer. The stick worked as effectively as carrots. Five stories and $7,500 later, Chester walked up the gangplank a free man. Many editors dislike making advances on the theory writers first spend the money, thereafter are rebelliously working to pay alimony to a woman no longer loved. Ross solved this ticklish problem by putting his best writers on a guaranteed drawing-account basis, as did DeWitt Wallace.

249

Authors frequently do not respond kindly to guidance. They prefer to learn the hard way, by writing, writing, writing—not a bad method. But to pursue that track you must possess old-fashioned stick-to-it-iveness—and learn as you go. And perhaps you must be a "born writer" to begin with.

Pliant or obdurate, writers are seldom grateful. To most, editors seem merely hard-handed parents forcing brilliant children to their will.

Some time after we took over the *Journal* we began to feel we must abandon typical women's magazine serials. The decision to raise the whole level of *Journal* fiction was dictated somewhat by our respect for our readers' taste; somewhat, perhaps, by sheer necessity. Radio's newly devised "soap operas," akin to much previous women's magazine fiction, had the added advantage of floating painlessly into the busy housewife's ear, as it were, on the Tide. The lower third, intellectually, of our potential readers, the ones who would gobble up such machine-made stories in magazines, now had a handier version that needn't even be read.

Upgrading our fiction wasn't easy. Agents wouldn't believe the *Journal* was turning its back on Kathleen Norris and Temple Bailey, current queens of the kitchen-sink school of escape literature. We pretty much had to do our own hunting, and improvement was necessarily gradual for there are not many Thackerays, Dickenses, Jane Austens, or Trollopes in any generation.

It was not until the later years of our editing that we found ourselves printing fiction by Rebecca West, Rumer Godden, John Marquand, Isak Dinesen, as well as the wry Hortense Calisher, the grainy Elizabeth Enright, to mention a few. James Michener's original South Pacific stories we discovered gathering dust on his book publisher's shelf (during wartime paper restrictions) and rushed them into print, turning over to the *Post* one or two which, we thought, suited better a man's magazine.

Not that our change for the better was noticed at first. *Publishers' Weekly* superciliously called typical "woman's magazine fiction" a novel we had just turned down. The editor failed to note that the novel he was then enthusiastically praising the *Journal* had just published. We thought it *was* woman's magazine fiction—at least for our magazine. I chided him by letter. He winced—but only for a moment. His needle dropped right back into the groove.

Rumer Godden's publisher was as skeptical as her agent that we could successfully print her slightly exotic novels.

"How," he inquired of me after a couple of strong Coffee House cocktails, "do you expect to interest millions of readers in Rumer Godden in your damned *Journal* when I can't even sell twenty thousand copies of her books?" But after our publication of Godden's *Fugue in Time* Sam Goldwyn made it into a successful movie as *Take Three Tenses.* We went on to print several novels and several of her delightful children's stories—*The Fairy Doll* was enjoyed by millions.

Even though Isak Dinesen was cool, her intricate prose occasionally difficult to follow, we published more of her magical tales than any other magazine, agreeing with Hemingway that Dinesen should have received a Nobel Prize, too.

Rebecca West couldn't believe, until we snatched it from her grasp, that we'd print *The Fountain Overflows* when she came over in the summer with the manuscript smoking in her hand, late for the book publisher's fall list. Canceling engagements, we read the novel all one rainy Sunday till Beatrice, raining tears, came into my study saying, "I want to be here with you while I finish this." We stopped presses to get it in the issue already printing. A short story of Rebecca's is the only manuscript I remember coming into the office whose comments from associate editors were simply "Yes! Yes!! Yes!!! Yes!!!!" On even the best manuscripts there was usually at least one dissent, one "If only—"

Skilled Hugh MacNair Kahler headed our fiction department, shepherding writers with a hard-earned sympathy gained as a suffering though successful author for the *Post*. A masterly letter writer, he often guided, by his gentlemanly awareness of the recipient's possible sore spots, my too brusque pen. Literary and scriptural allusions tripped off his tongue. In youth he had been required by a minister father practically to memorize the Bible from Aziel to Zachariah. So when hard pressed by some Fundamentalist shocked into Good Book denunciation of us for an editorial irreverence, I would pass the missive to Hugh with the scribbled words: "Bible him!"

At first we, perforce, did our own cutting—a difficult task, for as Anatole France points out cutting is itself a form of writing. Then Laura Lou Brookman walked into our office one day to become our invaluable editorial cutting edge and, finally, managing editor—a position she held until retirement. Delighted with Laura Lou's cutting, one grateful author offered—maybe threatened is the precise word— to marry her. But she edited him out of her life as briskly as she eliminated his excess verbiage—perhaps he spoke, as he wrote, too fulsomely. So brilliant was her cutting even dour Marquand grunted occasional thanks, though she had cut a few thousands of his cherished "he saids." Alec Waugh cheerily admitted that Laura's slashing a path with her editorial machete through his jungle of words helped make *Island in the Sun* a best seller.

Authors, being touchy, difficult creatures, were not always co-operative with our efforts to improve *Journal* fiction. Edna Ferber's yet-to-be-written works were discussed each time they became a gleam in her eye. Would we contract to buy her new novel, sight un-seen, with a purchase price set at say $75,000, she always wanted to know? We would not, we informed Miss Ferber, promise to publish any story or novel which we had not read. She thought this unflatter-ing to her high reputation; she was accustomed not to put finger to typewriter until she had a deal. We pointed out that authors some-times wrote poor books as well as good ones, a fact not usually ad-mitted by authors, even after the critics and the public have verified the fact. We wanted only the author's best, we told her, but we would pay, on acceptance, higher rates for the right to reject. We wouldn't, however, buy anything unless we liked it, just because it was by a "big name." Editorially, this is high-wire walking without a net.

She easily found editors more respectful. But, when she decided to write *Giant*, Miss Ferber, fearing it as controversial, warily approached us again. She suspected the *Journal* had courage for controversy. So, more tractable in this instance, she reluctantly agreed to submit *Giant* to us without a contract. After each submitted installment, she asked if we would not now, however, make up our finicking minds. Steadily declining to commit ourselves, we encouraged her to finish the book. Its controversial aspect—a good word for Mexican wetbacks in Texas as well as a rather bad word for some barbaric Texan medievalists—delighted rather than alarmed us. When the final page was in we bought it, though the ending was lamentably weak. *Giant* made a smashing movie after it had done very well in the *Journal*.

Miss Ferber, though basically of good heart, possessed an incendiary disposition. In final negotiations about *Giant* she furiously addressed a letter to me, "Listen Bub," pointing out she had known really great editors when I was just a "Bub."

The salutation rankled—pinpricks sometimes irritate more than deep wounds.

"Miss Ferber," I told Hugh Kahler, solemnly, "now gets about the highest word rate of any author in the world. Let's raise it even higher, putting a valuation of $5,000 on each word of Listen Bub, and pay her $10,000 less for *Giant* than we had in mind." Somehow this childish riposte—the $10,000 fine would not reduce Ferber to an Apple Annie—poulticed my bruised *amour-propre,* showing, I fear, I am mean-spirited at base. Also I knew that Edna Ferber would have been delighted, had she known, that she now had, indisputably, the highest rate per word of any author.

Margaret Mitchell never submitted *Gone With the Wind* to any magazine. The novel has been, I believe, among the ten best sellers of all time. On the general theory that when an author has written *Uncle Tom's Cabin, Ben Hur, Quo Vadis?*, he has frequently given his all, we were laggard in sending Stuart Rose, Kahler's mannerly and deadly handsome predecessor, to Atlanta to try to get her next book for the *Journal*. Miss Mitchell was as fond of horses as Stu, a gentleman rider, so, when we did send him, they got along famously over mint juleps as long as her next book was not mentioned. After several pleasant talks, Rose, nerving himself, took the fence.

"Might the *Journal*," he asked hopefully, "have first refusal of Miss Mitchell's next book?"

"What will Mr. Gould pay?" she promptly asked.

"Top money. He just wants your next novel."

Miss Mitchell quietly raised the bar, "Will Mr. Gould agree to buy anything I write, sight unseen?"

This high bar Stu knew he must refuse.

"Mr. Gould wouldn't buy a manuscript from Jesus Christ before he'd read it," Stu told her sadly. "Maybe not then."

Every magazine editor in the country, and some from abroad, had come begging for her next novel, Miss Mitchell told him, promising her millions of dollars. They'd made her life miserable with their importunities.

"And every editor has been willing to buy my next book sight unseen—if only I'll just sign a contract," she continued. "What's the matter with Mr. Gould?"

"I'm sorry, Miss Mitchell," Stu said sadly. "That's the way it is. It makes it hard for me. We don't believe just a name is enough. We have to like the particular story."

Margaret Mitchell probed. She'd like to be published in the *Journal*. She'd read it for years. But with everybody else begging for her new book—was Mr. Rose sure?

Mr. Rose was sure.

"Tell Mr. Gould, then," Margaret Mitchell said, "he's the only editor who has had the audacity to refuse to buy my next novel sight unseen. I may never write it. But if I do," she continued, smiling, "tell him the *Journal* will have first look."

An errant taxi driver struck Miss Mitchell down in the streets of Atlanta and killed her before she ever wrote that novel—if, indeed, she ever intended to do so. Could Margaret Mitchell have topped *Gone With the Wind*—a story people will be reading happily as long as there's memory of our Civil War?

Though not sure we'd accomplish anything, we decided to try to help beginning writers. Placing a talented young woman on our staff, Anne Einselen, in charge, we established what we called the discovery department—to unearth and aid newcomers.

Originally hired as a secretary, Miss Einselen had astute editorial brains and a tireless capacity for work. Moreover, unmarried, she had a mothering instinct, was unselfish without stint in helping infant talent.

Daily she scoured what magazine editors disrespectfully call "the slush pile"—manuscripts from unknown, unpublished, would-be writers.

The discovery department, in 1945, handled 150 unsolicited manuscripts weekly, by 1962, 500 manuscripts weekly, not counting poetry, which is as the sands of the sea, limitless. Miss Einselen, then an associate editor, had four assistants, each day, like herself, hoping for a miracle.

The miracle lies in suddenly finding one 8½ × 11 page, out of thousands of 8½ × 11 pages, which is pay dirt. There is no forewarning—gold is where you find it.

How do you find it?

Mark Twain said the difference between the right word and the almost right word is the difference between lightning and the lightning bug. Occasionally, a reader feels struck by lightning.

Many good editors have been good writers; in the case of Franklin, Willa Cather, Dreiser, better than good. They knew the agonies and joys. When the editor finds a manuscript of promise he must ask these two questions.

1. Is this someone who can use encouragement, hard-to-take suggestions, tough, realistic criticism?

2. Is this writer worth time and creative thought?

If "Yes" to both questions, something of value can come to both out of this communication. The beginning writer finds somebody cares. The editor is rewarded by new and better stories.

Most real editors enjoy buying an unknown's very first submitted story. As an aspiring author I had it happen to me. It happened to Beatrice. Some aspirants, alas, never again sell after their "first."

For it is an art to write a story. The money one earns seldom repays the hard labor involved. Writing doesn't look hard to the outsider. All of us have heard someone say, "Why, I could write a better story than that." They should try. They may succeed. Men and women have become writers under that stimulus—as did Rider Haggard, taking up a bet, with his *King Solomon's Mines*—but it's not the most effective prod. To write for money is certainly the best spur—it kept Chekhov, Balzac, and Shakespeare going. If you're writing just to become famous, it is unlikely you'll ever be—though there are exceptions to this rule, too.

What is a story? Our discovery department was sometimes challenged by aspirants of talent who failed to understand the objection "You haven't written a story." The beginner had created a fine mood, described something very well—but he had left the situation as he found it. Life, the movement of life, was missing.

Three words describe what most editors have in mind when they use the word "story": characters in conflict. Life, out of which fiction is born, is struggle from conception to the grave. A story must develop. Its end must find the imagined people in a situation different from their situation at its beginning.

Along the way we catch glimpses of character in moments of gaiety or misery, love or hate, courage or self-sacrifice, but, to hold the reader's interest there should be conflict—some obstacle to overcome. From Homer, Shakespeare, Tolstoi, right down to Hemingway and Ian Fleming, suspense is the magic ingredient.

We bought 110 stories, from 85 authors, about 50 of whom were men, through our discovery department. More than half of those 110 stories came from unknowns.

Many beginners believe having an agent provides an open sesame and can get the author a better price for his story. Not necessarily so. Wherever editors are genuinely interested in first stories—not all editors are—no difference in price exists.

When a writer is established an agent is invaluable. Prices get involved, then. Subsidiary rights become valuable. An agent saves the author time; he can negotiate unemotionally; turndowns don't destroy his confidence as they do the morale of some authors. The agent widens the market.

It might be helpful to explain why relatively few agents take on unpublished clients. Agents are brokers—they live by fees. They have to be sure of a reasonable profit if they are to stay in business. A beginner, even one in whom they may see a bright future, is a risk. Hard economics insist that they wait for a first appearance in print.

A few agents actively solicit manuscripts from unpublished authors.

They offer to read and criticize for a fee—usually a small fee, it is true. There is really nothing wrong with this kind of solicitation, unless it drifts into encouragement of hopes that never will be realized and thus becomes exploitation. Amateurs are hungry for praise, for direction. Hope is long-lived. So, casual counselors, who work with writing groups for a seasonal fee, or agents who advertise their reading services, usually flourish. There are always willing victims.

One such victim wrote asking help after years of paying a few dollars a week out of her nighttime cleaning wage in hope of getting her book of experiences ready for publication. The few pages she sent the *Journal* for an opinion were almost illiterate. Such persons should not be exploited. But no law can protect them. They simply lack common sense and the will to face reality.

Agents are not necessarily good literary advisers. They have one aim—to sell manuscripts. They're salesmen, not editors, though I've known one or two agents whose advice was worth any the best editor could give. But such talent is rare.

That basic requirements for storytelling do not change can be seen by reading the advice of Horace:*

> The ideal book is that which at the same time instructs and entertains; "he who has mingled the useful with the pleasant wins every vote." . . . Avoid words that are new, obsolete, or "sesquipedelian"—foot-and-a-half words. Be as brief as clarity allows. Go straight to the heart of the matter. . . . In writing poetry do not imagine that emotion is everything. . . . art is not feeling; it is form. . . . To achieve form . . . erase almost as much as you write; delete every "purple patch" . . . submit your work to a competent critic, and beware of your friends. . . . Study life and philosophy, for without observation and understanding even a perfect style is an empty thing. *Sapere aude:* dare to know.

Frequently asked to advise young writers, we quoted Horace, also said:

Art will find its way, make its own pattern, break most rules. It rarely asks advice and probably should ignore it. But if your desire is to be a tiny Trollope, minor Marquand, diminutive du Maurier, entertaining with plot and suspense, amusing by shrewd comment

* Translated and condensed by Will Durant in his book *Caesar and Christ* (Simon & Schuster, 1944).

on manners and customs, perhaps adding to human understanding by sympathetic or satiric portrayal of your town's mayor, preacher, or president of the woman's club, here are some suggestions which may prove helpful:

Don't be afraid of imitating. Great painters have learned by copying great paintings. Yeats owned his debt to Mallarmé through translations by Arthur Symons. Edith Wharton owed much to Henry James. Yet the originality of each came clear in time. Try copying. The material, we hope, will be your own and you will learn to handle your material by seeing how acknowledged artists handled theirs.

Write. Write a great deal. Don't toy endlessly with one story or idea. Balzac wrote bushels of manuscripts before one was accepted, living on centimes in an attic peopled by mice and the personages of his gigantic imagination. Writers learn to write by writing. Vitality of production is, in itself, a hopeful sign.

One excellent exercise for a would-be writer is to have a page of great literature read aloud, then try to re-express it in his own words. Comparison of his work with a master's will teach him to appreciate economy, vigor, precision.

Beware of wide words like *beautiful, marvelous, ugly.* Maupassant was told by Flaubert to find the exact adjective which would distinguish a certain Rouen cabdriver from every other cabdriver in the rank. Give the color of your heroine's eyes, voice, or laughter when you introduce her. She then breathes in a human shell. Often one special quality, gesture, trick of body, returned to like a musical phrase, will evoke her personality more than the most elaborate catalogue of features and proportions.

Every sentence you put in your story must have a purpose.

If you read a tale you admire, set down the plot in one hundred words. Putting the original in the attic, write the same story in your own way. Upon rereading both, you will easily be able to tell whether yours is as good as the model. If it is not, perhaps study will show you why. The first thing a story must be, said Trollope, is readable.

There are writing classes in universities and colleges throughout the country, many with good instructors. Some are, or have been, successful writers and experienced editors. Beginners with any potential can often be taught craftsmanship in these classes. What cannot be passed from teacher to student is the special endowment—of perception, of insight into another's situation, of art and love in choice of words—those qualities that make a writer out of a craftsman. That is why so many people experienced in the literary world sadly say nobody can teach anybody how to write—one has to be born with talent, as Babe Ruth was born to hit home runs.

Submit your writing directly to an editor. No agent, no teacher, no critic, no friend-of-a-friend can really influence that editor.

Miss Einselen's first "first," not long after the discovery department was started, gathered a crescendo of enthusiasm from assisting editors.

"A treasure—almost every child remembers this kind of teacher!" "One of the stories I'll never forget."

Hopefully, her face like a child's, not sure whether she'd found a diamond or a glass bead, she brought the manuscript to us. The writer whose "first" had caused such excitement turned out to be not a beginner but a columnist from another national magazine who had chosen to submit her first fiction "cold." (Later, she confessed to fear of trying this new field.) Miss Einselen had no way of knowing that day, however, that what had been picked out from the slush would someday be reprinted all over the world, in anthologies, in textbooks; that it would generate sequels and a collection of them in book form; that it would become a highly successful movie, and a play. We only knew we wanted to print it at once—"The Terrible Miss Dove," by Frances Gray Patton. What if Miss Einselen hadn't read her slush pile that day?

Everyone agrees that the best fiction is not written, it's rewritten. When revisions involve only minor changes—pruning irrelevancies, clarifying motives, accentuating the climax—an editor can often demonstrate what is needed by merely marking a few pages of manuscript. This takes patience and time, but is one of the things editors are for. But sometimes a story was so buried in bad telling we had to buy it and with the author's permission revise it from beginning to end, hoping that the beginner would learn more by this example than by paragraphs of advice.

This was the case with an imaginative, amusing, twice-too-long story whose time sequences and scenes were so confused by flashbacks and anticipations that the spell of the story was broken over and over again. The author seemed literally incapable of straightforward narration. But she had a true instinct for portraiture, and a wonderful sense of humor, qualities often deflecting a writer into diverting sidepaths.

Using only the author's phrases, in different sequence, dropping whole characters and expendable events, simplifying to gain focus (and working through part of a summer holiday) Miss Einselen carved out a story which received our final approval; but would the author be delighted or annoyed?

Some writers, usually beginners, would perish rather than change a word. They see all revision as lopping off arms and legs of a precious child, even though the editor may have sympathetically pointed out that what had been produced was a monstrous centipede rather than a well-articulated mammal standing on its own two feet. This writer, however, accepted our changes, with humor and gratitude—reward enough to the devoted, pencil-biting Miss Einselen. "Moon Walk" by Barbara Luther enchanted our readers. It was widely reprinted abroad. M-G-M made it into a movie, *A Ticklish Affair*.

And then there was what Anne Einselen, rejoicing in a young writer's joy—always spoke of as The Miracle.

As every beginner knows, or should know, he is required to follow certain basic rules for submitting manuscripts:

Double-spaced type on clean 8½ × 11 paper
Wide margins, both sides
No handwritten manuscripts
No blurry carbons
Numbered pages
Name and address on the title page
Return postage on enclosed addressed envelope
No multiple submissions (that is, submitting a manuscript to more than one editor or magazine at a time)
No advance letter

No telephone inquiry while the manuscript is being considered to
 see if it's liked
No request for detailed criticism

By respecting such good manners the author profits. Poor copy is
just as irritating to the editor as the pest who wants to talk about the
manuscript the pest has brought in by hand. Nothing in the publishing
code obliges editors to cope with either.

"But all rules are made to be broken," says Miss Einselen, recalling
her miracle. "We broke them many times, but never with better results
than on that summer day in 1950 when a letter came in attached
to a submitted manuscript."

Dear Editors [it said]:
 Segregation in the South poses many unique problems in the Negro
schools. The Negro teacher bears a responsibility to her students, un-
paralleled by that of any other, for though Negro children are typical of
children everywhere, they develop under greater handicaps and with less
outer aid.
 It is with these problems that the story I am submitting for publication
deals.
 SEE HOW THEY RUN does not seek to solve these problems, merely to
paint an honest picture of possible situations.
 Although I am a third-grade teacher in a Negro school, neither the
character nor the particular incidents have any basis in fact, within my
ken. I wish to point out, though, that they are actual possibilities.
 There are, it is true, many incidents of callousness, indifference, incompetence and negligence in the Negro system as there are in others. But
for every unworthy Negro teacher there are hundreds, who, consistently
overworked and underpaid, have through the years conscientiously sought
to fulfill their many obligations. With all their disadvantages, they do a
magnificent job.
 Please accept my story. It is my first submitted to any magazine. I must
confess that I don't know the first thing about preparing a manuscript,
and this was compiled in sweat and tears by the hunt-and-peck system,
but do read it anyway.
 I'm 26 years old and only now beginning to satisfy a lifelong ambition
to try to write. Isn't it wonderful how one can find time to do something
when the urge becomes strong enough? Need I say that I think the
Ladies' Home Journal is wonderful, when I'm entrusting you with my
first precious brain-child?

I shall be living in the mailbox till I hear from you.
Yours hopefully and sincerely,

MARY ELIZABETH VROMAN

The letter was handwritten. It was long. Attached was a snapshot of a pretty young Negro. She was smiling the same plea as the words she had written to some faraway editor whom she obviously thought receptive. Uusually, such letters made us cringe. They took unfair advantage, involving us, or trying to involve us, emotionally with the author before we had a chance to read his effort.

The manuscript's appearance was altogether unpromising—slippery, odd-sized, onionskin paper and single-spaced typing, hard on already burdened eyesight. It lived up to that description "sweat and tears by the hunt-and-peck system." Here was the offering of a rank amateur breaking every rule. No first reader would have been blamed for discarding it on sight.

But the letter's first word had squeezed an editorial conscience. (This was before the Supreme Court decision.) This young teacher was writing out some deep, terrifying experience of her own. Her story, with an unforgettable little boy, C. T.—that was all his name— was a document of courage and achievement written with poignancy never sentimental.

The story was printed by the *Journal* and reprinted many times. The movie made from it starred Dorothy Dandridge. There was a TV show as well.

"See How They Run" may have played its part in the events of this century as writings a hundred-odd years ago did before the Civil War. The short story won a Christopher Award. The young teacher was asked to write and to lecture and, hence, moved among people of all shades of skin and opinion. Her first impassioned plea might properly have been returned to her unread.

For Miss Einselen and for the author—a miracle!

> *The ideal book is that which at the same time instructs and entertains; "he who has mingled the useful with the pleasant wins every vote."*
>
> HORACE, *circa* 30 B.C.

21 ❧

You Must Work Your Passage

Editors, I suppose, will always brag. If your circulation is small, it is elite, discerning, avant garde. You illuminate new literary paths, beaming your intelligence upon them. You discover new forms, shatter outworn, hampering traditions. If your audience is large, you contend you inform millions, supplement high school and even college, in history, literature, political science, the arts. Both these stands, occasionally pompous, are often true. Publishing for the many or a few is almost necessarily educational. Occasionally, as education, it is corrupting—if it is false or exploitational.

While the *Journal* strove to entertain, we also wished to be practically useful. A Dr. Spock advised confused parents. Psychiatrists helped readers (many having no psychiatrists of their own) solve the relationship (or nonrelationship) of sex to their marriage problems.

We knew that our magazine must have range, the thoughtful as well as the frivolous, the lucid gem by Rebecca West or Isak Dinesen and Mr. and Mrs. North's latest lucid chiller; Edward Hopper and Al

263

Parker, Matisse near Coby Whitmore; fashion hard by Dorothy Thompson, who, square-built and handsome, herself interestedly followed fashion, as did those other two remarkable, creative intellects, Dinesen and West, all as steeped in feminine elegance as in other excellences which engaged their higher levels of attention.

Our advertising and circulation men were often puzzled. "Why don't you see that everything you publish is for everybody?" they asked.

We tried to tell them about the variety of human interest (perceivable in their own wives and daughters), the danger of the tried-and-true only, which can make radio and TV so monotonous.

Just as lawyers aren't lawyers only, but fishermen or power-tool craftsmen; as truck drivers can be hi-fi experts or Sunday painters, so women have their diverse enthusiasms, from needlepoint to poetry, from gardening to helping underprivileged children. Moreover, women, like most people, have a respect for what they might describe as the worthwhile—self-improvement or simply helping others.

Beatrice, believing no federal appropriation can ever replace human, neighborly effort to make a town better for children, for the old, the underprivileged, for the enjoyment of all its citizens, worked closely with Margaret Hickey when she headed a new department—Public Affairs. Widely experienced in volunteer work, her genius to be clear and cool in logic, warmly sympathetic about people, Margaret studied community projects throughout the country and reported on those which had a story to tell. A mother of three under five years, suddenly seriously ill, kept her family together with the aid of a well-run homemaker service. Unruly, unoccupied teen-agers were tamed by an imaginative youth center. These plans, successful in their towns, were then so carefully described they could be followed by other communities.

In "Political Pilgrim's Progress" the *Journal* told of young mothers drawn into local politics through concern over unsafe playgrounds, poor schools, dangerous streets, such activity often progressing toward a real involvement in the selection of good municipal and county candidates. We were able to explain to many women why simply voting in national and state elections is not enough, why grass-roots participation at the local level is important for all who would be good citizens.

A 25 percent increase in the women's vote occurred in the Presidential election of 1952. It is possible the *Journal*'s Political Pilgrims series helped bring this increase about. It certainly stimulated women to engage in politics actively in both parties—a movement that has had lasting effect.

A novel by an unknown, *Blackboard Jungle,* was submitted to the *Journal.* It shocked most of our editors. It shocked us, too, because we knew it was true.

A few weeks before, two able reporters, Barbara Benson and Glenn White, had returned with just such horrifying reports from a high school in Brooklyn. Young nonacademic boys were presumably being given vocational training there. But the school was referred to as a "dumping ground" by teachers as well as pupils. Attendance was sporadic, discipline almost nonexistent. Our editors were shocked by the cynicism of the boys, more shocked by the cynicism of the teachers. Here, the disciplinary problems, the nonreaders, marked time until they could escape at sixteen. The boys were cynical because they knew what they were learning was almost without value. Teachers were cynical because they felt themselves wardens rather than educators.

Blackboard Jungle's author, Evan Hunter, had taught in such a school in the Bronx. Fiction could tell what in factual report might have been too damaging to individuals, perhaps libelous. We hurried the novel, condensed, into the first issue we could catch. Some of *Blackboard Jungle* had to be left out for lack of space. Some had to be deleted to permit subscribers to receive the magazine legally through the mails.

The story was sensational because the conditions it described were sensational. It was unpleasant reading for gently bred women and decent men. Like *Uncle Tom's Cabin* it dramatized an evil—a condition many knew about, were talking about, but which hadn't yet been clearly perceived by the wide public.

Once *Blackboard Jungle* was published, school boards and parents began to face up to the problems it revealed. City newspapers printed accurate stories about "dumping ground" schools. Journalists factually verified what the book had fictionally revealed. Some reorganization of New York's educational system resulted. Even in its sensational movie version, some of *Blackboard Jungle's* essential truth was preserved. We were criticized for "sensationalism," too, but we felt that bad conditions would never be corrected without wide public knowledge and concern. As testimony to the book's basic validity the very title has passed into the language.

The *Journal* shared with its readers discussions on education with outspoken Whitney Griswold, then president of Yale; Sir Richard Livingstone, of Oxford; Robert Hutchins, roving *enfant terrible* of scholasticism; James Killian, M. I. T. president; Dr. Gallup; Clarence Faust, president of the Ford Foundation; and thoughtful articles by James Conant, Harold Dodds, many others.

"There sometimes seems a fundamental conflict between education and democracy," admitted Griswold. "Democracy says, 'Everybody is equal.' Education says, 'Some get 100, some get 60, and others flunk out.' It sorts the sheep from the goats. It says, 'You are qualified to go to college and you are not.' "

Poor reading skills, lowered standards, deterioration in the use of the English language, even by top college students, concerned these educators, as did the disruption of learning by lack of discipline, and they were not afraid to speak out.

"I can name three teachers not far from my home who have resigned in disgust from a public-school system because they were not able to discipline their classes," said Griswold. "They were insulted and even threatened with physical violence and when they tried to get support from the principal and superintendent for their discipline, they got none."

"To graduate pupils from high school without requiring effort and achievement I consider grossly unethical—evil," said John F. McNeill, principal of Erasmus Hall High School, Brooklyn.

Women, by and large, are truly concerned not only about education for their own children but about an optimum educational opportunity for all children, and women's magazines will continue to be one of the most valuable forums for discussing educational needs and urging action.

To amuse ourselves and our readers we even tried to revive an interest in manners, with only partial success—though clip sheets were avidly requested by hard-pressed high-school counselors, since today's rebellious young often consider the very word "manners" antediluvian.

"You can create a happy climate with good manners," said French poet, impeccably-mannered Louise de Vilmorin, echoing Emerson's "Manners are the happy ways of doing things."

But most of our panelists plumped for sheer kindness of heart as replacing "formal" manners, on the score that "manners" were only on the surface. "Just where they should be," Whistler had once retorted in a similar debate.

Supreme Court Justice Warren chatted with readers in our pages, as did Walter Elliot, Alfred Max and Chester Bowles, about how expansive, power-wielding Americans are regarded abroad. Governor Rockefeller, Billy Graham, and experts on juvenile delinquency and neglected children shared their views on these heartbreaking subjects. Public-affairs features gave variety and dimension to our magazine, attracted the more intelligent women, informed and interested many who were "average."

"Can This Marriage Be Saved?," suggested by quirkily original associate Glenn White, in each installment unfolded like a play. The injured wife voiced her accusations, the husband his; then the counselor asked questions, gave suggestions.

The marriages reported had actually been saved; the anonymity of the troubled pair was carefully preserved. Their verbatim words, skillfully compressed by Dorothy Cameron Disney, were drawn from the records of Dr. Paul Popenoe's American Institute of Family Relations. At the end of the woman's accusation her husband usually sounded like the heel she believed him to be, his least objectionable cruelty merely kicking his wife out of bed. As we heard the husband's story, our sympathies switched. If he had kicked his wife out of bed it had been for cause—why had he stopped there?

But then the marriage counselor spoke, summing up tirade and arraignment, pointing out gently that trouble-causing faults—jealousy, desire to dominate, or hypercritical attitudes—were found in each spouse. If one would try to improve, recognizing errors, the other might try also. In fact, both man and woman modified their faults. A marriage can be saved if one person, preferably both, *wish* to save it, Dr. Popenoe says. Without this desire, counseling is fruitless.

Sexual problems, of course, entered these accounts. In almost every instance, as conjugal criticism slackened, consideration grew and the sexual relationship improved. Couples whose struggles we portrayed had lived together, their marriage preserved with reasonable happiness, for some years.

I myself never read "Can This Marriage Be Saved?" without seeing, to a certain degree, some of my own most glaring faults and resolving mightily to correct them. Beatrice may have indirectly benefited— though I doubt my reform was complete or lasting enough to command her notice. But these human stories, drawn from the rewarding, unstereotyped material of life itself, helped many readers recognize their hitherto unadmitted failings—selfishness, stinginess, would-be superiority—helped them realize that, in marriage, to go halfway is not far enough. Maybe some relationships were improved.

"Tell Me Doctor," a two-column feature explaining a great deal about the intricate, marvelous, childbearing cycle, of which many women remain ignorant even while having children, ran for years. Our information was medically accurate, simply and clearly stated, never sensationalized in headline or makeup, primarily useful, written by a gynecologist of standing. The series, widely read, was helpful, as we learned from thousands of letters and comments.

Since doctors' humor can be grisly, and our first gynecologist fancied his light touch—what we, however, called his bedside lack of manners—Beatrice would never allow an article to go into the magazine, were she in Africa or the Crimea, until she had read and okayed every word.

Once, when she had been away, by mischance the article was not sent her. She returned, read the proof, stopped the presses.

"Fill the space with light verse or recipes," she said. "We cannot let this material seem unnecessarily anatomical, or exploitational of matters rarely discussed."

I had found nothing offensive—men and women are different.

But we were criticized by some for "Tell Me Doctor" 's clinical realism—specific and impersonal as a good physiology textbook.

One day a woman editor came to my office, half amused, quite angry. On the desk she dropped a piece of heavy white stationery bearing the letterhead of a manufacturer whose full-page ad appeared in the *Journal* each month.

I read: "Dear ——, How are your ovaries: Are you having any difficulties with your menstrual periods? . . .

The writer proved to be an irate *male,* head of his own firm, who objected to "Tell Me Doctor" 's exact wording and physiological detail being read by his wife in our theoretically proper pages. He threatened to stop advertising in the *Journal*. Our answer was:

Dear Sir:
Your wife is doubtless fortunate in having a family physician whom she can consult. Many young women have not that opportunity. It is for them and for the more accurate and complete information of all women that the column is printed.

It seems strange, in these days when *Human Sexual Response* makes the best-seller list, when Henry Miller, *Candy,* and *Fanny Hill* can be bought by pre-teenagers in almost any bookstore, that the *Journal* should have been criticized as sensational or pornographic for printing straight-forward, medically written articles on the physiology and psychology of being a woman, but this was so.

Some bright lad at *Playboy,* feeling that any mention of woman's generative processes was designed to titillate, apparently got prurient delight from this practical gynecological material. Our series brought a denunciation of the *Journal* as "Pious Pornographers" by *Playboy,* of whose piety there can be little doubt. Perhaps, being men, the Playboys were genuinely shocked.

Magazines fortunately do not, as commercial TV and radio have felt they must do, sell each story, each article, each poem even, to an advertiser willing to pay only for the number of people who will attend just that item. Since magazine advertising rates are based on total circulation, range and variety are achievable on magazines, as they are not on TV, which, in its numbers game, equates the child of four who has just learned to turn the ON knob with the Radcliffe graduate and the business executive of stature.

Too great advertiser control of any medium tends to bring results inconsistent with public good. TV and radio advertisers would like "everything for everybody." Not only does a dreary sameness result, since every item must be for the largest possible audience, but free discussion is often stifled. Criticism of advertising itself tends to languish. Misleading, even false claims can go unchallenged. In the next few years hundreds of Americans may die early if health hazards of cigarettes are minimized. Those who believe in the right of the public to know, and to have the best if they wish it, need always be concerned at any limiting of that right to know. Our country's pride in its free press should include all communications, not just newspapers, magazines, and books.

If all publishing were as advertiser controlled as are most TV and radio—all publishing, that is, newspapers, magazines, novels, history, poetry, save for a few subsidized university or foundation presses—the results may be not too fancifully imagined. No one could purchase a novel, a volume of poetry, or a history. He simply couldn't buy it. However, the book would be given him free but only if the advertiser deemed it would be widely enough read, and the attached advertisements effective enough in selling soap or toothpaste, so that the publisher could afford to give the poetry, novel, or history away. Such a cultural desert, if it could occur in the publishing world, would be somewhat equivalent to the present world of radio-TV.

Fortunately, American common sense appears about to break the shackles of purely commercial TV so that the great educational, cultural, and entertainment potential of our airways may be realized. Newspapers and magazines, too, must be ever alert to publish the best they can without keeping too close an eye on Madison Avenue's whims, fancies, and preferences.

As one who has spent a professional life dealing with audiences of millions, with constantly growing regard for their perception and intelligence, I can only hope that promising experiments in television broadcasting will not cut too harsh a line between the "popular" and the "intellectual"—between "culture" and "entertainment." Let us not dig this chasm too wide or too deep, as though different sorts of beings lived on each side of the rift. If we do, we ignore our common bonds. We're more alike than we're different, we Americans.

Because I have confidence in the power of truth and of the spirit, I believe in the future of mankind.

            —ALBERT SCHWEITZER

22

The First Lady

Our first editorial conference with Eleanor Roosevelt revealed her courtesy and tact more than ours, I fear [writes Beatrice, now tapping the typewriter]. Mrs. Roosevelt had come to our New York office to discuss possible improvements in her autobiography. Certain of the later chapters, hastily written, we felt were superficial and thin.

Mrs. Roosevelt arrived, stately in a plum-colored suit, her matching hat well anchored to well-waved, gray-brown hair. Stout shoes, sedately flat to the floor, gave a common-sense contrast to her rosy satin blouse, her rosy smiling face.

"Tommy" came too—Miss Malvina Thompson, faithful secretary, companion, friend, her shadow, really. Dressed like a brown wren, unobtrusive, silent unless her opinion was asked, Tommy soon revealed beneath her quiet a tart, astringent humor.

We began, as one always does in editorial conferences, with praise of the book—its honesty, the communicated emotion of the first portion. Mrs. Roosevelt, like any new author, beamed her delight. Our kind words gradually changed in tone as certain tentative questions were raised. Could we have an exact description of her mother-in-law?

Could she remember Franklin's first words when he realized he had polio? This picturing of a moment, this veracity of an instant caught by color, scent, or word, we told her, recreates life. Since she was listening intently, we began to expound. Our editorial blood rose, the warmup ended, discretion vanished:

"But this chapter is simply a listing of places you went and people you met," said Bruce. "It has nothing to say—in fact, it's terrible!"

Perhaps my dagger glance reminded him he was speaking to the First Lady of the Land.

"I mean, I mean," he hastily amended, "with a few more concrete details it could be much better."

But we did not then know our First Lady. Mrs. Roosevelt had pride and dignity but no shred of arrogance. Our brusque suggestions she accepted with courtesy; she quite honestly wished to improve her writing. Indeed, all her life, she earnestly strove to learn—to end her high giggle, improve her uncertain voice, make better speeches—even, for the sake of winter exercise, to learn the rhumba. Without a highly critical sense, not a natural writer, subject to excessive demands of people and travel, she had no chance for solitude and concentration, essential for good writing. Mrs. Roosevelt seeking peace and quiet might just as well have inhabited Grand Central Station's information booth as the White House.

Bruce had already visited her at the White House to discuss promotion for *My Story*. Arriving in the late afternoon for his talk, he was asked by the head usher to stay on for dinner and meet the President. Because of the known tension between the *Saturday Evening Post* and That Man in the White House, Bruce thought it perhaps wiser to refuse. Shortly, Mrs. Roosevelt's social secretary arrived to renew the invitation. Again he declined. But when Mrs. Roosevelt, in person, pressed him a third time, Bruce gave in, though he was not certain how amiably the President, a good hater, would greet an emissary from hostile Curtis—particularly one who had just paid his wife $75,000; for Roosevelt, who confessed an itch to be an editor and writer, had never earned much by his pen. Even later in his Presidency when he tentatively signed to do a column for *Collier's* after retirement, he was only to receive $75,000 a year, I believe.

Just before dinner was announced, the President rolled out of his office in a tiny wheelchair like a gallant knight charging from his castle gate, Bruce told me. The great bulk of his shoulders and his towering head so swamped the little vehicle it looked almost like something borrowed from a child. Wheeling the President sharply up to Bruce, his attendant, Arthur Prettyman, stopped the chair like a rider setting a quarter horse back on its haunches. The President, removing his jaunty white cigarette holder, shot out a long arm and a great hand. A broad, flashing smile snapped on like a green traffic light, as if they'd been friends for life. The President roared: "Hello, Bruce—Howaryuh!," establishing at first meeting the first-name relationship which has done so much to deformalize American social life.

Taken aback, Bruce mumbled something like, "Good evening, Mr. President." You could, Bruce related to me later, have knocked him over with a calling card. But before he recovered the President had been rolled on, propelled by a Prettyman intent on getting the President comfortably and not too noticeably settled at the middle of the oval table before family and guests, signaled by the head usher, filed soberly into the small family dining room.

Bruce's apprehensions were not unfounded, he soon learned. Unsettled, first, by watching the President crumble crackers into his soup with one single contraction of his great hand (how many times had Bruce's mother reproved him as a child for doing just that?) he was secondarily shocked when his unbelieving ears heard the distinguished FDR call to the butler's retreating back, "Butter!" in stentorian tones. In the midst of wondering, "What hath this, our Groton, wrought!" Bruce was made suddenly aware of the President's directly addressing him in a loud voice across the wide table where Bruce sat at Mrs. Roosevelt's right. In fact, Bruce seems to remember that Mrs. Roosevelt nudged him into attention, for Bruce, in conversation, is a twoser capable of completely forgetting everyone else in the room in the absorption of converse between just him and his immediate companion.

The President, it seemed, wanted Bruce to know, to really know, about the dreadful slums in the nation's capital—a shocking condition, indeed, that was evident to any journalist with average curiosity.

Listening politely, Bruce nodded his head, sensing, curiously, a growing animosity in the President's tone as he expatiated on the lamentable neighborhoods, so long neglected. Bruce wondered what his purpose could be in the long, doleful exposition, delivered almost as an accusation. Suddenly he heard a direct question:

"I suppose you never knew about that?"

Perhaps he was defending WPA, called boondoggling by the *Post* and harsher critics.

Bruce realizes a guest is supposed not to quarrel with his host. But he supposed, too, the President must have been told by his mamma not to make a guest uncomfortable by attacking him at table. And I'm sorry to admit that Bruce's temper is sometimes on short tether. And, in those early days, Bruce was still not entirely won by Roosevelt. But he contented himself with replying with, he assured me, masterly reserve:

"My predecessor, Mr. Bok, ran a series about such slum conditions in the *Journal* a generation ago, Mr. President. Bok called it, I believe, *The Shame of the Cities*. It is still, of course, a shame." (Even now no less so, after years of the New Deal, Eisenhower prosperity, and, now, the Great Society—all intent on erasing the shame as Bok had advised, but none more successful than the *Journal* had been.)

Since no further exposition seemed in order the President directed conversation to his right. Bruce obediently switched, too, wishing it were easier for him to say, "Yes, Mr. President. Yes, Mr. President."

Everyone left the table ahead of Mr. Roosevelt, before the difficult transition to his wheelchair, so Bruce never ascertained whether he was still on a first-name basis with FDR, as he hurriedly bade Mrs. Roosevelt goodbye to catch the next train home.

Eleanor Roosevelt visited our office many times in the course of our long association. Her directness and simplicity always astonished us. Once we spoke with enthusiasm of a certain successful play. "I'd love to see it," she said to Tommy. "But it's very popular. Do you suppose we could get tickets?" That any producer would turn handsprings to find her the best house seats never occurred to her; one wonders if she had not heard that when Queen Victoria sat down she never looked behind to make certain a chair awaited her bustle.

In that same conversation Clare Boothe Luce's play *The Women* was spoken of. This hard, satiric, very funny, even witty play about a group of malicious women had been a reigning hit.

Mrs. Roosevelt said, "After we left *The Women,* Tommy and I asked each other if we ourselves had ever known any women like the women in the play. We agreed that we had known *one.*"

Women like the women in *The Women* a woman like Eleanor Roosevelt, sincere to naïveté, good and believing others good, would scarcely have become acquainted with. If she had known them, she would have seen them in other terms, or another facet of their personality would have turned to her. Mrs. Roosevelt's play, if she had written one about women, would have dealt with a feminine group far less amusing, doubtless, than the harpies in *The Women,* but perhaps more recognizable as women by the majority of her sex.

Our first invitation to stay at the White House and attend a reception for the Supreme Court naturally seemed a great occasion. The silver-haired head usher's courteous greeting in the impressive hall, giving glimpses of the stately reception rooms and with its beautiful staircase sweeping upstairs; there our huge corner suite, vast old-fashioned bedroom with wide double bed sagging slightly in the center, a small bedroom or dressing room and large nineteenth-century bathroom alongside—all these inspired a little awe. The Roosevelt rooms we would learn to know, rooms unmodified by any interior decorator's hand, with furniture of diverse styles, worn but comfortable, slipcovers often awry, family pictures and memorabilia decorating the walls—pictures of weddings with bridesmaids in knee-length dresses and wide hats, children with dogs, boys in sailboats, larger boys holding tennis rackets. Mrs. Roosevelt, out when we arrived, had left word dinner would be at eight. Having come by train directly from the Philadelphia office, I put a few pins in my recalcitrant hair and prepared for a shower. Just then a knock at the door—Mrs. Roosevelt entered, greeted us warmly, asked if we would like tea sent to our room.

"Why, they haven't lighted your fire!" she exclaimed, and, before Bruce could intervene, stooped and touched a match to the kindling.

Mrs. Roosevelt's warm hospitality gave ease to an evening which, even so, inspired some constraint. Handsome in a white satin gown, she presided at a small dinner in the family room—the absent President doubtless resting against the evening's effort. House guests then assembled in a small parlor to await the always stirring "Hail to the Chief" as the President rolled in. In his wheelchair he went round the small circle, then on into the reception room where, shielded by greenery, he took up his standing position well-braced, but with the braces saving him little fatigue as he shook hands with members of the court and the many other guests filing past toward refreshments in the State Dining Room. Dancing in the East Room followed. It was an august evening.

But the pleasantest part of any White House visit was always breakfast in Mrs. Roosevelt's sitting room, a screened-off end of the second-floor hall filled with sagging chairs loosely covered in varied chintzes; a casual assortment of books, magazines, and newspapers; and everywhere more, unbelievably more, family pictures. This room opened directly into her suite at the left rear corner; the big chamber was fitted out as a private office, where she worked with Tommy. Mrs. Roosevelt herself, the President's lady, lived with little luxury in the smaller bed-dressing room, keeping her few well-chosen clothes in an old-fashioned wardrobe which could scarcely have been big enough for an average schoolteacher.

The President's rooms, bedroom and office, adjoined Mrs. Roosevelt's rooms along the hall. In the corridor sitting room, bright with morning sun, house guests, often including a cousin or a niece, assembled at nine o'clock around an oval table for a hearty eggs-and-bacon breakfast. Mrs. Roosevelt, wearing a trim, well-fitting, full-length, buttoned-to-the-neck housecoat in soft gray-blue or medium greens, poured coffee into enormous double-size cups. It was at this meal, if you were alone, or immediately after, if there were other guests, that one discussed work or future projects with Mrs. Roosevelt.

That first stay at the White House was followed by many more, but I must admit that, as most first visitors probably do, we succumbed to the temptation of writing several letters on our bedroom's supply of heavy white stationery headed in gilt "The White House." Wesley Stout, as tense a Roosevelt opponent as Lorimer, was still editor of the *Post*. Bruce could not resist his little joke, sending Wesley a White House letter, its sole message simply "Boo!"

As our working relationship developed into friendship, our admiration for Mrs. Roosevelt's magnanimity, her dignity with humility, her genuine devotion to the interests of others grew. Photographs maligned her. In a camera portrait done especially for the *Journal* to accompany her autobiography, even the talented Steichen caught only her homeliness and imperfections, the tension of a shy person fearing the camera, a sort of stately coldness. (Few photographers, Bruce says, can realistically catch on film the lineaments of a truly beautiful woman; they are always made to look like plastic dolls or premature old ladies of forty-three. It takes a painter to catch a woman's real beauty at any age, he thinks. Bruce and I once saw, in Paris, an exhibition of how one hundred famous painters portrayed their wives and mistresses. It was amazing to see what happens when the brush is tipped with love and the colors on the palette mixed with emotion— the loved face really flowers on the canvas. Dislike shows, too.) No photographer ever caught the warmth and responsiveness, occasionally almost a radiance, which made Mrs. Roosevelt's face so appealing to those who knew her well.

Her carriage erect and dignified, her hair always attractively done, in pale-colored evening dresses, with pretty, well-held neck and shoulders, she was handsome. In daytime wearing mostly well-tailored suits, usually in black with a white satin blouse, with a soft sable furpiece, she made a distinguished appearance. But her shoes stayed sensible, her hats stayed put to protect her hair from the wind as she whirled about the country intent on giving the nation a thorough and long-delayed spring cleaning.

But, after traveling to all parts of the country as her husband's reporter, making speeches, dealing with enormous correspondence, writing her column, she was always (at home) a considerate, a perceptive hostess. Guests, welcomed warmly, found their tastes and interests sought out and provided for. And she always managed time for a personal chat, which might take place on a walk, or over teacups in her study.

On an early visit, invited to bring Sesaly, then eleven, we were put in the historic Lincoln suite, with its huge double bed and walnut

Victorian table, whose four legs closed round a carved nest complete with four eggs. The President in his oval study showed her ship prints on the walls and overcame the little girl's shyness by letting her examine the very miscellaneous collection of small animals he kept on his desk—donkeys, of course, spaniels, squirrels, bears, even an elephant (presumably to be poked fun at)—and, eliciting from Sesaly the information that she too collected little animals, established a friendly bond between the great man and the little girl who, after half an hour, allowed herself to be rescued by Mrs. Roosevelt. At a small party in the family dining room, Sesaly came down in the glory of her best embroidered organdy dress, with pale green sash, to find a gold-crested place card for "Miss Gould."

Little Diana Hopkins, having recently lost her mother, was then sheltered through Mrs. Roosevelt's warm concern, with her nurse, on the third floor of the White House. Sesaly visited with Diana much of the weekend, and on Sunday the two small girls and a niece of Mrs. Roosevelt's drove to Mount Vernon in a White House car which, to the pride and joy of the young, did not halt at the ordinary car park, but swept right up to the door of that historic mansion, as though they were distinguished guests.

With Sesaly thus engaged, we went on one of many walks with Mrs. Roosevelt—she had a long stride—to and around the Washington Monument. When we were not discussing our own new project she talked with amazing frankness about her husband and Harry Hopkins, and some of their points of disagreement.

Bruce recalls Mrs. Roosevelt on that wintry, windy walk answering his question as to why the President, running for a third term to which there was much opposition, chose controversial Henry Agard Wallace for his vice-presidential running mate.

"The convention didn't want him," Bruce unnecessarily reminded. "Why did the President insist?"

"I asked Franklin that question," said Mrs. Roosevelt, without seeming in the least surprised at Bruce's asking it.

"He told me he chose Mr. Wallace because Mr. Wallace really understood what he was trying to accomplish. He didn't, he said, expect to live through his third term—" Mrs. Roosevelt was saying this as calmly as if she were talking about the blustery weather. "He wanted someone as Vice President who could finish what he'd started."

Some years later, following a long, casual talk in New York, Bruce, escorting Mrs. Roosevelt to the elevator, loitered a moment to remind her of that earlier conversation. "Why then was the President, for his fourth term, dropping Wallace for Truman?"

"Franklin," Mrs. Roosevelt said, "thought Wallace had had his chance. The public didn't want him. There was no use trying to make the country again accept him.

"And," Mrs. Roosevelt continued, "Franklin felt that this time he needed the backing of the regular politicians. Truman, a machine candidate, added strength to the ticket." One gathered that, perhaps because of his growing illness, the President was not too certain he would win a fourth term.

It soon became apparent that Mrs. Roosevelt's friends and guests were not the same as her husband's friends and guests. Mrs. Roosevelt, her childhood marred by an alcoholic father as she touchingly related in *My Story,* offered no cocktails whatever, although she served wine at formal dinners. And her guests rarely joined the President's cozy little group for late-afternoon refreshment. This was the period of the day when the President could fully relax with trusted intimates and his working family. Eleanor Roosevelt was often—and so considered herself—her husband's conscience, and apparently the President had a certain fear of his wife's do-gooder friends (among whom we, perhaps, were numbered). At least we were working early with Hopkins and others for a school hot-lunch program to benefit undernourished pupils and conferring later on war projects and aid to underdeveloped countries. Mrs. Roosevelt was quoted by Harry Hopkins as continually impressing on the President and on Hopkins himself that "we must not be satisfied with merely making campaign pledges, the President being under moral obligation to see his domestic reforms through. . . . She hoped neither the President nor I thought it was settled in any way by making speeches." There was no doubt that Mrs. Roosevelt's earnestness, her insistence on performance as well as promise, was often a sharp goad to her husband's less-exacting political scruples.

Although at the White House, the President's and Mrs. Roosevelt's friends and cronies ran on separate social tracks, still he and she were in daily communication. "I will speak to Franklin about it" was her immediate reply to any new proposal. By breakfasttime next morning one would have Franklin's views. Undoubtedly, though he teased her, often allowed her to be ridiculed by his little circle, and had his own less-rigorous cheering section, he recognized her value as shrewd reporter (disinterested as few other advisers could be), and also the vote value of the ardent admiration building around her.

Since a pre-dinner cocktail was never offered, many of Mrs. Roosevelt's guests, needing some lift before a formal meal, made their own arrangements. Even George Bye, her merry agent, was too awed to ask for ice, so surreptitiously served lukewarm martinis in his bedroom.

Once Bruce and I were invited to the White House over Saturday night (we were going out to a small dinner with Washington friends) to be on hand for a lunch party on Sunday and have a chance to speak to the President about one of our plans. That Sunday morning we were suddenly invited to stay on for the President's birthday party that evening following the performance of *Life with Father,* the entire cast coming down from New York. We were to sit in the President's box; some other guests probably had failed.

The honor of sitting beside the President was great, but most women will understand my feelings at that glorious moment—I had brought only a simple, second-best evening dress and had not seen a hairdresser. After the performance, when the lights went up, the audience—sprinkled with many old friends including Russel Crouse, co-author of the play and his wife, Alison Smith—rose to their feet, turned—the orchestra playing "Hail to the Chief"—and gave the President a thunderous ovation, while I shrank toward invisibility by his spotlighted side. Afterward the State Dining Room was lively with champagne and flowers, beautifully-set tables for eight, brief, amusing speeches from Howard Lindsay and Crouse.

In those days the Roosevelt's Red Room, Blue Room and State Dining Room were much as they had been through several administrations. Friendly in feeling, they seemed less done up, less elegant than under Jacqueline Kennedy. Flowers indicated housekeeping more concerned with people than appearances. Gladioli, the florist's delight, carnations filled out with babies'-breath, a dozen yellow daffodils sufficed. Upstairs Roosevelt sons dropped in and out. Their wives, or ex-wives with children, overflowed the halls. At pleasant informal Sunday-night meals in the family dining room, with a few intimates, the Morgenthaus or the Ickeses, a Delano cousin or a niece, scrambled eggs and cocoa were often served, reminiscent of the Sunday-night snacks of my youth. I remember Harold Ickes there with his younger, second wife—she railing against the stupidity of the mass of American voters.

It is sad to recall that this was a frequent theme in the White House in those days soon after the Supreme Court packing dispute. The Roosevelts, wounded by many barbs, victims even of some vicious slander, mercilessly attacked for their children's real faults or implied failings, had become defensive, on guard, almost fearful of "the common man," not trusting to the great good will and balance of millions of citizens never heard from except on election day.

It is curious that FDR should have remained so wary of the common man who, at crucial periods, gave him unfailing support. Before he would even move in what was widely considered a bold gesture in supplying over-age destroyers to Britain on a lend-lease basis—as one might lend a hose, he said, to a neighbor whose house was on fire—Roosevelt carefully gained from Dr. Gallup a quick poll's assurance that the public would approve, even applaud, his decision. Boldly, then, he made it.

Eleanor Roosevelt seemed to have a more generous faith in the common man than her husband, though she was still much criticized. However, she was angry with the press. She felt that small, youthful indiscretions of her sons were blown up out of all proportion, damaging their future. She often scolded the press to us for its almost vicious violation of family privacy. We agreed, somewhat. But, defending our profession, we reminded her there is no one press, but some irresponsible and some responsible publications. Government and other influential persons should distinguish, we said, ignore the bad and support the good. Too often, however, politicians pamper scandalmongering columnists and yellow journalists, who gain power through fear; leak news breaks to placate them; sometimes even end-run publications which can, without bribery, be trusted to be fair. The press, we insisted, should not be judged as a whole, as the legal and medical professions cannot be judged as a whole. Ambulance chasers, malpractitioners, demagogues, gossip columnists mar their professions, but by no means truly represent them.

Eleanor Roosevelt combined dignity with, at times, a lovable and touching naïveté. Her personal humility had its own greatness. Aware of her lack of obvious feminine beauty, she had perhaps decided, as many women have done, to be a valuable aid, a useful partner, instead of a cherished wife. Apparently she harbored few resentments. At least I remember her saying to us once, without any appearance of rancor, at a time when the President was about to use his mother's house at Hyde Park as a summer White House:

"I shall not be going to Hyde Park. Franklin has not invited me. He has asked Anna to be his hostess there this summer instead."

Her objectivity must have been based on many hurts. Fairly magnanimous about her husband's slights, Mrs. Roosevelt could not wholly extend this generosity to her mother-in-law. Once, in a long, twilight talk in Bruce's New York office, as the sun went down scarlet over the Hudson, and the dark-blue dusk of Manhattan became jeweled with lights, she spoke to us fully. Many of her children's problems, she felt, had come from a willful, capricious, interfering mother-in-law. One son, she told us, "smashed up a car and Franklin and I said that as a penalty—to make him more careful—we would not buy him a car for two years. His grandmother gave him one.

"She would sometimes say before all the children together [one son] 'is nicer to me than the rest of you. I think I will leave my money to him.'"

For periods when she was "not invited" to the big house (and perhaps for escape from that close mother-son relationship, so tormenting in her early marriage) Mrs. Roosevelt had her own cottage a short distance away at Val-Kill on what had once been a part of Hyde Park grounds. Furnished, as all her homes were, with odd bits of leftover furniture—Victorian sideboards, chintz-cushioned wicker rockers, fat, old armchairs protected at arms and head with crocheted mats—with books, papers piled high, snapshots everywhere, tea made on the spot, the house had a cozy, friendly atmosphere.

When she gave up the East Side town house and took a small apartment on Washington Square, her sitting room there had the same scattered, irrelevant air, as though all the furnishings no one else wanted had been crowded in. Sons came in, greeted her, raided the icebox, vanished again, as at the White House.

Eleanor Roosevelt had an adoring public, but she also had many critics. We received vituperative letters as we continued to print her articles and her column. "When are you going to get rid of Eleanor?" was a frequent bitter query from some acquaintance whose politics were more inbred than his manners.

Because we published Mrs. Roosevelt, and because an informal straw vote in 1948 revealed that several among our staff favored Wallace, running as a splinter-party candidate, red-eyed red-seer Westbrook Pegler accused us, in his column, of being Communists. (This was before it became libelous to hurl such accusations loosely, so he wasn't sued. Only a few cancelations resulted, showing the public's good sense.)

Mrs. Roosevelt was too aware of man's brotherhood not to support the Negro's aspirations for a juster economic and political life. And she was too respectful of human excellence not to befriend Negroes of intellect and achievement. Her stand infuriated many Southerners. Some of the letters were comic:

"Negroes lunching in the White House! Such people may be good enough for Eleanor Roosevelt, but they are not good enough for ME!"

Not the least of the criticisms of Mrs. Roosevelt in those days was that she was "selling" her husband's position by writing for money, while he was in the White House. Certainly there can be two opinions on this. Eleanor Roosevelt, always sympathetic, vulnerable to financial needs, would set aside money to help one of her secretaries educate a favorite niece, or to care for a friend or relative in illness. She aided many families in distress. She gave much to charity. So she needed money of her own. Unfortunately, too, her children were often pressed for money and demanding. This finally led to the *Journal*'s dropping her page. After many years of writing for us her question-and-answer column, she completed the second volume of her autobiography, on which we had first refusal. It was written much in the style of "My Day"—almost entirely an account, "We went there; we saw so-and-so."

My husband, never noted for gentle statement, in a letter, said: "You have written this too hastily—as though you were composing it on a bicycle while pedaling your way to a fire."

In answer to specific suggestions she did enrich a few paragraphs, added a few sentences here and there. But the book remained, except for a few good passages, very dull. Her son Elliott, acting as her agent in place of George Bye, who normally represented her, approached another editor, who offered $150,000 for the manuscript, as was, sight unseen. Elliott would get the 10 percent agency commission, $15,000. Urging that we had, in effect, refused the book, broken our unwritten contract by insisting on further work, Elliott persuaded his mother to resist further effort on the manuscript. So we told her to sell her book elsewhere if she wouldn't improve it, and her column, too. We felt Mrs. Roosevelt's stature was too great to permit her hasty, unrealized work that we felt reluctant to publish.

We were at least half in the wrong. Mrs. Roosevelt was too old then, too busy, too occupied in other matters, like the UN, which she perhaps considered more important, to alter a habit of years. We doubtless should have said "Yes" or "No" on the basis of her greatness as a person. Later, doubtless troubled by Elliott's intervention, she quietly sent Bye $15,000 as if he were entitled to the agent's fee after all.

Like most great people, Eleanor Roosevelt had her weaknesses and her failings. Many came from a trusting, naïve spirit. Her attitude toward her husband was not, perhaps, bitter, as Jonathan Daniels described it, but it was, quite justifiably, wary. Unloved at home, she was loved round the world. Her kindness, her forbearance, her deep belief in the worth of the individual human spirit, grew partly out of a Christian humility, "that low, sweet root/From which all heavenly virtues shoot." She has left a mark on her age; it was a privilege to know her.

*All men are ordinary men; the extraordinary men
are those who know it.*

—G. K. CHESTERTON

23

Figures in the Parade

On the wall behind Beatrice's New York desk hung a Renoir litho-
graphed portrait of a little girl seated, writing. Head bent low, arms
akimbo, the little girl strained with pencil, lips, and nerves. Beatrice,
amused, felt this effortful concentration expressed the editor at work.

As in most worthwhile jobs, much of editing is sheer drudgery.
An awkward phrase excised, another made livelier, a rambling, gauche
manuscript pruned to an inherent shapeliness—these achievements
fill an editor's life with a kind of joy. Artists and talented artisans,
engravers, lapidaries, good pastry cooks, equally feel the importance
of fine detail in their creative activity. I remember George Luks
finishing a little girl's picture, stepping critically back from the easel,
"Now, Bruce, the money touch!" His brush, poised like a dart, dotted
an electric highlight in a corner of the child's wide, exploring eye.
The artist turned away content.

Renoir's little girl, gripping her pencil, did give a fair illustration
of an editor's needful concentration.

But people who thought our life glamorous frequently exclaimed:
"You've been everywhere—seen so many interesting people!"

It is true that many personalities of the day pass by in parade before the editor—any editor—since he's necessarily somewhere near the center of what's happening.

General George Catlett Marshall stands out as one of the extraordinary men. He was one of the few who did not immediately hawk his memoirs for a large sum—a reticence greatly appealing to a jaundiced editor elbowed by personalities anxious to sell their stories for a profit. He struck into awe apparently almost all the great people of his day, including Churchill, who, despite clashes over strategy, admired him extravagantly for reasons less trivial than mine.

In his plain simplicity Marshall always seemed to recognize his kinship with ordinary men. I recall an anecdote he told a few in Washington. During the war, grounded by fog in Nova Scotia, he naturally went fishing. And the other side of the trout stream, as every fisherman knows, is where the big fish lie. So Marshall found himself gingerly picking his way across a high railroad trestle just as the one-freight-a-day came thundering around the bend. Hastily clutching a stringer, he let himself dangle from the trestle a long drop above the rock-strewn canyon torrent. As the train chugged over his head, he had time to wonder whether he could manage to swing his heavy hip-booted feet up and over the ties with his not-too-young legs.

Back in Washington, he told this wryly, as an old man's misadventure. There was no sense of the nation's danger as well as his.

After the war most people of consequence and some of very little rushed into print with memoirs of How Betsy and I Killed the Bear. Marshall refused large and larger sums progressively offered him, though he had only his military paycheck to live on. He pointed out to us why he would never write an autobiography. Unless he told the truth it wouldn't interest him. To tell the truth, as he saw it, might injure reputations, hurt some friends. And, not the Recording Angel, he might actually not be telling the truth when he thought he was.

One evening, dining with my old history professor, Arthur Schlesinger the first, at the home of Kenneth Chorley, who headed Williamsburg so long for John D. Rockefeller, Jr., I recounted my dismal failures to move Marshall. Didn't Dr. Schlesinger agree that Marshall should, somehow, be persuaded to set down his reminiscences before they were lost to history? Schlesinger's enthusiastic accord inspired Chorley. He began wondering aloud whether maybe Mr. Rockefeller —long an admirer of Marshall—might not finance the purchase of Marshall's papers for V.M.I. in exchange for Marshall's tape recording some of his memories to supplement the papers. And that is just what happened.

Unfortunately Marshall became ill after he'd dictated some thousands of words—like many he became fascinated with the tape recorder and forgot his decision not to become autobiographical— but he couldn't actually finish the job. Still, the resulting biography by Dr. Pogue contains valuable personal history direct from Marshall's lips.

Some other big fish we tried to net without success. During the *Little Princesses* negotiations we learned Queen Mary had kept a diary for most of her years. She was an extraordinary old lady, curious, almost nosy, ha'penny-wise, sensible despite her dreadnought hats. By now the royal family, realizing, though still angry with Crawfie, that her story had done much to win American sentiment, were growing more receptive to personal histories. We learned, "through Palace sources," that the Queen Mother would seriously consider writing her own life based on her diaries. Royalty like many political figures seldom spurn money if it can be swallowed like a ceremonial cup of tea; their receptivity to jewels presented by cheering Dominions is well known. Finally the Queen decided she was too old to make the effort, Lady Colville regretfully informed me. We then helped finance James Pope-Hennessy's biography of Queen Mary and published his fine book.

Queen Elizabeth as Dowager dallied for months with our proposal that she write her story. She preferred her endless games of solitaire. "The truth is," one of those close to her confessed at last, "she's too lazy"—an integral part, no doubt, of the Queen Mum's plump, enduring charm.

There are those who won't write; there are always many, frequently of high position, eager to tell all—for a substantial sum, preferably paid in advance.

In early New Deal days we had hoped Harry Hopkins would back our cherished project of hot school lunches. With his usual somewhat evasive charm, like a sprite who had stayed up all night, he countered by suggesting we advance a thumping sum on a not-yet-begun auto-biography. Such books, if commissioned, are often whipped together after a few interviews by professional ghost writers. Sometimes, but rarely, they succeed. Hopkins was perhaps justified by pressing needs —an ailing wife, a not-too-well-paid government position, in which he expended all his time and his health, and all his devotion in service to an immobilized President.

Big names, without a good story, mean little in a magazine. How-ever, being a stagestruck fan of all the Barrymores, I was easily won when Ethel, her beret the sea-under-sun blue of her eyes, read to us fifteen handwritten pages of the autobiography she proposed to write. Her first chapter was better than good—a childhood half-orphaned by trouping, casually amorous relatives, bound to the glory and drudgery of the theatre. Over lunch at our round marble table she cried in memory of that child and we cried in tribute to her acting. Herbert Bayard Swope, a friend of hers and ours, had urged her to do her autobiography and to tell the truth, regardless, she said. This is what she agreed to do. With contract drawn and advance paid, which we did only for her blue eyes and ensorcelling voice, the manu-script came in, chapter by chapter. After her youth, the story soon became a mere listing of plays she had starred in, with full quotes of all the nice things the critics had said about her, though they often, and she quoted, spoke ill of the play. We were in despair.

Hoping he might have influence with E.B., Beatrice called Swope, her one-time boss on the old New York *World,* to ask his advice.

"It isn't very good?"

"Alas, no."

"Does she tell a true story?"

"I fear not."

"She doesn't say anything about the drinking?"

"No."

Pause.

"Doesn't she even mention the dope?"

"No."

"I'll see what I can do."

But Swope proved unpersuasive, too. The story of a magical star's shining debut, tragic middle years—divorce, despair, drink, dope —then of her gallant fight back until she regained eminence on stage and film as the great character actress of her time—this dramatic tale was never told.

I sometimes agreed with Shaw that no one could or should tell the truth in an autobiography—though Shaw's *Thirteen Sketches* are autobiographically pretty close to the bone. Wilde couldn't even be truthful in his letters, but the truth to Wilde, I suspect, was just a perverse way of regarding unreality. Of course, it is impossible to know the ever-shifting truth when one sees it, or tell all the truth even if one were so inclined—one's memories move from grave to gay with sunshine, midnight, or a hearty breakfast.

Beatrice says that in writing autobiography one's choice is to be either indiscreet or boring. Ethel, to our regret, chose not to be indiscreet.

Among unreluctant autobiographers, we enjoyed our acquaintance with the Duke and Duchess of Windsor, though we didn't buy her story. We met them first at Margaret Biddle's splendid house in Paris, where we dined upon the vermeil service later given by Mrs. Biddle to the White House so our President can impress recently elevated African dictators with our democratic, gold-washed splendors. The Duke revealed his famous, rather weary charm, chatting after dinner with each lady in turn. Of Beatrice he inquired, to her surprise, about Walter Edge, former ambassador to Paris and governor of New Jersey, and his handsome, hospitable wife, Princeton neighbors. At their welcoming Georgia plantation he had (as had we) enjoyed shooting quail and turkey.

Among the strikingly dressed, well-jeweled guests that evening, the Duchess had contributed to Beatrice's comfort by wearing a short, simple, impeccably neat dark-blue satin—near twin to Beatrice's Hattie Carnegie own—the famous lady's elegance deriving from perfect fit, an excellent figure, and an almost lacquered look as to hair and face. The first to laugh at her own sallies, she seemed utterly to amuse the half-dozen men who hung on her not-too-subtle bons mots.

Having disposed of his own ghost-written autobiography, supervised by able Charles J. V. Murphy, to *Life* at a handsome figure, the Duke was anxious that his consort, too, should make a killing.

I'll admit I was tempted, and Cleveland Amory was proposed to "assist" the Duchess in shaping the book.

I am reminded of a story told us by Eve Curie, who, before she married attractive Henry Labouisse and became a plain American (though still beautiful), had been a member of Their Royal Highness' worldly Paris set. The Duke, chatting about their shared profession as authors, had asked Eve Curie whom she had to help her with her work.

"Oh, I don't have anybody," replied the author of many excellent books, including the biography of Mme. Curie.

"You mean," said the Duke, apparently astounded at this slavery to pen and paper, "you mean—you mean you just set it all down, yourself?"

Amory found his task difficult. The Duchess was highly reticent on certain sensitive points—what one might call the erogenous zone of her memoirs. Amory wanted the book to be reasonably accurate. There were other differences. Finally, he withdrew, to be succeeded by reliable Mr. Murphy.

On their next trip to New York the Windsors visited us in our small thirty-first-floor apartment, which Rockefeller Center had been persuaded to carve out for us, next to our offices. A *Journal* editor, we had been told, must await them at the curb as their car drew up at 1270 Sixth Avenue, conduct them to a reserved elevator, which must shoot them, with no other passengers, to our top floor (not easily arranged during the noon-hour bustle in a building housing its small village of obdurate Americans), and lead them directly to us, waiting. Fortunately, no curtsy or "Your Royal Highness" was asked for the Duchess as in their compliant European circles.

Again the Duchess arrived immaculate and ordered, every hair, every button, every fold of the skirt as exact as a doll's dress, her trim blue suit, creamy gloves, shining shoes and bag unaccented, impeccable. Both showed great charm, the Duchess a wide smile, an easy, warm, inconsequential humor. The Duke, having learned we had a house in the Bahamas, remembered the strong clans of Malones, Bethels, and Russels on our little island from his wartime days as Governor in Nassau. Fascinated by his easy memory of people and events, Beatrice asked him how he managed it.

"It's a lesson you learn," he said in his informal, disarming way. "You just bone up. History and geography of a new place from an encyclopedia. Someone, your secretary, perhaps, looks up the people you will meet, their interests, their work. It becomes a habit. It's part of the job." One thought a little sadly of years of training—so briefly used.

At our round marble table, under its crystal chandelier, over Scottish smoked salmon with cucumbers, fillet of beef and asparagus, our own three-fruit sherbet, we talked of the projected book. They would like it in the *Journal,* they said, because of the *Journal's* prestige. The fact that *The Little Princesses* had been published by us to later palace approval influenced them, I think.

The Duke explained winningly, ruefully, how very costly it was to do over an old mill into the country house outside Paris they longed for. I replied that the *Journal* would pay the highest price going for the book if, after reading it, we liked it. We could not make an offer sight unseen.

Women, naturally enough, always yearn to know how a charmer like Mme. Pompadour, Gaby Deslys, La Lupescu wins a King. The Prince of Wales had long been a favorite with the ladies. How had Wallis brought it off?

Self-made women like the Duchess obviously have a real problem in setting down truthfully the all-too-human details of their lives. But we felt an obligation not to present a picture of Wallis Simpson, late of Baltimore, as Rebecca of Sunnybrook Farm whose sweet manners and engaging innocence had just happened to attract the attention of the heir to the Realm as he passed the garden gate on which she was happily swinging.

Negotiations were continued by her lawyers, still coaxing us to buy before the manuscript was completed. We were amused when one of her agents, as a bonus to persuade us, offered to throw the Duchess in, too, as it were—her personality, that is.

"Couldn't she do a column on entertaining—decorating—and be a sort of hostess-representative for you abroad—entertain guests, big advertisers—that sort of thing? She has energy to burn. She's wearing the little man out."

I hated to deny purchasers of double-page color spreads the opportunity to enjoy Paris in the aura of this famed couple, but I was still not won. Our circulation manager, always interested in big names for newsstand placards, urged us to forget our scruples, and buy. *McCall's,* then edited by Otis Wiese, stood ready to catch her if we incontinently let the Duchess drop, he warned; her story would add half a million to *McCall's* normal newsstand sale, and *McCall's* had always been nearest us in newsstand leadership. If it would lift *McCall's* that much, $280,000—the Duchess's asking price for her memoirs—was not excessive. Had we believed in the story the Duchess wanted to sell, we would have gladly paid it. We said no.

The first installment of the memoirs, in which there wasn't a hair out of place, or a stocking seam crooked, shot up *McCall's* newsstand more than 200,000. Our circulation head sent me a memo about it.

The second issue told a different tale. Sales dropped. A shrewd public had sensed the story's emptiness. Before the series ended the newsstand advantage to *McCall's* had been wiped out.

Our circulation man neglected to send me a note on this interesting later development.

For though democratic Americans love to read about royalty, they can be discriminating in their tastes. Personal histories must have the breath of life in them to interest readers. They can be sensational, like Ethel Waters' matter-of-fact, shocking recital, or gentle and thoughtful like Mary Ellen Chase's quiet memories of a Maine childhood when mother darned stockings while helping children with their Latin. The reader must sense truth in the telling. If they are written for shock alone, or to cover up, they rarely leave a satisfied reader —more often the reader leaves them.

We never published Barbara Hutton's biography, "The Million

Dollar Baby from the Ten Cent Store," because it seemed to Beatrice too pitiful. Perhaps there was a moral in it about riches and happiness, but, after all, not many people have a chance to be ruined by accidental millions from grandfathers who struck it rich.

Ethel Waters' *His Eye Is on the Sparrow* was pitiful, too. But it was a narrative of courage and will overcoming every handicap life could devise. Ethel Waters had the devotion of a hard-working, loving grandmother, coming home on her Thursday off with a leftover pork chop in her pocket for Ethel, scrubbing her, scolding her, giving her that self-sacrificing concern without which a human being can scarcely grow into concern for others. The story was shocking with its opening sentence, "I was the child of rape." It told of a pretty young cousin's enforced prostitution, acquainted our middle-class millions with the wretched, submerged life of Negro millions in their slums. Our society is now reaping the whirlwind harvest of that sowing.

Numbers of stage and screen stars decided to tell all—but their all could be put in a thimble. We saw many merely sensational stories go without regret.

Lindbergh's early, cobbled-together *We* and his later, sensitive, almost poetic *The Spirit of St. Louis* revealed the contrast between ghost-written books, cashing in on momentary notoriety, and those which are the fruit of thoughtful living.

Having known and admired Lindbergh even before that cold, drizzly dawn on Long Island when a few of us watched him, alone, take off for Paris, I treasured—though not a hero worshiper or a collector—his thank-you note given me and a few others just before take-off. (Many editors, like Bok, *were* autograph gatherers—some editors were even suspected of buying poor manuscripts from famous persons just to enhance their collections. Perhaps I felt such collecting was too easy. An editor need only send a line to any noted person, saying, "Have you considered writing your life story?" Your store of signatures would be as large as your patience.) Admiring Lindbergh's courage, his practical good sense, I had saved his scribbled autograph. Later, as he became an isolationist, admiring Nazi power, I tore it up. But, after his gallant, unsung service with our Air Force

in the Pacific, I regretted my impetuous act. He remains a true hero
of our age. *The Spirit of St. Louis* was offered to the *Journal* first. I
should have enjoyed printing it. But its length was better for weekly
than for monthly publication, so we swung it to the *Post,* where it rang
the bell.

Our dealings with Mme. Pandit, as lovely as a gardenia slightly
creamy around the edges, made me certain that east is east and west
is west and on meeting are doomed to mutual obfuscation. Mme.
Pandit, then India's ambassador in Washington, assured us she would
let us publish her life story in the *Journal.* We agreed such a narrative
which would show India's life and needs might help our country understand India better during her struggle toward democracy. It would be
less political but more human, we thought, than Nehru's magnificent
autobiography, written in prison, telling of his distressed people in
their duel with the English, whom he respected so much and liked so
little.

Mme. Pandit, in Washington, told me she had, happily for us,
already written her autobiography during one of the lulls in diplomacy.
Interestedly watching her, white-sari-clad, seated on a fragile embassy
chair, slip off a golden sandal to toy idly with the scarlet toes of a
well-shaped foot, I said I'd be glad to take the manuscript back with
me to Philadelphia and read it at once. Unfortunately, she regretted,
the secretary who could lay hands on the papers was at the moment
out of the embassy. But she would mail it promptly to me on her
secretary's return. With a last admiring glance at her warmly beautiful
face and rosy toes, I took leave, well content with my luck.

For several ensuing years we negotiated for that manuscript, holding long discussions about its potential value in Indian-American relations. Steadfastly she assured us it existed. Once she telephoned me
at Hopewell from Pearl Buck's nearby New Hope home. The manuscript was on its way via her chauffeur. I should have it within the
hour. Half a day later she called again to explain that the manuscript
had inadvertently been tucked into a diplomatic pouch for London
consigned to her brother, but soon it would be back and in my hands.

We often saw the charming ambassador in Washington, in London,
and in New Delhi, where both she and her brother entertained us

handsomely at the prime minister's house and introduced us to everyone as the publishers of her forthcoming book.

We met Mme. Pandit's three lively, attractive daughters. I actually
touched them to make certain these creations, at least, were real.

Even Nehru must have believed his sister's affirmations about the
existence of her autobiography. He gave us luncheon—at a long table
beautiful with exotic fruits and flowers, the food delicious, among
guests the Lion of Kashmir. Beatrice, seated beside Nehru, saw his
face, sad, handsome, crinkling into laughter as he told her why he wore
a fresh rose daily, "for levity." The two most interesting sights for a
visitor in India, he said, were the tomb of Ut-Maud-ud-Daula, smaller,
more gemlike than the Taj Mahal, and the caves of Ellora and
Ajanta, so ancient, so sophisticated in their art.

As Mme. Pandit's story did not materialize, we assigned a writer,
Roger Butterfield, to "help her get it in shape," the euphemism editors
often use. In several conferences, often sitting on the floor, regarding
her toes distantly, she said, "I don't know why Mr. Gould has sent
you. The story is written." Butterfield finally withdrew, baffled.

I would have begun to believe that my own senses were at fault had
not her distinguished publisher, Dick Walsh of John Day, confessed
that he, too, had had the same puzzling experience. Repeatedly ready
to announce the book for fall publication, he found it faded away each
year in a mist, impossible to pierce, of promises and evasions be-
fogging the facts. I never saw a page of the manuscript. Like the boy
in the fabled Indian rope trick it simply climbed into the air and
disappeared .

Whether Mme. Pandit hoped to write something in an arduous
overnight session, whether she actually had a scattering of papers
she was not ready to release but thought of as her autobiography,
whether she had actually completed the book but did not wish to
show the manuscript I cannot say. I am still fogbound. Having recently
read Naipaul's *An Area of Darkness,* I have begun to wonder whether,
as he suggests, in certain oriental minds the desire to have something
true becomes so strong that the desired truth seems actual. Reality
is an illusion; illusion the only reality. An unpleasant fact can be so
unseen as to become untrue. Naipaul writes, for instance, of public

defecation along roads in Indian towns and villages, ignored, even denied as nonexistent.

To my knowledge Nan's book has not yet been completed. It should be interesting.

Something of this hysteria-producing atmosphere affected many phases of our work. I well remember when Katharine Newlin Burt, herself a successful writer, returned from a ragged day in New York as *Journal* contact woman with writers and agents there.

"I used to think publishing houses so stable: now I see they are built on shifting sands! It's all temperament and it's terrifying!"

Katharine, wife of that most delightful novelist friend Struthers Burt, had taken an editor's job during a drought in her creative inspiration in the commonly held belief that editors sit coolly and comfortably at air-conditioned desks while real workers in the vineyard labor and sweat to produce something pleasing to the editorial palate. Authors, I suppose, never think they are temperamental. But they occasionally recognize the quality in others.

Emotional writers like Paul de Kruif often airmailed their manuscripts at night and called up at nine-twenty the next morning to see how we liked them.

Handsome Benjamin Spock—the nation's pediatric daddy—as emotional as de Kruif and even more intent on reforming the world, was forever deserting his little charges to say his intense say about civil rights, peace, and later Vietnam. We were constantly trying to herd him back to the nursery, where he was superb—though not always persuasive in other matters. Bleeding if a line of his copy was cut, always fearing editorial distortion of his tender ideas, he was as difficult to dandle on the editorial knee as a baby who needs to go to the bathroom instanter. But for mothers he had written "The Bible." It is, I believe, America's all-time best seller. We had been lucky to get him for the *Journal*. We spoon-fed him compliments, when he was not on the soapbox, and guarded him like Fort Knox.

An author whose temperament ended in tragedy was Ursula Parrott, a lively, laughing girl in our early New York days. One Sunday late she had dropped down beside us in a Morton Street café bursting out, "Lindesay has left me"—a cry she was to expand into a best-selling, autobiographical novel, *Ex-Wife*. Its theme: "They used to buy me violets—now they bring me gin."

She went on to achieve blazing financial success as a magazine serial writer—early in our editorship bemoaning to us over lunch at the Marguery the fact that though she was earning $90,000 to $120,000 a year she was annually spending $150,000.

"I'm a fool," she said, "for a hard-luck story."

I suggested a lawyer handle her accounts, permitting her to cash no checks he didn't countersign. With great ingenuity Ursula charged things, wrote promises to pay, subsidized cousins, circumvented his every protective effort.

Many writers live from hand to mouth, glorying in a rich year (like Fitzgerald), incredulously starving the next—always believing the bonanza years are what the future will bring. Here again temperament counts—debts and discouragement do not foster creative effort.

Finally, Ursula's transient talent gone, several husbands divorced, the hangers-on of her prosperous days vanished, she wrote a woman friend she was sleeping by day on park benches, mopping office floors by night, trying, under an assumed name, to earn money enough for new teeth—maybe a new dress. Then she could stage a comeback. But before that comeback could happen she was just another anonymous number on an eventually identified corpse in the morgue.

Even members of our own staff were temperamental, having to be cozened into assignments, resenting editor's "interference" if the story seemed overlong or poorly organized. Good writers are rarely easy agreers. It all adds up to an editor's stress. One of the most difficult staff men, because of his regard for rules, was admirable John Werner, our relentless copy chief. His eye a precision instrument, he doggedly devoted himself to saving the *Journal* from those too frequent errors —in dates, geography, middle initials—which redden many magazine faces. Dedicated to facts, he believed writing, too, is governed by facts. Punctuation, grammar, diction must conform to rules. Ruthlessly he would reparagraph or repunctuate John Steinbeck, Roald Dahl, or even that precise stylist Dinesen, as well as many talented but more helpless beginners. We pleaded with him.

Commas, dashes, periods, verbless sentences even, were a writer's individual expression, we said. An author put it that way because that way accentuated his meaning. John was adamant.

There were rules. It was his duty to see that they were followed. Beatrice used a woman's wiles of coaxing, persuasion, flattery. John, with splendid male lack of malleability, resisted. If Zoë Akins wrote a long, commaless sentence (she used to admit she was dying of creeping parentheses), John Werner put in commas where he thought they ought to be. Finally, we had to issue an absolute rule. He respected rules. Changes could be suggested, but only as queries to the authors; only the author could okay them. Sadly, John resigned himself to this anarchy.

Daphne du Maurier, like Rumer Godden, never liked talking of a forthcoming novel—a little child with a secret. If one spoke of an unwritten story it felt betrayed, Katherine Mansfield had said in her journal. Suddenly, out of the blue, one of Daphne's stories would appear.

But Daphne nearly stopped writing.

"Why bother?" she said. "Income taxes leave barely a shilling in the pound." Why not retreat entirely to the quiet, almost mysterious life she lived at Menabilly? At a rare London luncheon at the Berkeley with her war-hero husband, Sir Frederick ("Boy") Browning, treasurer to Prince Philip, she moaned to us slightly about a command visit at Balmoral, her acceptance required by her husband's palace job. She preferred seclusion, woods, and sea.

In dealings with lawyers for Crawfie, I had learned that an unpublished serial could be given to a writer's child, saving much in taxes. Daphne, stimulated, continued working and set up a nest egg for each of her three with serials which did splendidly in the *Journal*. Another magazine sent an editor abroad with the sole instruction: "Tell Daphne du Maurier we will pay $25,000 more than the *Journal* for her next serial, sight unseen." Since we occasionally turned down a Du Maurier novel we thought not up to standard, this was dangerous for us. But the editor returned empty-handed.

A call on Mme. Chiang, wartime symbol of our oriental sister democracy, sharply contrasted with our informal White House experiences. Mrs. Roosevelt had suggested we see Madame to win her cooperation in our wartime project for leading women of the world. We were invited to call in her Waldorf suite. There conducted from stately room to stately room, we were passed on from aide to aide. At length, a young Chinese secretary led us to a fairly cozy inner sitting room, asked us to wait. Some twenty-five minutes later Mme. Chiang leisurely entered, handsome in a pale lemon-yellow brocaded gown. Even English royalty were more affable. It soon became apparent that Mme. Chiang was vexed.

Soon she explained, to our consternation, that she could not sell her writings for money, as Mrs. Roosevelt (whose guest she had just been in Washington) seemed pleased to do. She could take no money if she consented to our plan. With growing antagonism, to our horrified ears, she denounced Mrs. Roosevelt for profiting from her position in a materialistic U.S.—all this spoken with a curious toughness of American vernacular she could hardly have learned at Wellesley. As the talk continued, the cause of her resentment became plain. Although entertained with warmest hospitality in the White House and in Congress, she was more indignant at the wartime aid China was not receiving from the United States than appreciative of that already given. Since our project was abandoned later, we were never required to discuss it with Madame again.

Many of our writers, of course, were as courteous as officers of Chase Manhattan Bank to a big depositor, as faithful to their commitments, some even willing to admit that editors could be human. With a number of these broad-minded individuals we formed lasting, delightful associations.

Bill Benton, while vice president of the University of Chicago, contributed a series of short editorials to the *Journal* which proved that he could have made a straitened living by writing. Becoming a millionaire by neglecting that talent, he was one of those golden friends Tony Fokker spoke of who had a chartered-for-the-summer yacht, a great, square-rigged schooner, manned by Swedish youths learning to be shipmasters. It was a useless toy, however, without friends aboard to make Bill forget how luxuriously constricted is living on even the best boat. We floated on the Mediterranean with pleasant companions, Bernardine and Harry Scherman, friends from early New

York days before the Book-of-the-Month Club was even a gleam in his eye—Harry, whose taste, whose believing mind and skeptic's shrewdness, whose faith in middle-class intelligence have put more good books into more appreciative hands than any agency in our time. Bernardine, with curiosity, humor, and a contagious zest in sheer living, was doing a book column for the *Journal*. Both deepened every discussion by their disciplined, tolerant comment just as they widened every pleasure by their evident enjoyment of it. Like Bill, Harry was a self-made millionaire, his tastes and Bernardine's so serenely set in their impecunious youth that wealth was something they were more inclined to lavish on others than on themselves. In our interwoven lives the only serious criticism I have ever launched at Harry was that he would consult a watch at intervals while climbing mountains to be sure he reached the top on schedule, as he always did.

Adlai Stevenson was aboard. Since he was not above harpooning himself with the same trenchant wit which speared so many political adversaries, he made a delightful traveling companion. Like the Mets, Adlai possessed the odd quality of attracting most enthusiasm in defeat. His self-control, and personal discipline at the UN, under often difficult circumstances, set a high-water mark for that sometimes raucous tribunal—a tribunal you might say at war with peace. But on holidays that discipline was off duty. Rising early with the youthful crew, whose appetite for fried potatoes and sizzling sausages he matched pound for pound, he later would show up for a second cup of coffee when the nine-o'clock laggards sat down to sparser fare. Unfortunately, he was seldom seen aloft in the rigging working off his breakfasts as did the crew monkeys. Adlai could have been a fine actor. His mimicry, at a party, of one of our more vivid shipmates had a kind of good-humored savagery Robert Morley would have been pushed to excel.

Just as Bill liked women, challenged them, got on with them, so women liked, almost adored, Adlai.

Happily, Bill was a thoughtful host in more than luxury and delicious food during the two weeks for which his ordinary guests signed on. As the star of Bill's showboat, Adlai took the entire Mediterranean cruise. Always aboard was a devoted feminine friend, comforting, somewhat maternal, usually worshipful—one debarking, perhaps, in southern Spain as another charming stagedoor Jennie joined ship. Due to complications in Bill's ordinarily skillful logistics with the guest list, two feminine admirers were, for a few days, aboard at once; this produced a slight tension. It seemed to us that those hovering women gentled Adlai's arduous and devoted life of public service.

Bill, as avid in pursuit of knowledge as in pursuit of money, while wrapping us in comfort holystoned our neglected minds. Each day, watching the sunset slip into evening over the ship's taffrail, two guests who had spent the past twenty-four hours scouring reference books, including the Encyclopaedia Britannica, which just happened to be aboard, reported in detail at cocktail hour on history, fact, and legend about the next port of call, perhaps the population of Malta, the history of its knights—solid preparation for our rubber-soled, earnest trip of the morrow.

Bill was no more sparing of himself than he was of his guests. He was also a devoted reader of his own publications. As others were dressing for dinner he did a half hour's physical jerks on the deserted afterdeck, having persuaded his loyal wife, Helen, to sit beside him reading selected, worthwhile passages from one of his fifty Great Books, also, by chance, aboard.

Bill should have been in the periodical publishing business. With his shrewd mind, enormous energy, and genuine interest in the dissemination of information, he might have made an even greater contribution, if possible, to our times than his successful, more scattered activities achieved.

We boarded Bill's yacht once again a year later on a short voyage down the coast of Yugoslavia. Ambassador George Kennan and his wife, Annelise, with whom we were going on to Belgrade, were aboard. So were *Time-Life* publisher Henry Luce and his wife, Clare Boothe Luce. Clare, still beautiful, was fascinating to men like Bill and George, partly because of her informed grasp of world affairs and political maneuver, but partly because of her blue-eyed concentration on their every word. She had her own arts, often the most flattering one of all being "Tell me." Coolly, in the meantime, she pursued

Republican political ends which made her a Congressman from Con-
necticut and an ambassador to Rome; her further diplomatic career
receiving a fatal blow from the same horse which she suggested had
kicked Wayne Morse into opposing her. Her undeniable arts might
have landed her almost anywhere, except that, once in a while, the
perfected mechanism went slightly awry, the voice became thin and
the goal too obvious. She then had to retreat to the dressing room and
make up all over, as "little me." Women, like men trying their hardest
to become President, should pretend they are being really forced into
prominence—hypocrisy must pay its toll to femininity as well as to
democracy. A little nook where they can continue knitting while
rocking the baby is the sought-after image.

Henry, absorbed in books and papers, was silent much of the
time, but when he spoke his comments were pithy and stimulating.
We regretted we could not go on to the Isles of Greece in such
interesting company, but our trip with the Kennans through the
mountains of Montenegro, picnicking on the way, visiting ancient
Byzantine churches, was an experience not to be missed.

Back in Princeton, Robert Oppenheimer, fondling a book as John
Gilbert might have fondled Garbo, startled me by murmuring reverently, "This is a first edition of Mendel's law."

He had taken the slender volume down from a shelf at the Institute
of Advanced Study to show it to Walter Elliot, whom Harold Dodds
and I were informally conducting around the Princeton campus. Why,
I wondered, awe for a first edition on the part of a great mathematician presumably interested only in facts, unvarying in any edition.

"What difference," I asked, "does it make to you whether it's a
first or a fifth? The facts are the same."

Unabashed, continuing to caress Mendel, Oppenheimer tried to
explain. "I guess—well, being close to this first edition brings me
closer, somehow, in spirit to Mendel's times, the actual moment he
conceived his law."

"How does a mathematician," I asked, "make his discoveries—is it
all carefully thought out—or more a sudden inspiration?"

"More," answered Oppenheimer, "like a poet, perhaps. Shakespeare
probably never worked out his poetry word by word. The lines must

often have just leaped into his mind. I think mathematicians are like poets. They get an idea. Then they set out to prove it. That's about the way it happens."

"I've always been interested, too," I continued, seeing that he was in an answering mood this Sunday, "whether knowing so much about the universe that is complete mystery to the common brain makes a man believe more or less in God."

Oppenheimer sucked on his pipe as if he would draw the answer deep from its bowl. It was some time before he replied.

"Well, I don't know," he finally admitted. "Einstein believed in God, I should say. Niels Bohr doesn't, I think."

Einstein, I knew, felt something like Goethe that "the universe is the living garment of God."

Oppenheimer did not say what he believed—he was born a Jew; when he died his funeral was a secular memorial.

Beatrice's mother held religious views similar to Einstein's as revealed in the little book I helped her to compose in her ninetieth year, just before she died,* her thoughts at ninety surprisingly interesting to the young.

Walt Disney was a magical companion of many days, even as he engagingly postponed writing his half-promised life story for us. Our friend Ruth Moore first learned of Disney's death from the headlines of a fellow commuter's paper. She begged an instant's look (her husband, Fred, had long helped in Disney's financing), explaining: "I am proud to say Walt Disney was my friend."

"Madam," her neighbor said, handing over the paper, "Walt Disney was everybody's friend."

An enviable epitaph.

* *Conversations on the Edge of Eternity*. Morrow, 1965.

Life happens differently every day.
—OUR FIVE-YEAR-OLD GRANDSON

24 🐌

We Lived Here

During these years of hard work, of ranging travel—as Bruce and I sought new scenes, pursued people for their ideas and the pleasure of their company—our farm at Hopewell, of course, remained the center of our real life. How much of oneself a house absorbs. How its very walls reflect our history.

Here our daughter grew up. From here she was married in an austere Quaker service to a young man who contributed not only cheerful intelligence to our family life, but a further auburn strain to assure that no grandchild was less than a redhead. Here she returns to visit with her children, who enjoy, as she did, the open fields, violets and milkweed, animals, things growing, life turning.

From the wise age of three Sesaly loved the farm. "It is quiet here," she announced, rejecting New York's roar. She loved the raucous chickens, the sudsy thud of milking in a barn often mysterious by lantern light. Russet cornfields invited exploration of their magic aisles.

Even during Depression years we usually had a high-school girl, happy with food and lodging and a very few dollars, to help with housework so we remained free to write. To one of these, an awkward farm girl, religious and kind, I owe two charming compliments, both relayed by my husband:

"I always thought Mrs. Gould must have done domestic work as a girl; she is so understanding of someone who does for her."

"Mrs. Gould is the finest woman I've ever known who was not a Christian"—that is, we did not go to church regularly, as she did. Like Winston Churchill, Bruce has always been more a buttress than a pillar of the church, giving support from outside.

When my father's shattered affairs were settled, my parents moved to an old, whitewashed stone house on the broad-flowing Delaware, its purchase price salvaged from the collapse of his Iowa properties.

Our house, now ours, grew and changed as our lives did. The two square farm parlors became a long living room. Federal chests, walnut rockers, and maple beds from Bucks County and Trenton secondhand shops supplemented our scanty store. A small, fat, red-plush sofa costing $4, brought home roped to the back of the ancient Velie, was greeted with hooting laughter by my husband. Thoroughly cleaned, its springs tied up, my husband's jeers ignored, it was slipcovered in soft green to match the carpet, stood proudly beside the corner hearth in the hall. It stands there still, now more expertly upholstered in prim-patterned violet calico. Painted a soft pink, the dining room turned dining room again. The old kitchen became our daughter's playroom, its ancient chimney made to draw, its small stair curling round to her bedroom above. The windmill pump gave way to more reliable electricity, and several miniature bathrooms were squeezed into odd corners and under roof slants. One is called the Thin Man still. In what had been back sheds, housing old boots, snow shovels, washtubs, a modern laundry and kitchen grew, blessed, because windows were small, with a skylight above which white clouds scud and star patterns wink.

Seedlings grew to massed evergreens. A small apple orchard set out when Sesaly was eight grew tall enough to walk under in bewitching fragrance during her courting days.

Throughout these years undoubtedly my job gave me more fun than solitary writing might have done. Editing brings a fascinating, strange array of people near and there is pleasure, too, in exacting work. My "career"—an overimposing word—was extremely enjoyable to me. Whether it was equally good for my daughter I am not sure.

I still regret those days she returned from school to a house empty except for paid helpers. I still question those out-of-town trips, even though my mother and father were generous in coming to stay or taking Sesaly when our trips devoured weekends. (Doubtless this is why I have perhaps an exaggerated respect for the utility of a handy grandmother today.) And until Sesaly went away to school we did not keep a New York apartment, commuting on fatiguing trains three days for me, five for Bruce to a house where the nursery governess longed to recount problems and hurt feelings.

"You say Peachy is supposed to be here to take care of *me*," my child rebelled one day. "Really, she has nothing to do. I have to take care of *her*."

And, later, a sequence of lively young girls, companions after school hours, were often found detachedly reading, bored, eager to be off about their own lives. When generous Negro helpers came to our house its atmosphere grew warmer. The kitchen became friendly, smelling of cookies.

If I could have chosen my own pattern I would have stayed at home until our daughter was older. But of course life is never entirely arrangeable. It was then that opportunity offered, that my husband needed me.

As I see my daughter's five, giggling, quarreling, playing on a friendly street, often with three or four neighbor children trooping in, I am glad their mother is there. What career can equal this? Mom is at home, to praise art, offer snacks, hear news, patch hurt knees, hurt feelings. A small child's problems cannot always be deferred till after supper or settled, by appointment, on Saturday or Sunday. And so much of a family's beliefs and principles can be conveyed in random moments—while a button is sewed on, over a cup of cambric tea, after a bicycle tumble; while hearing about a friend "who isn't nice to me any more" or about a frightening bully down the street. Talk is fruitful when the mood to talk is there. My daughter survived with standards unimpaired, but became more bookish perhaps than she otherwise might have become. Surviving well, she cherishes no career ambitions for herself.

It was a pleasure, always, to work with my husband—stubborn and nettly, often (I, too,), intensely opposite in so many things— who lightened any disagreement with his humor, gave more than generous credit to my part-time contributions and, perhaps because he is so masculine, allowed me always to be a woman—in my editorial attitudes, in shirking, when necessary, my working job for those things important to a woman—allowing me, for instance, to take a clear month as each of Sesaly's first three children were born, when she and her promising husband, Ted, lived in a young, bustling Midwest town where hospitals were overcrowded and help, either for nursing or cleaning, was starkly unavailable. I doubt whether for me my work would have been possible with anyone but Bruce—and on any but a part-time basis. But it brought stimulus and enjoyment.

Happiness is a different thing.

It comes in remembered gleams. Our first visit to Sesaly at camp— my carefully chosen button-down-the-front green linen dress, brown-and-white shoes, conservative Panama slightly dipped over one eye, white cotton gloves, one modest string of pearls. My reward: "Oh, Mummy, you look so nice," after warm embraces. "You look just the way a mother ought to look."

Or, again, when the public-health nurse (in Muskegon) came to teach a very new mother, after only three days in the hospital, to bathe a very unfamiliar infant, aided only by an anonymous, work-aday grandmother with skills long forgotten—"Sesaly, you're so lucky your mother can be here—most mothers are working nowa-days."

A little girl coming softly early to my bedside: "Can I snuggle?" Her small boy, red-haired, too, clutching the same stuffed dog— stuffing new, calico skin new, but the same—peering round the same door: "Can I snuggle?"

So reality lies in our big old house, growing rather worn, with room early for my parents, and later our young marrieds, coming back with a baby, two, suddenly five children; exploding everywhere,

fascinated by Mama's books and dolls, dressups in the attic, and by
Bruce's dictating machine; picnics, pine cones, a brook to fall in.

Our early walnut table from Morton Street with hard refectory
chairs around it is now in the playroom. How many greedy children's
milk and cookies has its bare old wood offered? How many gay party
meals, also, with friends overflowing from the dining room. Six
people there, too crowded, heads to heads, talking, talking barely
room for plates and glasses:

> Your hands once touched this table and this silver
> And I have seen your fingers hold this glass. . . .
> . . . . Your touch upon them will not pass.

Here my mother dressed in gray-blue lace for her ninetieth birthday
party—shared with ten-year-old Dean, born on May 19 when his
great-grandmother was exactly eighty years old—the first time I ever
heard my spirited mother admit, far less brag about, her great-age.
Together, they made an exact one hundred. We called it the party
of the century.

Our long, narrow blue living room, faded by sunny light from three
sides, is cozy for tray dinners for two before its fire, really wakes up
with companionable talk, or when music and dancing in the playroom
set the walls throbbing and fun flows throughout the house.

George Kennan, poet as well as historian, bending mischievously
over his guitar, strumming gypsy tunes in unambassadorial merriment
—nearby his gay, distinguished wife, Annelise.

Baroness Karen Blixen, old, frail, polished and ill, her elegance a
repudiation of age and illness; at a New York publishing party a
wide dramatic hat of black monkey fur had accentuated her bone-
thin face, her shadowed haunting eyes; in Princeton she dressed
appropriately in golden tweeds, gold-turbaned, for a golden fall day.
So fragile one questioned whether she could continue breathing, she
began in our playroom to recite her tales to an audience from the
university, gathering strength and magnetism as she spoke till she was
the frail, glowing center of a spellbound room.

Our old house has welcomed Rumer Godden, her eyebrows black
wings over mysterious, perceiving eyes, sharing memories with hand-

some Bob Goheen, Princeton's president, whose youth with missionary parents was also spent in India. Harold Dodds, Bob's predecessor, humorous, responsive, so enjoying good, amusing talk that he will often speak "against himself" in a spirited discussion—like a good debater appreciating two points of view; his contained wife, Margaret, giving an early impression of formality, almost sedateness, masks a merry, untrammeled self. She, when President Johnson's widely pictured gall-bladder scar was mentioned at a sedate ladies' luncheon, remarked tartly, "Aren't we lucky it wasn't a prostate?"

There come Rensselaer Lee and his Stella, serene as the evening star, but more warmly shining. Rens, fastidious, humorous, his mind a treasure house of art and literature, for years headed Princeton's department of art and archeology. In Rome, "I want you to see one picture, just one Caravaggio here, then we'll have lunch high over the city and a little wine." Poetry lives in his mind, instantly summoned to enrich a conversation—as of my mother in her final years he quoted Yeats:

> An aged man is but a paltry thing,
> A tattered coat upon a stick, unless
> Soul clap its hands and sing, and louder sing
> For every tatter in its mortal dress.

Rebecca West, beautiful, with overpowering dark eyes and a lightning-swift mind, terrified me during early acquaintance. She seemed never to forget a picture she had seen, a book she had read, or a person she had known (so many of all). She could summon at will all the relevancies of this vast experience into one swift and pertinent, often devastating sentence. Happily she is also interested in good food, attractive houses, French dressmakers. And, a wonderful gossip, she uses gossip in its best way, not for malice or spite but in a continuing attempt (valid for a writer, but valuable, too, for us all) to understand human character. "Now why do you suppose he left her?" The answer, never malicious, though quite possibly sharp, a score of complex possible motivations brought to light and weighed. From her store of persons, their life stories followed with a writer's perception, her conversation can give all the pleasure of a good novel, since in life, too, stories have their beginning, their climax, and often the terrifying conclusion, learned in childhood, "As ye sow so shall ye reap." Henry Andrews, Rebecca's courtly banker husband, knowledgeable in literature and art as well as finance, enriched many conversations.

The George Gallups, neighbors in the Bahamas as well as in Princeton, seem almost a part of our house, having known it since its early-plumbing days—he with his questioning mind, always seeking better ways, new solutions, so that when he is trying to sail an Abaco dinghy he refuses a teacher, makes his own rules, finds the why of old ones. "In sailing you learn by your mistakes," he says, ruefully rubbing his ear, hard-clapped by a jibing boom. His try-for-yourself methods and his scientist's refusal to warp findings for monetary gain have made "Gallup-poll" almost a single word, respected in much of the world. His wife, Ophelia, generous friend, masks clear intelligence and piercing humor under her quiet, warmly-responsive, dove-gray manner.

In our house, for years kept clean, waxed, and shining by the sterling, admired qualities of Mrs. Hixson, I have known, too, a cook, Julia John, crippled with agonizing arthritis, who pours forth a stream of love in soups and pies, and in cakes and cookies, "not for meals—just for eating," when children are about. Who, in occasional sultry rages, not against us but against brooding Things, treats her iron frying pans as enemies, with clamor, but who puts love into toast that is always hot, an egg that is quietly ready exactly when you are ready for it. And I have been pleased to consider one of my cherished friends for twenty years a Negro housekeeper whose dignity, courtesy, and tact match a diplomat's—proud, honorable, and kind, with beauty too—Mary Sullivan.

Memories linger in our house, of beloved dogs, of amusing cats —the greatest, that golden, gentle Sappho, growing rather worn as she produced, with two suitable husbands, 110 golden Persian kittens, all beautiful, all like their mother, gentle and gay. A fan of blue-eyed yellow puffballs followed us on summer evenings over green grass; for our entertainment their mother taught them to tussle and leap, to climb trees, to toy with captured mice. That famous race had a waiting list, never exhausted; kittens were finally scattered like stations along the Pennsylvania Railroad—Washington, Baltimore,

Wilmington, Philadelphia, Trenton, Princeton, New York, Boston. Long after Sappho's peaceful, rueful end, unknown persons telephoned or wrote, "Have you any more of those marvelous . . ."

So, in our house, we laughed with Ogden Nash, with K and Walter Elliot, and Sir Denis Browne, from whom wit exploded like a roman candle. With writing friends we have probed human motives in relaxed talk, exploring politics, our neighbors, and the mysteries of existence, the meaning of God.

We have enjoyed handsome young neighbors, in Hopewell and Princeton, generous to their seniors in tennis, in friendship, in fresh viewpoints, sharing the gaiety of elastic young bodies and elastic minds. Others, long unseen, are in my mind as I write. "To know of someone here and there, whom we accord with, who is living on with us, even in silence—this makes our earthly ball a peopled garden," says Goethe. So, to me, my friends seem a bouquet—vivid anemones, purple, mauve or red; spicy carnation pinks; sturdy black-eyed Susans; humorous nasturtiums—joyous as a scented, flower-filled border in June.

My parents' capacity for admiration doubtless shaped me. Like Camus I believe there are more things in men to admire than to despise. I have found myself rarely with people who were malicious, envious, ignoble—though all have foibles.

> The soul selects her own society,
> Then shuts the door.

Like a sundial I, perhaps, mark only the sunny hours. The dark hours I forget; the sun shines on so much.

Holidays are shared with friends, children, and grandchildren. In the Bahamas a turquoise sea, white-ruffled, beats at the east side of our cottage and on the west a calm harbor shows off orange and purple sunsets over quietly stirring boats. Seagrape flowers scent our outdoor dinners, and moons grow larger and oftener. In Martha's Vineyard, from our terrace, we see the Elizabeth Islands rise, fog-veiled or sunny above rocks, woods, and ocean. On clear evenings, perched in a large climbable oak, the tree-top chorus, singing redheads, divert our cocktail hour; in autumn, huckleberry, wine-red on headlands, outlines the dark bright blue of the Sound, our Vineyard retreat perhaps never discovered had not generous friends, Ruth and Fred Moore, shared its unspoiled beauty with us. But we return always to the old house, still holding old fragrances, its potpourri of so much living.

In the final chapter of her autobiography, Simone de Beauvoir, great writer friend of the greater Sartre, rails at fifty-four at growing old, bemoans the loss of power, love, and beauty, compares her wrinkled face in the mirror with the face she remembers from when she was twenty, a whole life before her—says, as her concluding words, "I realize with stupor how much I was gypped."

It is true that a woman's life often seems to impose limitations, either upon intellectual or worldly achievement (perhaps more limitations on worldly recognition than upon intellectual fulfillment itself). Florida Scott-Maxwell says in *Women and Sometimes Men* that a woman needs always to know just what is in the refrigerator at that moment. Rebecca West observed years ago that the cream of a woman's energy is taken every morning by fifty small questions, tasks and interruptions before she can sit down to her major tasks.

The present day is woman's province; men have tomorrow also; perhaps that is why they are the seers and dreamers as well as the builders. Lunch cannot be postponed a day or two while one concentrates on world-shaking endeavor. Lunch, nourishing body and spirit, links one, however, close to life itself. "What good soup!"— A tray for an invalid. "I feel better." These are rewards for interrupted hours.

I remember my mother's youngest sister, pretty as a girl, with great blue-gray eyes under dark brows, engaged to a young man struck down by polio. Crippled, he withdrew from the marriage. She lived on as a spinster librarian inclined to melancholy, reminiscence, regret. When she was old, her mind hazy, she would wander through the house crying, "Where is my baby? Where have they put my baby?"

The cry, in a way, of so many as we grow older, "Where is

my . . .?" That something that life seemed to promise, some aim realized, some dream, of perfect love, perfect happiness, of finding answers to mysteries—where is the fulfillment of that promise?

Women perhaps are fortunate; they have their babies in a realer sense than men have theirs. Possibly, women are less likely, in later years, to give this cry of incompletion. Having always had interesting work, and a rewarding family life too, I feel doubly grateful.

Thinking over in busy days the life I have lived, there are two minor qualities for which I can testify, along with the greater ones we somehow take for granted. My husband says he is sentimental. He is. And what delight this heart-lifting quality gives. How fortunate to have it house-close. How endearing every tear at the movies, at a choked reading aloud of "The Death of the Hired Man."

As for me I am hopelessly naïve. I gush over historic ruins, young children in graceful play, each sunset lurid scarlet or cloud-dimmed to palest rose. Nor do the words "What a beautiful sunset!," uttered in happy peace, seem to me more trite than that oft-repeated "Praise God, from whom all blessings flow!"

As I have been thinking over our life in this old house, the many blessings I enjoy here, the blessings I would wish for my grandchildren, I would like to say to them: "If your desires are to do things, you are more likely to be happy than if your desire is to have things."

Cadillacs become junk, but skies and stars are there as long as one has eyes to see; the roar of the sea, music, and friendly voices exist as long as ears can hear.

Companionship enjoyed with laughter is delectable fruit. So I would wish for my grandchildren the character, the courtesy, and the ability to admire (with—oh, desirably—a whiff of humor) which will make possible for them the respect and friendship of those people they like and regard (to be worldly for a moment, good posture, grace of body, attractive attire are in themselves endearing).

I hope they will have courage, courage to try again, never to compromise with what they think is right, though a friend might be lost or a job be lost in the choice. (For a man with courage, there is another job and a stauncher friend.) I will always remember my mother's unconquerable words "I can do *anything* I must."

Bruce says to his grandchildren, "Keep your eyes on the stars; your feet will find the cobblestones." I wish for them satisfaction in work, in problems solved, silver polished, knowledge shared, a cake well baked, a child taught.

For me a husband fortunately met (but recognized, I claim, by shrewd perception), coming in no Ivy League attire, no material goods in hand, a husband boundlessly generous in supporting a wife's sometimes shaky ego (never guilty of that marriage-dooming cruelty of nibbling away a partner's confidence in small criticisms, in compliments unsaid)—this marriage has been life's greatest gift. How I would like to teach my grandchildren, before this important choice, Stella Benson's words, "Call no man foe, but never love a stranger."

The greatest sin of all is to lose faith in one's fellow man.
—JOHN DEWEY OF HIS NINETIETH BIRTHDAY

25

We Say Goodbye

All companies rise and fall with the dynamism of their leaders. Sons do not necessarily inherit, together with stock control, the intelligence, imagination, and courage of their forebears.

It is impossible, I suppose, to participate in the dwindling of a great publishing company, where opportunities were generously given, where happy years were spent, without pondering the reasons for decline. Did the downward slide lie in policies?—in men?—how much in one's own wrong decisions, in one's inability to persuade others to different, perhaps better, decisions?

Looking back over the bumpy road of life and the ups and downs of my career—amusing and satisfying, varied and fruitful in so many ways—I realize, rather late, a glaring fault in my character. I lack humility.

The ability, even the desire, to conciliate in order to win is hardly a part of my nature. I tend to feel a policy I believe in is so obviously right that a person who opposes it is, to speak mildly, a dolt. I am not sure I mask this feeling. Perhaps it becomes apparent to the other fellow. This attitude, I belatedly realize, is scarcely winning.

316

An early example of this lack of tact still amuses me, though I am aware my behavior was less than ingratiating. But from Curtis, Bok, and Lorimer I had inherited the testy tradition that the editor is not to be interfered with.

One day, when I was very new, I received from Cary Bok, in Maine, a critical telegram—my response was an automatic "Hands off."

His message lamented that the *Journal* spoke of Franz Schubert as a musician when all the world knew him as a famous composer. This error not only damaged Curtis' high reputation for accuracy but reflected on Cary's known encyclopedic knowledge of matters musical.

Our copy chief, Jack Werner, showed me defensively a fairly long article in an encyclopedia for musicians. Franz Schubert was, indeed, a famous composer. But there was another Franz Schubert, noted enough as a violinist to merit continuing fame, to whom the *Journal* article clearly referred. I instructed my secretary to telegraph the entire encyclopedia's piece on Franz Schubert, the violinist, to Cary—collect, and at day rates.

I was never sure, as years went by, and I became only slightly wiser, that this episode had improved my relations with Cary.

Early on, Mr. Lorimer had suggested to me that I be groomed as president of Curtis, to succeed, or actually replace Walter Fuller. Fuller, a clear-headed, intelligent man, steeped in the ethics of the Curtis tradition as long-time company secretary with the founder, had been chosen by Mr. Curtis to succeed to the presidency. But Lorimer believed Fuller had the virtues of the-second-in-command rather than the dynamism required to hold our turbulent company on a strong course.

Before he sprang this surprising suggestion on me, Mr. Lorimer had often told me how much he disliked being president. The time-wasting business problems of paper, of manufacture, of ink production, which must vary with the weather, of circulation policies and advertising personnel took too many precious hours away from what he really enjoyed—the imaginative business of planning, creating (and in some instances himself writing for) the great magazine he loved. Moreover, he assured me, an editor had more fun and dealt with more interesting people than businessmen usually had access to. In this I agreed, and I managed to convince him I did not wish to be considered for the presidency. Already ill of cancer of the throat —though unaware of it—he didn't force the point.

As I look back, I sometimes think I am fighter enough so that, had I been chief executive, I would have torn the company apart rather than participate in the slow, gradual, and sadly predictable decline. Perhaps this is only my old arrogance roaring and shaking its mane. I am quite certain that, with the increasing complexity of publishing, one man could not have been president of Curtis and continued to edit the *Journal,* and editing a magazine is a career I would not have missed. Moreover, I could easily have made the worst president Curtis ever had. Since no one can tell what might have happened, I cannot regret my choice.

I then believed that, as long as an editor had full control of his publication, overlordship as to its promotion and advertising policies, a determining say in its distribution and manufacturing problems, then no business-department attitudes could affect him. This had been Curtis tradition; and at Curtis successful editors had always had more power than advertising or business heads. But the publisher-owner, perceptive enough to put the editor first, had gone—and control was fractured. A good editor needs a good publisher—primarily to see that the heads of advertising, circulation are determined able men; secondarily to balance the always conflicting pressures between them. I should have realized from the theatre that "control" can be nibbled away in tiny fragments, some of them described as "cooperation" or "going along."

A strong, editorial-oriented publishing head is frequently the only one who sees the magazine as a whole. Without this omnipotence diverse departments tend to squabble among themselves since their aims are different. Especially is this true in promotion. The advertising department's job is to sell advertising—and if in so doing it presents the magazine's audience as so many sheep being led to the seller's market, it is unable to perceive the betrayal this may seem to astute readers. Circulation men selling the magazine as a whole to subscribers have a yearning for big, well-known names—Edna Ferber, the Duchess of Windsor, Jackie Kennedy (the quality of the manuscript they leave to the editor). To get a big newsstand sale they like to attract other than regular buyers. Therefore, they crave something provocative or sensational. In an uncensored circulation ad even a worthy Dr. Spock article on teenagers can be promoted to seem to offer the forbidden or titillating, cheapening a loved magazine's image to its most enthusiastic readers. Yet it is the enthusiasm of the multi-reading, oft-returning audience that advertisers buy. This intangible but very real spirit of a publication should never be distorted for short-term gains.

The business department, too, needs an editorial-oriented publisher for, since the business department's business is to balance its books and see that there is a profit, it not unnaturally looks with skepticism on too great aggrandizement of the editorial role. "All those people just sitting around there thinking up ideas!" A costly gamble like *The Little Princesses* can affright them. They labor to get good color printing reasonably. The best at any price is what the editor desires. Views as to paper differ. Editors want quality, businessmen price. Only a publisher who puts the quality of the magazine first—as Curtis, Lorimer, and to a certain extent Mr. Fuller did—can keep a clear vision among all these pressures.

An old, solid institution perhaps appreciates its own past and present leadership too much. Its "prestige" becomes crystallized, more real and perceptible within the company than to the competitive world outside. Its success and prosperity seem to affectionate insiders to be frozen, unchanging, and unchallengable.

To such loyal company men things will always go on as they have. New departures, if any, are to be approached timidly.

And timidity likes imitation, fears originality. In the booming postwar years when some branching-out was cautiously considered, the branching-outers felt safer in trying to copy established success.

Curtis, under Fuller, decided to put out a picture magazine. "Like *Life,* only better" was the guideline. It wasn't easy to better *Life,* as *Look* was discovering. Months and hundreds of thousands were spent in dead-secret attempts to design a successful, highly imitative picture weekly, magazine "X" it was called, and then abandoned. The projected editor, Ted Patrick, was abruptly drafted to save already troubled *Holiday,* which he made a brilliant magazine.

Ventures under Robert MacNeal, later, were equally unoriginal. *Brides Magazine* was doing well—why shouldn't Curtis publish a "like, only better" version? This, and a similarly ill-fated *TV Guide* imitation, failed after a few costly issues. The president did not accept any responsibility for these failures. "Our circulation department told me they could sell such magazines. Apparently they couldn't," he sidestepped.

The opinion of Curtis editors was consulted on none of these projects. They were planned solely by business and circulation men; as copycats their doom might have been foreseen.

After these failures caution and economy became more marked.

Having opposed policies we considered the opposite of vigorous, such as holding back *Journal* circulation to protect the *Post*'s leadership, while allowing *Life*'s total circulation to pass first the *Post*'s, then the *Journal*'s ("We're too smart to get in a disastrous circulation war," said management), I began to regret my lack of persuasive powers. Our suggestions, also, that the Curtis board be enriched by including one or two men of wide experience and success in the field of public opinion (men like Dr. Gallup, Scherman, Benton, Rubicam, Ogilvy) were regarded as so critical as almost to constitute active disloyalty. Since these men were all friends or acquaintances (which is why we knew their capacity and character), it is possible some felt we were simply trying to ensure a board favorable to our own venturesome ideas, often described as brash.

We had always said to ourselves we would retire at fifty-five, while the world was still wide and fair to explore. By then, however, it seemed more necessary than ever to try to persuade our company of the need for dynamic policies. Lively, imaginative competition was being met with caution. We were told that the *Journal* print order could not be increased because advertisers would not support a larger circulation.

It was impossible to persuade management that *Life,* and later *Look,* cutting subscription rates, determined to lead in circulation, were confident that, with good promotion, advertising would rapidly follow. Madison Avenue seldom inquires anything but "Who's first?" It was the expressed view of our officials that such reckless slashing of subscription and advertising prices would simply cause other companies to go broke. They sat back and waited for this to happen. The *Post,* losing first place, with promotion less skillful, lost advertising dominance to its livelier competitors.

Traditionally Curtis had believed its prestige was such that both *Post* and *Journal* could maintain higher advertising rates than competitors. This was not rational—it was simply an emotional holdover from years of undisputed success. When others cut advertising rates drastically, *Journal* rates remained as high as ever. Not unnaturally, advertisers preferred a lower price with the bonus of higher circulation. But it could only be a matter of time, our people felt, until such rash bookkeeping would cause collapse. Any slide rule, any column of figures would show that these procedures simply weren't sound business, MacNeal pointed out. Curtis' standing, its long-established, well-loved publications were certain to carry us through. Complacently, we would watch others lose millions through such ill-judged cut-rate policies. To make up for dwindling revenues, economy, it was decided, was the way to weather this temporary crisis.

So all possible minor retrenchments—thinning paper, watering inks, downgrading color printing—reduced, and partially destroyed, the former beauty of our magazine. Curtailing editorial pages—as it became apparent that advertising was indeed declining—further limited readership appeal.

While other publications deluged Madison Avenue with aggressive promotion campaigns, *Post* and *Journal* promotion budgets were sharply cut. Promotion should not be too competitive, it was decided. The word "First" regarding newsstand or total circulation must never be used by the *Journal.* It might spur on the fighting spirit and lavish spending of our rivals.

For instance, though *McCall's* had announced and advertised its determination to pass *L.H.J.* on the newsstand in 1960, the *Journal's* newsstand sale actually exceeded *McCall's* in all issues but one. Our promotion agency prepared a clever ad showing twelve *Journal* covers, one with its shamed face turned to the wall, thus dramatizing our single month's loss of supremacy in our year-long, continuing leadership—a good-natured brag.

MacNeal, by this time a prisoner of his own indecision, forbade the promotion department to run it. We don't want to increase antagonism, was his view.

It was inconceivable to Beatrice and me that such cautious policies would be adhered to when the very life of the company seemed at stake. But, by this time, the business department had the full ear of ownership. Comfortable with figures, finding strength in balancing the budget, it waited in its cyclone cellar for the tornado to pass over. Morale in the advertising department was shattered. Circulation men, more confident—circulation on both magazines held up astonishingly well—asserted that if the *Journal* print order was increased the *Journal* could be "let out" to eight million without strain. This was vetoed, as risky, by MacNeal. With already declining advertising, would advertisers pay higher rates for even more circulation? In spite of smaller books, with fewer editorial pages, even with poor paper and poorer color printing, *Journal* newsstand, because of editorial content alone, remained high, well above competition, our cheering circulation men reported. Our competition flooded the newsstands and accepted a higher rate of returned copies. Women still seemed to prefer the *Journal*.

Cary Bok, representing his family as majority stockholder, had served in the business department. He respected the business mind. Not well, he now spent most of his time in Maine. He was frequently unavailable for consultation, yet with a hesitant management he exercised, even in absentia, great power, chiefly of a negative sort. In the disorganized company, the will to take any strong decisions seemed entirely lacking. Penny-pinching seemed to Bob MacNeal the only solution. Demoralized, he found it possible to say to Beatrice and me, in 1959, "Our —— department is terrible" and two years later in 1961, having made no changes, say to Mary Bass, "You know our —— department is the worst in the field."

When our suggestions were listened to politely and politely ignored, when it became abundantly apparent that Curtis was too proud to fight, we found someone who seemed likely to rise to competitive challenge in the time-honored way—by sheer determination to come out on top.

Beatrice and I interested a man of wide public interests—a proven success in business, skilled in promotion—who agreed to buy into Curtis with the hope of bringing new life to its board, its business, and its publishing methods.

Through friends in Wall Street, another interested group, of equally high reputation, with unlimited financial resources, was also inspired, by us, to look into Curtis affairs. We pushed them both forward as possible purchasers before Curtis found itself on the ropes.

While these negotiations were going on, and as long as Curtis did not actually turn down our candidate's proposals to buy the *Post* and the *Journal,* or the company itself, we withheld our resignations. Our interested Wall Street group started discussions, but their representative was repulsed so coldly, he said afterward, it was almost as if he'd suggested something criminal in asking for the privilege of examining the company's worth. The other man's offer to buy was after some months formally withdrawn because Cary Bok delayed, then refused even to see him, let alone discuss terms.

A poignant moment was revealed to us, later. Nellie Lee Bok (wife of Curtis, Edward Bok's older son, a lawyer and judge, who had never participated in any way in the company but was a substantial stockholder in the Curtis trust) told us of standing in Curtis' hospital room, where he was recuperating from one of a series of severe, eventually fatal, heart attacks. With tears in her eyes, fingernails clenched in her palms, she heard Curtis, weak and ill, try over the telephone to persuade his obdurate brother, Cary, at least to see our candidate who was offering to buy the entire company, or if preferable to buy only the *Journal* and the *Post.* The interview was never granted.

When all these efforts failed, we realized we, at least, could do no more. Regretting our lack of persuasive powers, we submitted our resignations to take effect in a month.

We would miss, we knew, the keen enjoyment of our profession, the pleasure of working with able, enthusiastic people—many more than mentioned here. It had been fun when a vivid story leaped out from ill-typed pages; fun to bring the unexpected to millions— Margaret Mead's *Male and Female*; Bill Mauldin's bristly, earthy story of his war; John Steinbeck, persuaded he could write for the masses. We were proud of the skill in our craft which enabled us to win the trust and exuberant affection of our readers. The communication between us like a strong tide flowed out to them in the magazine and flowed back to us in messages, newsdealers' reports, and letters. Ruled drugstore sheets, prim printed stationery expressed similar messages, not always as memorably simple as the one on thick, engraved paper from Cartier topping my pile one morning: "Dear Journal, I love you!" It amused Beatrice when, during the war, Sir William Haley, editor of the London *Times,* told her, "My wife always has two *Journals* sent—one by sea, one by air—to be sure she never misses an issue."

America had come to our desks: "I have to barbecue a pig next Friday." "I need a wardrobe for a summer trip to Africa." "Tell me how to tell my parents—" or "I decided to keep the baby, not give it out for adoption. How can I support my child?" (Our editors got her a job as housekeeper to a married doctor pair. She is now married herself, with more children.) "You should do a truck driver's family in 'How America Lives.' It's so romantic. Even in the middle of the night—when my husband comes back from a trip—we cook a steak and drink wine." "Help us start a Youth Center in our town." "You bring good art to ranchers in Montana." "My daughter has just married and gone to Philadelphia—you are my only friends there. She's terribly lonely and unhappy—I'm afraid her marriage may break up. Couldn't one of you just drop in?" We did—but the bride had already gone. M.D.'s thanked us for "Tell Me Doctor." College instructors praised our articles on education. From Uganda— "I try my best to copy Wilhela Cushman's fashion pages in our local stores." And just plain people wrote, "Dear Journal—You are my friend."

Readers from India, Norway, Italy, Thailand, Zanzibar came to the workshop, longing to meet fashion and food editors, see our well-planned kitchens, marvelous washers, dryers, and ironers, magical, almost, in countries where many women still flogged their wash in rushing streams. The *Journal,* they told us, brought America to their door.

To those who had always longed to see the world, the *Journal* gave a vantage point. Through "How America Lives" they dipped into homes in every income and calling. As usual, the average proved to be exceptional. Readers were not uniform, like matches in a box. People, just ordinary people, were too individualistic, too cranky, too long in goodness or too short in malice or too thick in stubbornness to be made up into neat packages.

Our readers saw how sparely England lived during the war with fortitude, even humor. How France lived after liberation eating carrot soup, cooked carrots and potatoes, apples for dessert, cheered by hoarded wine. How Italy lived blighted by Mussolini. They saw fear in post-Stalin Russia, beauty and misery in India, flies clustering black on the eyes of apathetic infants. They saw a young woman in Africa walk "through lion country" her baby on her back, to learn to read, to learn elements of sanitation for her village. Readers were entertained at St. James's and by Chiang Kai-shek in wartime China. Through Margaret Hickey, they learned what women were doing to make their towns better in Gary or Sacramento—and in Hopewell, New Jersey, where our neighbors were our readers and severest critics.

It had been amusing to be the only people who slept the night, thirty-one empty stories high, in Rockefeller Center. "Aren't you frightened?" people asked. But the dark hours hummed with the activity of friendly elevator men, work crews waxing, polishing, sweeping, emptying. If wakeful, one could hear the regular step of the night watchman like a medieval tower guard reassuring, "All's well!" I always told guests, "We live over the store."

To our entertainment room for luncheon—the Empire State tower glinting clear in sunlight, stately ships floating down the Hudson to the world—or in the gray-blue twilight, as jeweled lights of Broadway gradually seemed many-hued fireworks against a darkening sky, people came from all over:

Daphne du Maurier, elusive as smoke. Marquand, gruff, dry, pompous, humorous, and acidulous as his books, Lippmann, his thoughtful face marked with magnanimity, growing handsomer with age, his Yeatsian soul still clapping its hands. Kit Cornell, beautiful, warm, quiet offstage as any good wife, while her producer husband, Guthrie McClintic, took stage center in hilarious mimicry. Anne Lindbergh, delicate and shy, pretty as a Japanese fan, poetic in talk as in her books. Lady Reading, still guiding her Women's Voluntary Services, sharing her skills in personal, humanized help to the ill and the aged. Florida Scott-Maxwell, a Floridian turned British subject, an actress turned wife, mother and Jungian psychiatrist, in her eighties, her worn, beautiful face clear and fine as an old Roman coin, whose brilliant *Women and Sometimes Men* makes Betty Friedan's complaining of woman's lot sound shrill as she wails against things as they are, against the cycles of the moon.

Dorothy Thompson came often, especially in her later years, when, lonely, she grew to rely on our friendship and counsel. In her book of *Journal* columns, *The Courage to Be Happy,* dedicated to us, she wrote magnanimously: "A conscientious and perceptive Editor is a writer's truest friend," a thought not echoed by all writers.

After Sinclair Lewis and Dorothy Thompson parted, Dorothy was never able to explain why she had married that fabulous Main Streeter with the Sahara thirst. Perhaps for much the same reason Françoise Gilot lived with Picasso—neither egocentric man would let his chosen victim be until she'd succumbed to his need to be cared for.

Handsome, with commanding blue eyes and a powerful body, Dorothy longed to be womanly and was, but continually betrayed this desire by a wish, also, to be definitely intellectual, and assertively, table-poundingly right—qualities not always winning with the opposite sex. Her third husband, handsome artist Maxim Kopf, had a serenity against whose calm Dorothy's more didactic moments lost their force. Until his death this marriage brought her joy.

Louise de Vilmorin, elegant French novelist and poet, in ravishing Paris clothes, came to speak at a forum on manners, her own so perfect, so formal, so mannered, everyone else at the table, including acerbic English humorist Malcolm Muggeridge, huddled in defensive, democratic simplicity, rejecting all forms, opting for pure American kindness or heart as the best "manners" of all.

Memories linger about our beautiful entertainment room, transformed by designer-friend H. T. Williams from an office cube to dusk-blue elegance, with dark, polished, marquetry floor for instant dancing when we felt in the mood, one blue wall carved like a Coromandel screen with brilliant painted field flowers against its dark lacquer. The room heard many thoughtful discussions, much gay and lively talk.

We turned over the editorship of the *Journal* to Curtiss Anderson, chosen by us a couple of year before as a possible successor, gratified that our final issue (March, 1962) continued to have unquestioned newsstand leadership in its field. And our circulation head later informed me its total circulation was the largest in *Journal* history. We had fulfilled Miss Madeira's precept, while Sesaly was at her school, "Finish in style."

Anderson, an intelligent young Middle Westerner with sound publishing traditions, proved too independent for the new Curtis management which seized control of the company some months later, after a stock-market raid and a threatened proxy fight. He resigned.

Now after several other editors, John Mack Carter has taken over, just as the fourth *Post* editor has succeeded Ben Hibbs—following ructions which had the whole publishing world aghast when it was not laughing. Both magazines, it is hoped, will steer into calmer waters.

We resigned with gratitude for wonderful opportunities given us, with pride in what the *Journal* had accomplished in education, in maternal and child health, in partial conquest of venereal diseases, in awakened community and political responsibility among women—in sheer literacy offered to many. The *Journal* had been a power, not in itself, but because of its remarkable audience, the women of America, who, if spoken to in a way which touches their concern, have capacities for work, for altruism, which should never be underestimated. "Everything comes out of the people," says Whitman, "everyday people, the people as you find them and leave them; people, people, just people."

We resigned with regret for things we had left undone.

Beatrice has always been sensitive to child abuse, child neglect, because of young powerlessness—and, practically, because children callously treated grow up to damage our society. As a young murderer recently said, "We hate the world." Thousands of American children are willfully injured or killed every year by their parents. Hundreds of thousands more grow up brutalized by neglect. Deserted or corrupted, often wards of the court, they move from inadequate institutions to indifferent foster homes, in emergencies housed in jails—often returned to alcoholic or drug-dimmed parents because suitable shelters are lacking. To rescue these rootless, affectionless waifs, laws would have to be changed, money spent, the public taught *to care enough*. Beatrice's greatest regret for our days on the *Journal* is that we were not able to do more with this problem.

We are, of course, an inconsistent society—and need a modern Montesquieu to point out our absurdities in a new and biting *Persian Letters*.

We spend billions on a Great Society and leave thousands of children beaten, starved, tied to bedposts, irreparably damaged. An African village might be kinder.

We moan lack of "home influences" yet often make intelligent young women feel they betray their expensive education by spending their days in the home, instead of doing something "worthwhile."

We fail to educate our disadvantaged young in the tools of learning and are surprised when, at fourteen, they reject the process of learning with which they cannot cope.

Many psychiatrists assure the urgent young that premarital sexual satisfaction is their right, without stressing the dangers and responsibilities of that right. And as the young are always anxious to find endorsement from their elders for their own desires, and as birth control measures are not infallible, we bewail the fact that more and younger teen-agers become promiscuous and pregnant annually. Impetuosity is the attribute of youth; restraint the learning of age. Age abrogates responsibility if it does not contribute its balance to the scale.

We permit violence in solving labor disputes. Even teachers, images for youth, claim false sickness to gain usually well-deserved pay rises. We tolerate a callous brutality in movies, even greater violence in TV fed to three-year-olds, are surprised when unoccupied, aimless youth erupts into violence.

We know that cigarette smoking is dangerous, and hesitate to warn our youth, in every ad, on every package. Our democracy founded on free expression, on a free press, muffles some of this freedom for commercial ends.

Truly, here is the material for many magazines to come.

We regretted too leaving our apartment, with its view of the world, where so much of the lighter side of our work was centered. Women's interests they are called, and most important to women. Here Beatrice found Louella Shouer's recipes good, proven at innumerable small luncheons or dinners, served by tiny, tripping, faithful Annie Kelly, always smiling. Here Margaret Davidson (who had courageously helped persuade manufacturers that women's cherished household machines were as entitled to careful servicing as any Volkswagen) in her homemaking department had tried new devices in our laundered, waxed, and polished rooms, had passed on those worthy to our readers.

Here Beatrice selfishly chose the loveliest of *Journal* clothes—dresses made up and photographed, to aid home sewers, under Nora O'Leary, genius in fitting color and material to design.

"Could this be let out a little, Nora dear?" she would suggest—then wore Nora's dresses at parties in London and Paris, at tiaraed dinners at Holyrood Palace, less regal ones in New York, and before the often more discriminating eyes of friends in Princeton.

Here our too busy life was sheltered and soothed by two delightful secretaries, of velvet-glove efficiency, Margaret Beall and Bertha Fischer. Here, after five, Wilhela Cushman brought us, for cover ideas, for fashion pages, boxes of hats from Emmé, the latest handbag from Paris—a Wilhela Cushman so fanatic about fashion she will surely choose Paris in place of Heaven as her final reward. So perceptive was she that, while I was temporarily hospitalized in Boston, and Beatrice, commuting there and running the *Journal,* was getting our daughter ready for boarding school, Wilhela said, "Let me help with her shopping." Two days later Beatrice returned to find Sesaly delightfully wardrobed, in suit, coat, and evening dress of modest price and great charm—garments Sesaly felt certain she had selected herself, with Mrs. Cushman merely standing by.

Enchanted hours, working and living—because editing is life distilled—hours rich with friendship, laughter, devotion to creative effort —they will be with us always.

On the last night spent in our New York apartment, we had seen a play with Rebecca West and Rensselaer Lee, and Rens had come up with us for a visit and nightcap. At midnight, we heard a knock on the door. Our friendly night cleaning woman of many years, Mary Stevko, with whom we had exchanged news and pictures of children and grandchildren evenings as we came in after concert or theatre, stood there in her working dress.

"I've just heard you were leaving. I had to say goodbye."

She and Beatrice embraced with tears, and through Christmas cards we still watch her children grow and she, ours.

Next day, as we made our final trip down from the thirty-first floor, the elevator man said, "We're sorry to see you go. We'll miss you. We liked to see you going out in the evening. You always seemed to be having such a good time."

We were. We did. We are.

Format by Katharine Sitterly
Set in Linotype Times Roman
Composed, printed and bound by The Haddon Craftsmen, Inc.
HARPER & ROW, PUBLISHERS, INCORPORATED